A Comprehensive Guide to the Causes, Treatments, and Prevention of Eating Disorders

THE Eating Disorder SOURCEBOOK

Third Edition

Carolyn Costin

M.A., M.Ed., M.F.T.

New York Chicago San Francisco Lisbon London Madrid Mexico City
Milan New Delhi San Juan Seoul Singapore Sydney Toronto

The McGraw-Hill Companies

Library of Congress Cataloging-in-Publication Data

Costin, Carolyn.
The eating disorder sourcebook by Carolyn Costin. — 3rd ed.
p. cm.
Includes bibliographical references.
ISBN 0-07-147685-7
1. Eating disorders. I. Title.

RC552.E18C67 2007
616.85'26—dc22 2006036808

6 7 8 9 10 11 12 13 14 15 16 17 18 19 QFR/QFR 1 5 4 3 2 1

ISBN-13: 978-0-07-147685-0
ISBN-10: 0-07-147685-7

McGraw-Hill books are available at special quantity discounts to use as premiums and sales promotions, or for use in corporate training programs. For more information, please write to the Director of Special Sales, Professional Publishing, McGraw-Hill, Two Penn Plaza, New York, NY 10121-2298. Or contact your local bookstore.

This book is printed on acid-free paper.

Contents

Acknowledgments

MY TEACHERS HAVE been many, and my anorexia was one of the best. I am grateful now for so many important lessons learned at an early age—lessons I continue to do my best to pass on to others. My work and this book would not exist without my past and without the many incredible, lovely people who have enriched my life and thus these pages. This book is dedicated to you all.

- To my clients and their families, who share deeply, struggle valiantly, and teach me well.
- To my colleagues in the field, who endure my endless quest for knowledge, clarification, and understanding and who continue to provide it.
- To all my staff members who are my friends and comrades in this war against eating disorders. Thank you for your dedication and for suffering through my absences necessary for writing.
- To my roadies—the people who take care of me, find my lost notes, read my rough drafts, bring me coffee, rub my shoulders, and encourage me to keep writing. You know who you are. You make it possible for me to do all that I do.
- To my dearest friends, who allowed me to put not only this book, but over the years many things, before

watching the sunset with them, even though it should always be the other way around.

- To all the people who have read *Your Dieting Daughter* and the previous editions of *The Eating Disorder Sourcebook*, especially those who let me know that my writing meant something and was worth continuing.
- To my husband, Bruce, and my dog, Gonner, the best teachers of all.

Contributors

In the following chapters, I was fortunate to work with several contributors. These coauthors helped me out tremendously by adding their expertise. Their addition has made this sourcebook a richer resource of information.

- **Chapter 12: Enough About Your Mother, What Did You Have to Eat Today?** The following registered dietitians coauthored this chapter: Marcia Herin, Karen Kratina, Diane Keddy, Rebekah Mardis, Erin Naimi, Francie White, and Kim Wyman.
- **Chapter 13: Medical Assessment and Management.** Richard L. Levine, M.D., professor of pediatrics and psychiatry, Penn State College of Medicine; chief, Division of Adolescent Medicine and Eating Disorders, Penn State–Milton S. Hershey Medical Center; and Philip Mehler, M.D., chief, General Internal Medicine, Department of Health and Hospitals, Denver, Colorado, coauthored this chapter.
- **Chapter 14: The Psychiatrist's Role and Psychotropic Medication.** Timothy D. Brewerton, M.D., DFAPA, FAED, clinical professor of psychiatry and behavioral sciences, Medical University of South Carolina, coauthored this chapter.

- **Chapter 16: Alternative Approaches to Treating Eating Disorders.** Coauthors for this chapter were Carolyn Coker Ross, M.D., M.P.H., head of Eating Disorders Program and Integrative Therapies Department, Sierra Tucson, and Hamlin Emory, M.D., psychiatrist at Monte Nido Treatment Center, Malibu, California, private practice, Beverly Hills, California.
- **Chapter 17: Increasing Awareness and Prevention.** Michael Levine, Ph.D., FAED, professor of psychology, Kenyon College, coauthored this chapter.

Introduction

THIRTY-SEVEN YEARS AGO, when I was 15, I went on a diet. By the time I was 17, some 40 pounds lighter, and still losing, something was terribly wrong. The first doctor my mother took me to told her that I might be trying to lose weight to hide a pregnancy. The first therapist I went to suggested that if eating made me feel guilty, perhaps I should try eating by myself. The only psychiatrist I ever saw tried to get me to drink a regular Coke in his office so he could watch. None of these professionals had ever heard of anorexia nervosa, much less had any knowledge of how to treat it. Finally, in 1973, my mother found the first book written about the subject by Hilda Bruch called *Eating Disorders: Obesity, Anorexia Nervosa and the Person Within*, which was geared for professionals and had only a small section at the end on a strange syndrome of self starving called anorexia nervosa. This was the beginning of understanding—for myself and the world at large—that there was actually a name for these thoughts and behaviors I had. My morbid fear of weight gain was an actual illness and others suffered from it too.

The field has come a long way since then. Once I recovered and eventually began treating eating disorders, I decided to write a book. At first I hesitated, because I thought, "Who will be interested except people with anorexia and their moms, and how many of those could there be?" but soon I started pouring out the pages.

Before I finished, Hilda Bruch's book for the public *The Golden Cage* was published, and I thought, "That's it, the book on eating disorders has been written!" I dropped my book project and did not pick it up again for another decade and a half when I finally wrote the first edition of this sourcebook. Now there are a plethora of books, too many to keep up with; several journals devoted solely to eating disorders; and approximately seven hundred journal publications on the subject every year. Eating disorders are mainstream in our literature, our media, our legislation, our homes, and our group consciousness. A well-respected colleague, Richard Gordon, is writing a book on the history of eating disorders and interviewed me for the project. How interesting and what an honor to be included in such a book along with Hilda Bruch herself and many other prominent people in the field. I too have come a long way. From disordered, to recovered, to therapist, to author, to lecturer, to clinical director, to executive director, to coeditor of *Eating Disorders, the Journal of Treatment and Prevention*, and National Eating Disorder Board trustee.

What You'll Find in This Updated Edition

I am grateful that the *Eating Disorder Sourcebook* has been so popular and helped so many people over the years. I have heard from sufferers and family members, educators, and clinicians who have told me how much they valued this book. So when I was approached to write an updated edition, I asked myself, "Is there much to add that is new, especially since the last update in 1999?" I knew the research developments could be summarized quickly.

New Medical Treatments

In the area of medication, some initial research has shown that an antipsychotic medication called olanzapine (Zyprexa) may be useful in treating anorexia nervosa, which is promising since this illness is very difficult to treat. However, the excitement has been tempered by the drug's serious side effects, including diabetes. Furthermore, people with anorexia often will not take it. They look it up on the Internet and see its weight-gain properties along with other side effects and, well, that's that. Fluoxetine (Prozac) is still the most common medication prescribed for bulimia—and some initial research garnered excitement that it may be effective after weight restoration to prevent relapse in anorexia. However, the excitement has faded as new trials showed this not to be the case.

In clients with binge eating disorder (BED), topiramate (Topamax) has been reported to reduce bingeing compared to placebo. For this reason it was also used with individuals suffering from bulimia with some efficacy, but it is also a problematic medication that causes nausea, loss of appetite, insomnia, tingling, and possibly even kidney stones. Several selective serotonin reuptake inhibitor (SSRI) antidepressants have been reported to significantly reduce bingeing in this population but only one medication, sibutramine (Meridia), also reduced weight compared to placebo.

More research needs to be done and none of these medications is considered the definitive treatment for these disorders. There is also no definitive treatment for the loss of bone density seen in anorexia even though we have several new studies and suggestions for treatments that are presented in the chapter on Medical Assessment and Management.

New Psychological Treatments and Research

In the area of psychological treatment, we have learned that cognitive behavioral therapy seems to perform better than other treatments—for bulimia nervosa, in particular—but then again it might not, especially in the long run. Even when it does perform better than other treatments studied, up to 70 percent of individuals in some studies still experience symptoms. Newer approaches, such as dialectical behavior therapy and interpersonal therapy, are getting attention. However, the really exciting new discovery involves the promising results of using a family-based approach with adolescents who have anorexia, which is described in Chapter 11. Originally called the Maudsley method, this model puts parents back in charge of getting their teen with anorexia to eat. The research done on a very specific application of this approach has shown a high degree of success lasting through the five-year follow-up. This is exciting stuff, and every clinician, client, and family member should be aware of it.

Etiology

Researchers now report that it appears that eating disorders do have a genetic component to them. The field is buzzing with excitement, but the media has unwittingly exaggerated the claims. What exactly this will all mean is unclear. The research is from small samples, there are actually mixed results, and many assumptions are being made. There are many who believe that we will never find the genes for eating disorders partly because we have never found the genes for any mental illness, chemical dependency, or obesity for that matter, and it is not because we haven't been looking.

Even with a genetic predisposition, we know that it will take an environmental trigger to set it off; we must continue to research these triggers, such as sexual abuse, attachment issues, the current cultural pressure to be thin combined with the fear of fat, and the societal expectations of women particularly since the 1960s all of which are discussed in Chapters 1 through 5. Men get eating disorders too, but a young woman today with an eating disorder, whether in the United States, Europe, Hong Kong, China, India, or South Africa (the list is growing), is actually, at least initially, praised and reinforced for taking the current westernized cultural norms to an extreme and even dangerous form. Eating disorders are about food and weight but they are also about much more.

The Heart and Soul of This New Edition

So what is in these approximately 350 pages? As I began to write, I realized that there was, in fact, a lot to write about—a decade's worth of additional information since the first edition. This includes 10 additional years of working with clients and their family members on a daily basis, either in my outpatient practice, day-treatment program, or residential setting in Monte Nido, which I opened the same year in which I wrote the first edition of this book—a decade of working in the trenches. Imagine Jane

Goodall's exponential growth in understanding chimpanzees after every additional decade of experience. A silly analogy maybe, but the truth is I have almost three decades of field research in treating eating disorders, which I brought to bear in the writing of this book.

Although I am not a researcher in the academic sense, I have collected more than 30 years of data. So this time around I'm giving readers all of the important information required in a sourcebook—a brief history of eating disorders, standard clinical diagnoses and criteria, what to look for in terms of psychological and medical assessments and monitoring, and what to do if outpatient treatment fails. However, there are many eating disorder books that include this material. Therefore, the real heart and soul of this book—my emphasis on what is new—lies in the enriched information provided on the art and technique of treatment. This edition includes significant factors and strategies that have helped people recover. I give examples of topics I use in individual, group, and family sessions, as well as assignments I give to clients.

I am also more forthcoming in this edition about what I have learned personally. This book is full not only of facts but opinions. My opinions are based on countless hours of experience with what does and does not work. Some information is taken from the last edition, but much more is changed. I use new case examples and new journal entries and quotes from clients—not just about their illnesses, but about what they think works in treatment.

Some Thoughts to Keep in Mind When Reading This Book

In the text, I alternate using the words *patient* and *client*. There are clinicians in the field who prefer one or the other. For example, physicians regularly use the word *patient*, whereas therapists often use *client*. I also use female pronouns approximately 90 to 95 percent of the time. This reflects the percentage of females to males who get eating disorders, which you will read about in Chapter 2. I also avoid using the terms *anorexic*, *bulimic*, or *binge eater* to describe people unless the material was from a quote or contributing author. These terms imply identity, which is a mistake and should be avoided when referring to or working with people who have an eating disorder. A person suffers from bulimia nervosa, she is not a bulimic; and I am not Carolyn Costin, a recovered anorexic. I am Carolyn Costin, who once *suffered from* anorexia nervosa.

For the last 30 years I have not dieted, starved, weighed myself, or valued how I look over who I am. Even so, calling myself recovered is to some a bold statement. There are those who believe that eating disorders are genetically caused diseases from which one can never really be recovered. My goal in this book is to make sure that with the zeal for the evidenced-based, scientific paradigm—fueled in part by the search for a medication solution to eating disorders—we do not overemphasize genetics and underplay the still serious etiological factors of our culture's obsession with dieting and thinness and each person's underlying psychological issues that contribute to their eating disorder. I do not believe we will find the genes or drugs that cure eating disorders any time soon. The chemical dependency field is still looking and they are many years ahead. Therefore I am making sure (as best I can) that the field keeps things in perspective and readers are duly informed. We must continue to search for all causes of eating disorders, biological or otherwise.

In regards to the evidenced-based paradigm, the research on treatment approaches is tainted with too few studies, too few subjects, self-reporting, researcher bias, a lack of long-term follow-ups, and more. Too often treatment protocols and decisions are guided by one or two studies that are reported over and over. I know that we have to start somewhere, and I am not against research, but I am cautious and wonder why certain areas of research are left out. Research that I think is exciting does not come out of the eating disorder field but is applicable there.

There are now numerous studies being discussed in books such as *The Heart and Soul of Change* and *The Heroic Client*, discussed in Chapter 8, which show that rather than a certain treatment approach, the alliance between the therapist and client is a better predictor of outcome. This is an area that resonates with me and is due much more attention from the field. I encourage readers to research this area and anything else I say in this book that seems controversial or off track. There are credible data for all of it. This is especially true for the information on genetic research, described in Chapter 4 and in the chapter on alternative approaches to treating eating disorders, Chapter 16. There were so many things I wanted to include regarding alternative approaches, such as detailed information on meditation, massage therapy, equine therapy, and yoga. I have seen some very impressive psychotherapeutic work done in all of these areas. Unfortunately, the scope of this book would not allow it. For more information on these topics, I refer readers to my short guidebook *100 Questions About Eating Disorders.* I did contact two individuals who are progressive, alternative, and integrative thinkers and clinicians who stand out in their field. They each bring a different dimension to the alternative treatment chapter and provide a plethora of citations to back up what they have to report.

Lastly, when colleagues asked to look at rough drafts of the chapters in this book, no one was interested in the one on prevention. It is sad, but I have also noticed at the last few eating disorder conferences that the workshops on prevention had the poorest attendance. This reveals something about the current state of affairs. I think many people don't believe that they can do anything about preventing eating disorders because it feels too big. But then I am reminded and remind others about the women suffragettes. They started in small groups all over the country and were not deterred by those who said, "It can't happen," or "You are never going to be able to change things." These women worked for changes that perhaps would not happen in their lifetime, but in their daughters' or granddaughters' lifetimes. That is why I believe in and continue to work on prevention every day—for both eating disorders and body dissatisfaction. I work on the prevention of valuing appearance over substance. What a world we would have if we could change just that one thing. We can do it; women did get the right to vote.

I know that, like me, people with eating disorders can be cured and healed. I have been fortunate to see this happen countless times. However, to help individuals afflicted with eating disorders fully recover, we must help them understand how they have given up all of their strivings and longings for an obsession. We must help them see how their internal conflicts have shifted from the real and vital issue of their own development to the symbolic issue of the size of their bodies and the amount of food they eat. What was written about one of the first documented eating disorder cases, a patient known as Ellen West, can be said about any woman suffering now: "Her rage, which arose initially because of the restrictions imposed upon her self-development, is now directed, through her body, at the 'inner self' which hungers for its development. It is a costly and tragic reversal . . . her obsession with her body is, fundamentally, an expression of violence towards her soul." Part of our treatment must focus not just on the care and feeding of the body, but on the care and feeding of the soul. When people are reconnected with the soulful aspects of life, reconnected with true meaning and joy, the need for eating disorder symptoms will diminish.

We still have a lot to learn about eating disorders and the individuals who have them. In the meantime, every individual who has an eating disorder should be treated with a multidimensional approach involving nutritional, biochemical, psychological, and spiritual perspectives. An understanding of the importance of all of these areas is necessary for those suffering from eating disorders, their significant others, and the people who treat them. My purpose in this book is to provide a summary of the current knowledge in the field and to examine the continuing mystery we still must deal with of how someone could binge or starve themselves to a ruined life or even death. In addition, I hope to provide the available information on how, by whom, and in what manner these disorders can be prevented, dealt with, and overcome.

1

From Diet to Disorder: Problems and Prognosis

DISORDERED EATING IS alarmingly common, and having an eating disorder is often seen—except by those who have one or their family members—as a diet strategy, a phase, or a trendy thing to do. In 2005 a television comedy series called "Starved" included scenes in which eating disorder behavior was mocked and shown to be, according to the producer, "tragically comic." In one episode, a character pours detergent all over a dessert to avoid eating it, then later retrieves it from the trash for a binge. Another scene portrays a policeman who's been diagnosed with bulimia letting a deliveryman out of a ticket in exchange for Chinese food, on which he then binges and purges in an alley, accidentally vomiting on a homeless man. Is this funny? Is it entertainment? Would we accept a comedy about a skid-row alcoholic or heroin addict?

Groups such as the National Eating Disorder Association (NEDA) and the Association of Anorexia Nervosa and Related Disorders (ANAD) led a public outcry. Sponsors pulled out under the pressure, and the show was cancelled. Both "Starved" and the grassroots organizations that protested against it are evidence that eating disorders are now part of our culture and are increasingly earning respect as illnesses rather than lifestyle choices as the Pro Ana (short for *pro Anorexia)* websites would have us believe. As difficult as it is to understand the growth of websites promoting this illness, their proliferation proves that eating disorders have come out of the closet and into our living rooms, and few of us can remain unaware or untouched.

Elementary school girls continue to starve and purge as an acceptable method of weight loss. Binge eating disorder (BED), although still not yet listed as a separate diagnosis in the *Diagnostic and Statistical Manual for Mental Disorders, Fourth Edition* (*DSM-IV*), is increasingly discussed as an illness. Sadly, eating disorders have become mainstream on both ends of the spectrum. In our current cultural climate, instead of asking, "Why do so many people develop eating disorders?" one wonders, "How is it that anyone, especially a female, does not develop one?"

Are Eating Disorders More Common Now or Have They Just Been Hiding?

The first hint that eating disorders were a serious problem came from Hilde Bruch, who in 1973 introduced the first major work in the field, *Eating Disorders: Obesity, Anorexia Nervosa, and the Person Within.* This book was geared toward professionals and not readily available to the public. Bruch followed it up in 1978 with her pioneering work *The Golden Cage*, which continues to this day to provide a compelling, passionate, and empathetic understanding of the nature of eating disorders, particularly anorexia nervosa. With the book and television movie *The Best Little Girl in the World*, Steven Levenkron brought an awareness of knowledge of anorexia nervosa into the average home. And in 1985, when Karen Carpenter died from heart failure due to anorexia nervosa, the picture of the emaciated singer haunted the public from the cover of *People* magazine.

Since then, women's magazines and television journalists have presented us with stories of people who we thought had everything—beauty, success, power, and control—but who were lacking something else, as they began to admit that they too had eating disorders. Olympic gold medal gymnast Cathy Rigby revealed a struggle with anorexia and bulimia that almost took her life, and several others followed suit, including Gilda Radner, Princess Diana, Sally Field, Elton John, Tracy Gold, Paula Abdul, and more recently Mary Kate Olson, Felicity Huffman, Jamie-Lynn DiScala, and Portia de Rossi to name just a few. In her recent autobiography, Jane Fonda describes having led a double life suffering secretly from anorexia and bulimia throughout most of it even with all of her success and fame. Talk shows on eating disorders continue to feature the media's fascination with every possible angle one can imagine: "Anorexics and Their Moms," "A Ten-Year-Old Boy with Anorexia," and "Eating Disordered Twins."

Similar to chemical dependency in the 1970s and 1980s, eating disorder treatment is a growing business, with hospital and residential eating disorder programs rapidly on the rise. Large corporations are now "investing" in this industry as a result of their market research. This can only mean that it is a growing problem. The passage of the federal Mental Health Parity Act fueled the growth of this treatment industry by mandating that insurance companies cover major mental illness just as they would physical illness. However, the legislation allows each state the freedom to determine what constitutes a major mental illness, and eating disorders are most often left out. To date, only 12 states (California, Connecticut, Delaware, Maine, Maryland, Minnesota, Rhode Island, New York, North Dakota, Vermont, Washington, and West Virginia) have state-mandated insurance coverage for the treatment of eating disorders, but the pressure is on to change this. To further exacerbate the struggle, for the most part, only medically necessary cases of anorexia nervosa and bulimia nervosa—as diagnosed under *DSM-IV*—are insured for inpatient day treatment and sometimes even outpatient settings. Clients with atypical or less severe cases often get no coverage at all.

When people ask, "Are eating disorders really more common now, or have they just been in hiding?" the answer is both, however, the overall trend shows that the number of individuals with eating disorders has been increasing continually since their recognition, paralleling society's growing obsession with being thin, losing weight, and fear of fat.

Is It Disordered Eating or an Eating Disorder?

Eating disorders may seem more common today because even though individuals who have them are reluctant to admit it, they do so more readily than in the past. People are more likely to know that they have an illness, the possible consequences of that illness, and that they can get help for it. The trouble is they often wait too long. Determining when problem eating has become an eating disorder is difficult. There are far more people with eating or body image problems than those with full-blown eating disorders. The more we learn about eating disorders, the more we realize that individuals may have varying predispositions to developing them. A person's particular genetic makeup may account for a heightened sensitivity to the current cultural climate, thus increasing the likelihood that he or she will cross the line between disordered eating and an eating disorder. But when is this line crossed?

Diagnostic Criteria for Eating Disorders

To be officially diagnosed with an eating disorder, one has to meet the clinical diagnostic criteria delineated in the current edition of the *Diagnostic and Statistical Manual for Mental Disorders IV TR* (2000), but the specific definitions therein do not encompass all of the syndromes health professionals treat. In fact, the *DSM-IV TR* criteria can be confusing, complicated, and restrictive.

There is an ongoing, passionate discussion among experts in the field about changing what is considered by many to be an outdated system of classification. The current *DSM-IV TR* diagnoses for eating disorders include anorexia nervosa (AN); bulimia nervosa (BN); and eating disorders not otherwise specified (EDNOS), which includes binge eating disorder (BED) as well as a variety of subclinical or more appropriately "atypical" eating disorder presentations. Clinicians and researchers alike are proposing alternatives to this model for a variety of reasons. One model proposes a general diagnosis of "eating disorder," with a corresponding list of symptoms or features from which the clinician can choose. This would alleviate the problem of changing the diagnosis when clients develop new symptoms or gain or lose a certain amount of weight.

Furthermore, the severity of an eating disorder has historically been measured by how well the client meets the full diagnostic criteria. Clinicians in the trenches know that this is not the reality. I once treated a young woman who began dieting when she weighed 200 pounds. At the time of her first visit, she was eating only 300 calories a day and had lost 70 pounds in one year. She was fearful of eating, could not eat with anyone or in public, was terrified of gaining weight, and met all the criteria for anorexia nervosa except that her weight was 130 (she was 5′4″). This young woman had one of the most entrenched eating disorders I had ever treated, yet with a diagnosis of EDNOS, I could not get her approved for residential care because she did not meet criteria for anorexia or bulimia.

Changes in official diagnostic criteria happen slowly. There are ongoing debates and calls for more research. Eventually we will have more clarity, but the clinical descriptions taken from *DSM-IV TR* are the currently accepted standards.

Cases of Anorexia Nervosa

Despite its increase over the last decade or so, anorexia nervosa is not a new illness nor is it solely a phenomenon of our current culture. For an interesting history of this illness, read Joan Brumberg's *Fasting Girls: The History of Anorexia Nervosa* (1989). The case of anorexia nervosa most often cited as the first in the medical literature was that of a 20-year-old girl treated in 1686 by Richard Morton and explained in his work *Phthisiologia: Or a Treatise of Consumptions* (1694). Morton's description of what he termed *nervous atrophy* or *nervous consumption* sounds eerily familiar:

> I do not remember that I did ever in my entire Practice see one that was so conversant with the Living so much wasted with the greatest degree of Consumption, (like a Skeleton only clad with Skin) yet there was no Fever, but on the contrary a Coldness of the whole Body . . . Only her Appetite was diminished, and Digestion uneasy, with Fainting Fitts, [sic] which did frequently return upon her.

The *DSM-IV TR* Diagnostic criteria for 307.1 Symptoms of Anorexia Nervosa

A. Refusal to maintain body weight at or above a minimally normal weight for age and height (e.g., weight loss leading to maintenance of body weight less than 85 percent of that expected, or failure to make expected weight gain during period of growth leading to body weight less than 85 percent of that expected).

B. Intense fear of gaining weight or becoming fat, even though underweight.

C. Disturbance in the way in which one's body weight or shape is experienced, undue influence of body weight or shape on self-evaluation, or denial of the seriousness of the current low body weight.

D. In postmenarcheal females, amenorrhea, i.e., the absence of at least three consecutive menstrual cycles. (A woman is considered to have amenorrhea if her periods occur only following hormone, e.g., estrogen, administration.)

- *Restricting Type:* during the current episode of Anorexia Nervosa, the person has not regularly engaged in binge-eating or purging behavior (i.e., self-induced vomiting or the misuse of laxatives, diuretics, or enemas).
- *Binge-Eating/Purging Type:* during the current episode of Anorexia Nervosa, the person has regularly engaged in binge-eating or purging behavior (i.e., self-induced vomiting or the misuse of laxatives, diuretics, or enemas).

The first case study in which we have descriptive detail from the patient's perspective is that of a woman known as Ellen West (1900–1933). Ellen committed suicide at age 33 to end the desperate struggle that had manifested itself through an obsession with thinness and food. Ellen kept a diary that contains perhaps the earliest record of the inner world of an eating disorder sufferer:

> Everything agitates me, and I experience every agitation as a sensation of hunger, even if I have just eaten.
>
> I am afraid of myself. I am afraid of the feelings to which I am defenselessly delivered over every minute.
>
> I am in prison and cannot get out. It does no good for the analyst to tell me that I myself place the armed men there, that they are theatrical figments and not real. To me they are very real.

Like Ellen West, people suffering from anorexia today exhibit rigid control of their "out of controlness," making an effort to deny or to purge not just food but yearnings, ambitions, and sensual pleasures. Emotions are feared and translated into somatic (body) experiences and eating disorder behaviors, which serve to eliminate the feeling, needing aspect of self. Through their struggle with their bodies, individuals with anorexia nervosa pursue a mind-over-matter mentality, perfection, and mastery of self—all accomplishments that our society praises and applauds. This, of course, entrenches these patterns into the very fabric of each individual's identity. Indeed, people with anorexia nervosa seem not simply to have this disorder but to become it.

The term *anorexia* is of Greek origin—*an* (meaning "privation" or "lack of") and *orexis* (meaning "appetite")—indicating a lack of desire to eat. It was originally used to describe the loss of appetite caused by some other ailment such as headaches, depression, or cancer, where the person actually doesn't feel hungry. Normally, appetite is like the response to pain, beyond the individual's control. Ellen West and others like her are not suffering from a loss of hunger but from hunger and a denial of it that they cannot explain. They may eventually develop a true lack of appetite, but for the most part, it is the strong desire to control their appetite that is a cardinal feature. Thus, the term *anorexia* alone is insufficient because people afflicted with this disorder have not just lost their appetites. In fact, they long to eat, obsess and dream about it; some of them even break down and eat uncontrollably. Rather than losing their desire to eat, those suffering from anorexia report spending 70 to 85 percent of each day thinking about food but denying their bodies even when driven by hunger pangs. They often want to eat so badly that they cook for and feed others, study menus, read and concoct recipes, and go to bed and wake up thinking about food. They simply don't allow themselves to have it; if they do, they relentlessly pursue any means to get rid of it.

The full clinical term, *anorexia nervosa* (lack of desire to eat due to a mental condition), is a more appropriate name for the illness. This now-common term was not used until 1874, when British physician Sir William Gull used it to describe several patients who exhibited all the familiar signs we associate with the disorder today: refusal to eat, extreme weight loss, amenorrhea (absence of menses), low pulse rate, constipation, and hyperactivity—all of which he thought resulted from a "morbid mental state." Other early researchers pointed out individuals with these symptoms and began to develop theories about why they would behave in such a fashion. In 1903, psychiatrist Pierre Janet describes the case of Nadja, who exhibits mixed features of an eating disorder, including an obsession with thinness. Janet described the syndrome by explaining that "it is due to a deep psychological disturbance, of which the refusal of food is but the outer expression."

People with anorexia nervosa are afraid of food and of themselves. What often (but not always) begins as a determination to lose weight, progresses and transforms into a morbid fear of gaining any weight—even when it is necessary to maintain life. A relentless pursuit of thinness takes hold. These individuals are literally dying to be thin. Being thin, which translates to being in control, becomes the most important thing in the world.

In the throes of the disorder, people with anorexia are terrified of losing control, terrified of what might happen if they allow themselves to eat. This would mean a lack of willpower, a complete "giving in," and they fear that once they let up on the control they have imposed on themselves, they will never get that control back. They are afraid that if they allow themselves to eat, they will not stop, and if they gain one pound today or even this week, that they are now "gaining." A pound today means another pound later and then another and another until they are obese. Physiologically speaking, there is a good reason for this feeling. When a person is starving, the brain is constantly sending impulses to eat. The strength of these impulses is such that the feeling that one may not be able to stop is powerful. Self-induced starvation goes against normal bodily instincts and can rarely be maintained. It is also one reason why 30 to 50 percent of individuals with anorexia ultimately end up binge eating and purging food to the point of developing bulimia nervosa. This is why researchers are looking for differences in the biology of individuals who develop and maintain anorexia.

People with anorexia fear, as crazy as it may seem when looking at them, that they are or will become fat, weak, undisciplined, and unworthy. To them, losing weight is good and gaining weight is bad—period. With the progression of the illness, there are eventually no fattening foods but simply the dictum that "food is fattening." The "anorexic" mind-set seems useful at the beginning of a diet when the goal is to lose a few unwanted pounds, but when dieting itself becomes the goal, there is no way out. Dieting becomes a purpose and what can be referred to as "a safe place to go." It's a world that serves to help cope with feelings of meaninglessness; low self-esteem; failure; dissatisfaction; the need to be unique; and the desire to be special, successful, and in control. Individuals with anorexia create a world in which they can feel they are "successful," "good," and "safe" if they can deny food, making it through the day while eating little, if anything at all. They consider it a threat and a failure if they break down and eat too much, which for them can be as little as 300 calories or less. In fact, for some people with anorexia, eating any food item of more than 100 calories can cause great anxiety. They often prefer two-digit numbers when it comes to calories and to their weight. This kind of overcontrol and exertion of mind over matter goes against our understanding of all normal physiological impulses and instincts for survival. Of the eating disorders, anorexia nervosa is the most tenacious, the most deadly, and the most rare.

Signs of Bulimia Nervosa

The term *bulimia* is derived from Latin and means "hunger of an ox." It is commonly known that the Romans engaged in binge eating and vomiting rituals, but it was first described in medical terms in 1903 in *Obsessions et la Psychasthenie*. Psychiatrist Pierre Janet described Nadja (the woman mentioned earlier), who engaged in compulsive binges in secret. In today's terms, Nadja seems to have suffered from what we call body dysmorphic disorder and perhaps anorexia nervosa, binge/purge type. But Janet's descriptions were the earliest writings on the bingeing accompanied by some kind of behavior to try and compensate for it, two of the key diagnostic patterns required for a diagnosis of bulimia nervosa. Compensation is most often accomplished through purging by vomiting or taking laxatives but restricting food, excessive exercising, and other methods are also now commonly used.

People who meet the other criteria for anorexia (e.g., 15 percent below normal weight) who binge and/or purge and normal-weight individuals who purge but do not binge are often improperly diagnosed with bulimia nervosa. Without frequent binge eating, a diagnosis of bulimia is incorrect. It is the frequency and intensity of the bingeing and thus the lack of extreme weight loss that separates people with bulimia nervosa from those with anorexia nervosa who binge and/or purge. Many people with bulimia nervosa have thought patterns and experience symptoms similar to those of anorexia nervosa. The drive for thinness and the fear of being fat appear in both disorders, and while body image distortion is present in bulimia, it is usually not to the same degree as in anorexia nervosa.

People with bulimia often restrict their caloric intake to try to keep a weight that is too low for them to maintain without experiencing symptoms of semistarvation. Some are at or above normal

The *DSM-IV TR* Diagnostic Criteria for 307.51 Symptoms of Bulimia Nervosa

A. Recurrent episodes of binge eating. An episode of binge eating is characterized by both of the following:
   (1) eating, in a discreet period of time (e.g., within any 2-hour period), an amount of food that is definitely larger than most people would eat during a similar period of time and under similar circumstances.
   (2) a sense of lack of control over eating during the episode (e.g., a feeling that one cannot stop eating or control what or how much one is eating).

B. Recurrent inappropriate compensatory behavior in order to prevent weight gain, such as self-induced vomiting; misuse of laxatives, diuretics, enemas, or other medications; fasting; or excessive exercise.

C. The binge eating and other inappropriate compensatory behaviors both occur, on the average, at least twice a week for 3 months.

D. Self-evaluation is unduly influenced by body shape and weight.

E. The disturbance does not occur exclusively during episodes of Anorexia Nervosa.
   - *Purging Type:* during the current episode of Bulimia Nervosa, the person has regularly engaged in self-induced vomiting or the misuse of laxatives, diuretics, or enemas.

- *Non-Purging Type:* During the current episode of bulimia nervosa, the person has used other inappropriate compensatory behaviors, such as fasting or excessive exercise, but has not regularly engaged in self-induced vomiting or the misuse of laxatives, diuretics, or enemas.

weight but still experience starvation symptoms due to their continual efforts to restrict and or purge food intake. Individuals with bulimia nervosa live in a world between compulsive or binge eating, and purging or starving, pulled in both directions. Some refer to themselves as "failed anorexics," because they have repeatedly tried to control their weight by restricting intake and have been unable to do so. They end up bingeing and then, out of anxiety and desperation, use purging or some other compensatory behavior to make up for their overeating. On the other hand, many individuals with this illness describe themselves as being driven to binge even with no prior restricting. They resort to purging after dieting fails. Lastly, there are those whose motivation for bingeing is the act of purging.

Initially, purging and other compensatory behaviors often serve to calm individuals with bulimia and ease their guilt and anxiousness about having consumed too much food or gained weight. As the disorder progresses, a person with bulimia will purge or compensate for eating even normal or small amounts of anything they consider bad, fattening, or off limits—and eventually any food at all. The behavior can become extreme, and binges of up to 50,000 calories a day have been recorded. Purging is so pervasive on college campuses that a major university even posted signs in dormitory bathrooms pleading, "Please stop throwing up, you're ruining our plumbing!"

The early behaviors in bulimia nervosa, which appear to be related to dieting and weight control, eventually become a means of mood regulation in general. Sufferers find solace in food and often in the purging itself. The act of purging becomes powerfully addictive not just because it controls weight, but because it is calming, serves as a way of expressing anger, or helps the individual cope in some way (albeit destructively). Eventually the binge/purge behavior becomes an addiction in the sense that the person does not need to be triggered to do it; but rather the behaviors become a normal part of daily life. In fact, the person with bulimia seems to have difficulty regulating or modulating mood states and therefore often uses a variety of coping mechanisms, such as drugs, alcohol, shopping, and sex. It is common to hear statements such as "I binge on men" or "I went on a shopping binge."

Social functioning and adjustment among individuals with bulimia varies greatly. Unlike those with anorexia, people with bulimia are not easily identified and are often able to be successful at work, in school, and in relationships, while keeping the bulimia a secret. Clients have disclosed their condition to therapists after successfully hiding it from everyone, including their spouses, sometimes for as long as 20 years. Others become so entrenched in the behaviors—bingeing and purging 20 or more times per day—that they have little or no ability to perform on the job or in school and have marked difficulty with relationships.

People with bulimia are almost always distressed by their behaviors and simultaneously amazed, surprised, and even horrified at their inability to control them. In contrast to those with anorexia, individuals with bulimia most often talk as though they were not in control of it, as if they were possessed by something or had an evil twin. They are alarmed at the things they hear themselves saying or what they have written. It is not uncommon to hear statements such as "I feel that there is a monster inside of me" or "I tell myself not to binge, but something comes over me and I can't help myself."

People with bulimia often appear more motivated entering treatment than those with anorexia because they feel out of control, taken over, and even possessed and want help getting back in control. However their motivation may be generated only by the desire to become better at dieting or controlling their weight. People who focus on bingeing as the root of their problem—the thing to be ashamed of and to control—commonly express a strong desire to stop bingeing but a reluctance to give up restrictive eating. So they continue to assert their efforts to overcontrol their eating, thus setting themselves up again for a binge. Although most people now know what bulimia nervosa is, few ever realize its life-consuming devastation.

Signs of Binge Eating Disorder

Individuals who binge eat and do not resort to some form of purging or restriction fall under a different category known as binge eating disorder (BED). Binge eating has certainly been around for centuries. The case of Laura published in 1949 was a dramatic description of this disorder (Linder 1955). Binge eating was observed and reported in studies on obesity in the late 1950s by Dr. Albert Stunkard of the University of Pennsylvania. In the 1980s, additional studies on obesity and bulimia nervosa showed that many people in both populations have binge eating problems without the other criteria for bulimia nervosa and therefore should come under a separate category since these individuals were different from those who compensate for the bingeing. In the past, these individuals were often referred to as compulsive overeaters, emotional overeaters, or food addicts. Originally a research group headed by Dr. Robert Spitzer of Columbia University proposed that a new disorder called "pathological overeating syndrome" be used to describe individuals who binge eat without engaging in behaviors such as fasting or some form of purging to lose weight. It was also important to distinguish them from obese individuals who did not binge. Obesity is a medical condition and not a psychiatric diagnosis. Finally, in 1992, the term *binge eating disorder* was officially introduced in the *International Journal of Eating Disorders* (Robert Spitzer 1992). In 1994, the term was included in the *DSM IV.*

Although the research is scarce, it suggests that approximately one-fifth to one-third of the people who present for the treatment of obesity meet the criteria for BED. In the *DSM-IV TR*, binge eating disorder is not officially recognized as a separate eating disorder but is included as one of a number of syndromes in the category "Eating Disorder Not Otherwise Specified," which will be discussed later. However, BED is also listed in *DSM-IV TR* in a category for proposed diagnoses and includes diagnostic criteria to aid further study.

Binge eating is described as part of the diagnostic criteria for bulimia nervosa, but it is the central feature in BED. The binge eating patterns in BED are longer than those found in bulimia; binges can last entire days as opposed to hours and the bingeing needs to have existed for six months or more instead of the three months required for bulimia.

Distinguishing people who overeat from people with binge eating disorder is like distinguishing dieting from anorexia; it is a matter of definition and degree. The criteria in the sidebar help determine when someone has crossed the line into BED.

The following is an excerpt from the diary of a person with binge eating disorder:

> When I start eating, I can't stop. I don't know when I'm hungry or when I'm full anymore. I really don't know; I can't remember what it was like to know. Once I start, I just keep eating until I literally can't take another bite.

DSM-IV TR Research Criteria for Binge Eating Disorder

A. Recurrent episodes of binge eating. An episode of binge eating is characterized by both of the following:
   1. eating, in a discrete period of time (e.g., within any 2-hour period), an amount of food that is definitely larger than most people would

eat in a similar period of time under similar circumstances

2. a sense of lack of control over eating during the episode (e.g., a feeling that one cannot stop eating or control what or how much one is eating).

B. The binge eating episodes are associated with three (or more) of the following:
   1. eating much more rapidly than normal
   2. eating until feeling uncomfortably full
   3. eating large amounts of food when not feeling physically hungry
   4. eating alone because of being embarrassed by how much one is eating
   5. feeling disgusted with oneself, depressed, or very guilty after overeating

C. Marked distress regarding binge eating is present.

D. The binge eating occurs, on average, at least 2 days a week for 6 months.
   Note: The method of determining frequency differs from that used for bulimia nervosa; future research should address whether the preferred method of setting a frequency threshold is counting the number of days on which binges occur or counting the number of episodes of binge eating.

E. The binge eating is not associated with the regular use of inappropriate compensatory behaviors (e.g., purging, fasting, excessive exercise) and does not occur exclusively during the course of Anorexia Nervosa or Bulimia Nervosa.

Many of these people suffer from debilitating eating patterns often cued by the need for self-soothing rather than by physiological cues. Such patterns usually, but not always, produce weight gain and even obesity, a symptom upon which physicians, dietitians, and other health professionals often focus their attention, without inquiring about possible binge eating patterns or overeating as a form of psychological self-medication. However, it is also very important to emphasize that being overweight or even obese is not enough to warrant the diagnosis of BED. There are a variety of causes for obesity. Some overweight individuals graze on food all day long or eat high-calorie foods but do not binge. Researchers in weight control and obesity are increasingly discovering evidence that biological predispositions may also play a role.

Some professionals are of the opinion that there are two distinct subcategories of binge eating: deprivation-sensitive binge eating and addictive or dissociative binge eating. The deprivation-sensitive category appears to be the result of weight-loss diets or periods of restrictive eating, both of which can lead to binge eating episodes. However, the addictive or dissociative category is related to self-medication or self-soothing rather than a reaction to prior restricting. Such individuals may report feelings of numbness, dissociation, calmness, or a return of inner equilibrium after binge eating.

BED treatment focuses on binge eating, compulsivity with food, an inability to control food intake, and the use of food as a method of coping with anxiety or other underlying issues and dieting or deprivation which leads to bingeing. Weight loss in the treatment of BED is a very touchy and difficult issue, and attempts to lose weight before resolving any contributory psychological, emotional, or relational issues will most likely result in failure. Eating disorder therapists often shy away from any discussion of weight loss as a goal, having been sensitized to this danger by years of working with individuals with anorexia and bulimia for whom the goal is to get the focus off weight. Professionals are also worried about sounding like they are weight prejudiced or creating bulimia or anorexia in clients with BED. These are important issues to consider but so is weight loss for people whose health is in jeopardy. An experienced and sensitive clinician has to negotiate these difficult nuances with each individual. To date, most studies that report successful treatment of BED are unsuccessful in the area of weight loss.

More research is necessary to understand this illness, find proper treatments, and prevent the ongoing inappropriate treatment of binge eating disorders solely with weight-loss diets and exercise programs. These types of recommendations may exacerbate the disorder and tragically fail clients who need more extensive help to recover.

Eating Disorders Not Otherwise Specified

Aside from BED, there are several other variants of disordered eating that do not meet the diagnostic criteria for anorexia nervosa or bulimia nervosa but nevertheless require treatment. *DSM-IV TR* places these atypical eating disorders in a category commonly referred to as EDNOS, or Eating Disorders Not Otherwise Specified. In this category are syndromes that resemble anorexia nervosa or bulimia nervosa but fall short of an essential feature or symptom duration, thus precluding either diagnosis. Also in this category are eating disorders that may present quite differently from anorexia nervosa or bulimia nervosa, such as BED. The diagnosis of EDNOS is used as a kind of catchall category.

According to several sources, roughly one-third of those who present for treatment of an eating disorder fall into the EDNOS category. In fact, the current estimates reported at several eating disorder conferences I attended in 2005 and 2006 are even higher. Unfortunately, as noted earlier, a diagnosis of EDNOS is insufficient to obtain insurance coverage under many circumstances, and, as a result, most cases of EDNOS are still undertreated and underappreciated. Even though they don't meet the full diagnostic criteria for one of the major eating disorders, individuals with EDNOS need help.

DSM-IV TR V Diagnostic Criteria for 307.50 Eating Disorder Not Otherwise Specified

The Eating Disorder Not Otherwise Specified category is for disorders of eating that do not meet the criteria for any specific Eating Disorder. Examples include:

1. For females, all of the criteria for Anorexia Nervosa are met except that the individual has regular menses.
2. All of the criteria for Anorexia Nervosa are met except that, despite significant weight loss, the individual's current weight is in the normal range.
3. All of the criteria for Bulimia Nervosa are met except that the binge eating and inappropriate compensatory mechanisms occur at a frequency of less than twice a week or for a duration of less than 3 months.
4. The regular use of inappropriate compensatory behavior by an individual of normal body weight after eating small amounts of food (e.g., self-induces vomiting after the consumption of two cookies).
5. Repeatedly chewing and spitting out, but not swallowing, large amounts of food.
6. Binge-eating disorder: recurrent episodes of binge eating in the absence of the regular use of inappropriate compensatory behaviors characteristic of Bulimia Nervosa.

What *DSM IV TR* Can't Tell You: The Inner World of an Eating Disorder

Diagnostic descriptions and criteria are important, but to truly understand the inner world and life of a person with an eating disorder, one must hear directly from that person. I ask all my clients to write an essay titled "My Worst Eating Disorder Day." I am continually shaken by their accounts. The client in the following example has anorexia nervosa, binge/purge type, and exercise addiction (which I will discuss further in Chapter 3); therefore, I chose her essay because she exhibits symptoms associated with all of the disorders.

Assignment: Worst Eating Disorder Day

> I have a hard time remembering a worst day. Toward the end, all of my days were about the same, so I will just pick a recent memory. Friday I went out with people from work for happy hour. We went to a Mexican restaurant. After a couple of beers and just a few chips, I became so hungry for what the others were eating—nachos, lots of chips, and salsa—that I gave in. I knew all I had to do was go home and throw up, so go ahead and enjoy.
>
> When happy hour was over, I immediately went to the grocery store. Since I was going to bring up what I had eaten, I might as well eat more. I bought goodies and went home to "indulge." Oh, what tasty food. But as I got fuller and fuller, I realized what I had to do. I vomited thoroughly for about 10 minutes. After each "session," I felt better and better. I continued to eat and vomit for a long time, periodically weighing myself. Usually at night on a Friday, I would take five or so Benedryl and some other type of medication so

that I could sleep through as much as possible of the next day . . . if I was asleep, I couldn't eat. Plus, there were fewer hours the next day to be tormented by food issues. But since I was vomiting, I decided not to take more than a few sleeping aids.

The next morning I got up after about 10 hours of sleep and immediately weighed myself—I had lost five pounds. I felt so good. I had enjoyed food and did not gain weight from it! So the next step to survive the day and be productive at work was to exercise. I ate an energy bar and began. First, floor exercises. Next I went out for a run, wanting to run two and a half hours. When I started out, I seemed out of balance. I would run a few steps then become uncoordinated. I had experienced this many mornings before, but this time it didn't seem to go away as fast, but after the first 30 to 40 minutes, things started to stabilize. After an hour and a half, I had to slow down, as I started becoming weak. No matter what, I had to keep going. I felt bad then but knew how good I'd feel later. This was always my way of pushing myself more. If I stopped, the rest of the day would be ruined. I wouldn't be productive. And what would I stop at tomorrow, and the next day? No, I couldn't let myself wimp out and start a "giving in" cycle.

Eventually, after two and a half hours, I was running so slow that I couldn't get my heart rate up, so I had to stop and do another aerobic activity. I got on my eclipse machine and started to exercise. At first my legs were so weak and hurting that I had to take breaks every couple of minutes for the first 10 minutes. I was getting madder and madder, realizing the more I gave in the more determined I was to exercise longer. I hit the three-hour mark. But since I wimped out so much at first, I needed to exercise a few more minutes.

Once I hit the three-hour mark, I started calculating that if I exercised on the eclipse about 15 more minutes I would be at three and a half hours. Next I took a diet pill so it would start working before I finished my whole exercise routine. I finished up with some weights and more floor exercise, ending at the four-hour mark. The whole time I was looking forward to going to the salad bar and getting a salad, without dressing, as now that I had exercised I could enjoy it without feeling guilty. Sometimes after exercising I would be beyond the point of feeling. I didn't allow myself to feel pain, as this might be a catalyst to stopping, something I was not going to tolerate. I showered and headed out the door, grabbing a diet drink. I got the salad take-out so I could eat it all evening long (over a period of time, not all those calories at once) as well as buying a six-pack of 20-ounce diet drinks. This would give me seven to have at work. If I became hungry, I would allow myself a few crackers. If those didn't work, I would take more diet pills.

I was always exercising to the last minute then quickly putting on limited makeup and driving like hell to get to work on time, often speeding at 60 in a 35-mile-an-hour zone. Then as time went on, I took the makeup in the car with me so I could put it on driving or when at lights. That allowed me to exercise those five minutes longer. Then it got to the point I just quit putting on makeup. I would work out to the last minute and throw on my clothes, often buttoning the blouse on the way into the car or when I started down the street (driving my car with my knee so I could fasten the buttons).

Often I would see blood in my vomit either from vomiting, period, or from cuts I had created in my throat from my fingernails. So I decided to cut the nail on the finger I "needed" to at least decrease the blood from that. When the burning in my chest got bad, I started finishing off the binge with frozen yogurt. That way I would have a coating as it came back up. Once in a while I would go out with someone to eat (maybe two times per month), but I made sure I was back home within one hour so I could vomit up what I had eaten. At night I would often sleep only a few hours before waking up hungry. So I would get up, weigh myself, and then decide if I could get a few crackers.

Toward the end of the weeks before coming to Monte Nido, I remember saying, "I am just existing. I am trapped in a prison I can't get out of." And the only thing slowing me down was that my body was beginning to wear down with no reserves.

Eating Disorder Statistics: How Common Is the Problem?

Citing several sources, the National Eating Disorder Association reports on its website that in the United States, as many as 10 million females and 1 million males are fighting a life-and-death battle with an eating disorder such as anorexia or bulimia, more than those suffering from HIV/AIDS. Even though these are alarming statistics, many people with eating disorders may not classify as officially recognized cases and therefore are not included in the studies, for example, people who suffer from various forms of EDNOS. We are a society of EDNOSs. Being a female in America seems synonymous with being on a diet, and the dieting has become more severe and more entrenched, starting at younger ages. Dieting is also considered a major risk factor for developing disordered eating and eating disorders, so we need to continue to look at body image dissatisfaction and dieting behavior in our society and to work on the prevention of eating disorders from this angle.

To understand how common fully diagnosible eating disorders are, researchers look at prevalence and incidence. *Prevalence* means how many people, out of 100,000, in a given population, have the disorder. *Incidence* means how many new cases are developed in a given time period. Definitive statistics on the prevalence and incidence of eating disorders are impossible to come by and the existing research provides conflicting data. In reviewing various sources, I ended up far more confused than before I started. The research is beset with problems in sampling, methods, assessment, definitions of key terms, and reporting.

The first epidemiological study on bulimia was not conducted until 1981. In one study that looked for cases of bulimia nervosa (Whitehouse et al. 1992), it was "found that 50 percent of the cases of BN determined in the community were unknown to their general practitioners, despite referrals made for complications of bulimic pathology in half of these hidden cases." Eating disorders are thought to be underreported, because of the fear and shame connected with these disorders, as well as the lack of resources. Many studies deal with people who are in treatment, although treated cases represent a minority of all sufferers. Other studies using population screening are flawed because of poor response rate, a lack of sensitivity in screening instruments, and inappropriate sample sizes.

The most consistent overall finding is that the rate of anorexia nervosa is much higher in adolescent girls than in any other segment of the population. It also appears that the incidence of eating disorders (especially bulimia nervosa and EDNOS) is increasing in other countries; in all areas of the population, including minorities; and in other age groups. A review of all the studies in Keel and Klump (2003) and Gordon (2000), points to an increase in the incidence of anorexia all over the world especially between 1970 and 1985.

Prevalence rates for anorexia are still hard to come by. The most widely cited estimate is from a study conducted in the 1970s by Arthur Crisp in England citing one case of anorexia for every 150 to 200 adolescent girls (Crisp 1976), which is consistent with studies of American college students. As Gordon (2000) points out in his discussion of prevalence, this would mean that in America we would have approximately 120,000 cases of clinical anorexia, which may not seem like much until severity and lethality is taken into account for what would otherwise be healthy young girls.

A study with a thorough methodology and a high degree of credibility that was conducted by Dr. Alexander Lucas, a psychiatrist at the Mayo Clinic in Minnesota, found that the overall prevalence for anorexia nervosa was 306 per 100,000 for females and 22 per 100,000 for males. The Lucas study took place over a 50-year period from 1935 to 1985 and used records from the Mayo Clinic and the surrounding community of Rochester, Minnesota. As for incidence rates, for females 10 to 19 years old, the incidence rate of anorexia from 1935 to 1939 was relatively high but fell to a low in the 1950s, began to increase in the 1960s, and rose to a peak in the 1980s. The incidence for females between the ages of 20 and 59 remained more for less stable. It is interesting to note that on the average the incidence rate increased by 35 percent for every five-year period beginning in 1950 and ending in 1984 with a sharp increase in cases from 1980 to 1984. Lucas suggests that changing trends in fashion over the 50 years may account for the somewhat cyclical incidence of anorexia nervosa.

Studies on bulimia nervosa suggest a significant increase in this disorder since the 1970s. In his book, *Eating Disorders: Anatomy of a Social Epidemic*, Richard Gordon says, " . . . the sudden ascendancy of bulimic syndromes seems nothing short of spectacular." Evidence suggests that bulimia was becoming common on college campuses as early as the mid-1970s, and clients were being treated in significant numbers when Gerald Russell wrote his seminal paper on this syndrome in 1979. Over the last three decades studies on the prevalence of this disorder have varied indicating it to be anywhere from 2 to 7 percent of the populations studied. As mentioned earlier, data on bulimia are fraught with problems. Also, the definition of bulimia nervosa is vague and has changed over time. Nevertheless, all of the research I pored over, including that from Keel and Klump (2003), suggests a significant increase in the rate of bulimia over time. It is interesting to note that this increase coincides with the increasing idealization of thinness during this period.

The epidemiological patterns that emerge on anorexia and bulimia suggest evidence for an increase of both eating disorders in the United States and other cultures. However, modern western culture may play a more central role in the etiology of bulimia compared to anorexia. Several studies indicate the incidence of bulimia nervosa to be as much as three to five times higher in urbanized areas and cities than in rural areas, whereas rates of anorexia nervosa seem to be independent of urbanization (Brewerton 2004 and Keal 2005). As mentioned earlier, this suggests to some that the development of bulimia is affected more by cultural ideals or norms. In other words, bulimia is not found in individuals with no exposure to western ideals, such as the idealization of thinness. As for anorexia, however, it is interesting to note that both historically and in other cultures, there are some cases in which refusal of food is reported to be motivated by factors other than weight loss (Bell 1985 and Lee 1991, 1993). However, in other cultures, clients with eating disorders who deny a desire for weight loss as a factor might not be telling the truth about this.

Prevalence and incidence rates for BED and other eating problems that do not fit neatly into the category of anorexia or bulimia are not often studied and are hard to come by. Brewerton (2004) tentatively reported a prevalence rate of 1 percent and stated that there was not enough incidence information to summarize. Keel (2005) reported that BED affects 0.7 to 4.0 percent of community samples, and more women than men have it. For example, in weight control programs where BED is often found, women with BED outnumber men by 1.5 times, and in other community samples, the ratio of women to men with BED is closer to 60:40. However, this is a far cry from the disparity seen in the ratio of women to men with anorexia and bulimia. In his book, Gordon (2003) discusses studies that have shown prevalence rates for these subclinical eating disorders is as high as 13 percent. These and other studies support a spectrum notion for eating disorder behaviors that we must be keep in mind.

Can People with Eating Disorders Fully Recover?

Eating disorder clients can recover fully. However, clinicians, clients, and loved ones must understand that full recovery can take many years and that it is not possible to predict at the outset of treatment who will be successful. The field is currently struggling with recovery definitions. For example, what exactly does it mean to say someone is fully recovered? Does it mean, not meeting the *DSM-IV* criteria or complete absence of any symptoms and, if so, for how long? As yet, we have not come up with any definitive answers. Some believe that people with eating disorders can never be recovered but can be in remission, similar to recovering alcoholics. Even though this may apply to some individuals, it is ludicrous to lump everyone into this category because we know there are countless people, like myself, who are recovered from their eating disorder and have been for many years. (See more about "Recovered Versus Recovering" in Chapter 8.)

The following features may improve a client's chance of full recovery: early onset of the illness (if treatment is sought without delay upon diagnosis), early intervention, fewer simultaneous or "comorbid" psychological diagnoses, infrequent or no purging behavior, and supportive families or loved ones.

Most medical consequences of eating disorders are reversible, but some conditions may be permanent, including osteoporosis, endocrine abnormalities, ovarian failure, and obviously death. In regard to death rates, anorexia nervosa, bulimia nervosa, and certainly ENDOS are rarely listed on death certificates. Physicians are more likely to attribute cause of death to heart failure or some other medical issue even though the eating disorder caused the heart to fail. This makes it almost impossible to determine death rates associated with these disorders. I know of parents who have fought to have anorexia nervosa or bulimia nervosa listed on their daughters' death certificates. Some have won this battle; others have not. Family organizations such as the National Eating Disorder Association's Parent Family Network (PFN) are actively trying to remedy this situation.

Anorexia Nervosa Outcomes

The mortality rate for anorexia nervosa is reported to be higher than that for any other psychiatric disorder. Early studies reported starvation as the leading cause of death, whereas more recent research has identified suicide as the leading cause (Nielsen, et al 1998). However, the conclusion that suicide has overtaken starvation as the chief cause of death may be misleading. First, early intervention may be decreasing the percentage of starvation-related deaths by keeping weights higher. Second, the diagnostic criteria for anorexia decreased from 25 percent to 15 percent of expected weight, thereby significantly increasing the number of diagnosable individuals who are closer to normal weight and less likely to die from starvation.

The original American Psychiatric Association guidelines for the treatment of eating disorders reported that 44 percent of hospitalized populations of individuals with anorexia have "good" outcomes (i.e., weight was restored to within 15 percent of recommended weight and menstruation was regular) four years after the onset of illness. "Poor" outcomes were reported for 24 percent, whose weight never approached 15 percent of that recommended and whose menstruation remained absent or sporadic. "Intermediate" outcomes, somewhere between those of the good and poor groups, were reported for the remaining 28 percent. A survey of recovery rates in various studies throughout the 20th century (Steinhausen 2002) reported that approximately 46 percent of patients recover, 33 percent improve, and 20 percent remain ill.

Other noteworthy findings from various sources, including Strober 1997 and Keel 2005, include the following:

- Recovery time is lengthened significantly among patients with disturbances in family relationships. Long-term prognosis may have more to do with developmental aspects and relationships than was previously thought.
- When full recovery includes complete remission of all diagnostic features of the illness, average recovery time takes 20 months longer.

- Relapse after full clinical recovery (not just weight) is relatively uncommon, while nearly 30 percent of the patients discharged from a treatment program prior to clinical recovery have relapses.
- A compulsive drive to exercise present at the time of discharge is a predictor of a long-term chronic illness and a poor outcome.
- Being asocial prior to the eating disorder is a statistically significant predictor of poor outcome. This has also been linked with poorer outcomes in other studies (Strober 1977, Hsu 1991).

These findings may be useful when presenting the case to families and insurers that a client should stay in treatment for a longer period of time to focus on reducing compulsions to exercise and improving family and social relationships prior to discharge.

Bulimia Nervosa Outcomes

Although bulimia nervosa can take a lengthy, costly, and damaging course, a review of the current data indicates that death rates for this illness do not appear to be high. Suicide attempts are as common in bulimia as in anorexia but appear to result in death less often. This may be explained by speculation that individuals with anorexia may be more physically compromised and are therefore less able to survive suicide attempts or that people with bulimia make less serious attempts.

Combining results of various studies (Keel and Mitchell 1997), it appears that approximately 50 percent of patients with bulimia nervosa recover, 30 percent improve, and 20 percent continue to meet full diagnostic criteria. However, long-term follow-up of individuals with bulimia indicates that after 10 years only 10 percent will continue to meet the full criteria for the disorder.

These findings support the conclusion that anorexia nervosa and bulimia nervosa are illnesses from which one can recover, but the length of time needed for recovery may be as long as 10 years. Further research is critical if we are to improve these recovery rates.

Binge Eating Disorder Outcomes

Since BED was only introduced into *DSM-IV* in 1994, long-term outcome studies are scarce. At the time of this writing, there were two studies with durations of five or more years. These two studies indicate that, like bulimia and anorexia, individuals who have BED can recover over time. Continuing research on binge eating disorder will provide further data and additional insight into this syndrome.

Eating Disorders and Other Coexisting Diagnoses

Eating disorder clients (and/or their family members) are often diagnosed with other psychiatric syndromes—particularly affective, anxiety, obsessive-compulsive, and substance use disorders. To better understand and treat eating disorders, one needs a knowledge of and skills for treating these preexisting and coexisting (comorbid) disorders.

The comorbid condition may either have a causal relation to or become exacerbated by the eating disorder. In terms of discussing causal relationships, comorbid disorders of any type develop in one of two ways. Either one disorder precedes the other and is therefore assigned a portion of the "blame," or they both develop in response to some third independent factor. For example, some people may have developed an eating disorder at least partially as a coping mechanism in response to their depression or another disorder, while others are depressed because they can't control their eating disorder. Sometimes it is too difficult to tell if there is a truly separate comorbid disorder until weight has been restored or until other eating disorder symptoms and behaviors have subsided. In either case, these conditions have to be taken into account and treated. Although the scope of this book cannot include specific recommendations, the following sections can help identify common comorbid conditions.

Eating Disorders and Affective (Mood) Disorders

The relationship between eating and affective disorders has been studied intensively, and the resulting body of evidence suggests that comorbid depression exists in a high proportion (approximately 50 percent) of individuals seeking treatment for anorexia nervosa, bulimia nervosa, and binge eating disorder. Research reveals that the eating disorder more often precedes the depression and that eating and depressive disorders are not manifestations of a common underlying genetic vulnerability.

Seasonal affective disorder (SAD) has received increased attention in the field of eating disorders, particularly in regard to bulimia nervosa. Clients with SAD demonstrate bulimic-like symptomology (problems with eating, weight, mood, and sleep) and vice versa. Neurobiological factors recently implicated in the development of SAD and other depressive disorders such as serotonin dysfunction may be involved, and light therapy has shown some efficacy in the treatment of patients with SAD and bulimia nervosa.

Eating Disorders and Anxiety Disorders

Brewerton (2004) reported that various studies indicate a lifetime prevalence of anxiety disorders in approximately one-third to two-thirds of individuals with anorexia or bulimia. Two anxiety disorders in particular, obsessive-compulsive disorder (OCD) and social phobia commonly occur with anorexia and bulimia. Studies have shown anywhere from 10 to 66 percent of clinical samples with clients who have anorexia also have OCD, and one-fourth to a little more than one-half have social phobia. The rates for bulimia sufferers are similar, with OCD occurring a little less frequently. Treating OCD and/or social phobia, whether they are the cause or the result of the eating disorder, is important for recovery to occur.

Another anxiety disorder, post-traumatic stress disorder (PTSD), has also been associated with eating disorders and sexual abuse. This is discussed in the next section.

Sexual Abuse, Trauma, and Eating Disorders

Early research looked for a cause-and-effect relationship between sexual abuse and eating disorders; however, the interaction of multiple factors and variables made such an approach too simplistic. For someone who was sexually abused as a child, the nature and severity of the abuse, the functioning of the child prior to the abuse, and the response to the abuse all contribute to whether this individual will develop an eating disorder or an alternative means of coping. Other influences are nearly always present, and although searching for a clear causal relationship is like searching with blinders on, it is equally absurd to say that because the sexual abuse is not the only factor, it is not a factor at all.

Well-designed national studies by Dansky et al. (1997), Brewerton et al. (1999), Fairburn et al. (1997), Wonderlich et al. (1997), and others have supported the idea that childhood sexual abuse (CSA) and other forms of victimization are risk factors for the development of bulimic pathology among women. A number of additional studies, all reported by Brewerton (2004), support these findings. Clinicians across the country have encountered countless clients who describe and interpret their eating disorder symptoms as being connected to early sexual abuse or other victimization. People with anorexia have described starving and weight loss as a way of trying to avoid sexuality and thus evade or escape sexual drive, sexual feelings, or the attention of potential perpetrators. People with bulimia have described their symptoms as a way of purging the perpetrator, raging at the violator or themselves, and getting rid of the filth or dirtiness inside of them. Binge eaters have suggested that overeating numbs their feelings, distracts them from other bodily sensations, and results in weight gain that "armors" them and keeps them unattractive to potential sexual partners or victimizers.

Histories of sexual trauma and/or abuse exist in the eating disorder population, especially among those who have had PTSD and those with purging behavior. When working with someone suffering from an eating disorder, it is necessary to inquire about and explore any abuse history and to discover its meaning and significance, along with other factors contributing to the development of disordered eating or exercise behaviors. The area of trauma and abuse is so prevalent in eating disorders and the topic so broad, that readers should refer to other books in this area for further information and understanding. See *Sexual Abuse and Eating Disorders*, Schwarz and Cohn (1996) and *The Trauma Model*, Ross (2000).

Eating Disorders and Substance Use Disorders

Substance use disorders and bulimia frequently co-occur within individuals and within families, but recent research indicates that these conditions do not share the same genetic vulnerability. It has also become clear that disorders that include bingeing and purging, regardless of diagnosis, are associated with higher levels of substance use disorders, whereas restricting anorexia is not. One review estimates that approximately 24 percent of individuals with bulimia experience alcohol abuse or dependence. Although alcohol use in anorexia is not as common, this combination results in the highest death rate.

In the last 10 years, I have seen an increasing number of clients with anorexia and bulimia enter treatment with a comorbid substance abuse problem that involves stimulants. Drugs such as cocaine and methamphetamine are increasingly used to curtail appetite and lose weight rather than to get high. Drug treatment programs often miss this fact. Celebrities who have obvious eating disorders are unfortunately ending up in drug rehab for this reason and because it is more acceptable to have a drug problem than an eating disorder.

Stimulant use is not new. Throughout my career I have seen clients with anorexia and bulimia use over-the-counter agents such as diet pills, No Doz, or caffeine pills. What is new is the growing number of individuals who use prescription drugs for this purpose. People are getting doctors to prescribe attention deficit disorder medications such as Ritalin or Dexedrine and using these medications improperly, even snorting them for their appetite-suppressant and weight-loss effects. Some of these people actually have attention deficit problems but abuse their medication and/or lie about the side effects. Others lie to doctors about having attention problems in order to get these medications for weight loss. Furthermore, some clients buy these drugs from other individuals who are being prescribed the medication but choose to sell it to the ever growing market.

Eating Disorders and Self-Harm

Although self-harm (also known as self-injury) is not a *DSM-IV* category but rather a behavior occurring in individuals with varying diagnoses, it is important to list here because of the prevalence of self-injury in the eating disorder population. One study found that in a sample of self-injurers, 61 percent reported a current or past eating disorder (Conterio and Ladder 1998). Eating disorder clients in general have a unique relationship to self-harm, as their behaviors can be viewed in that light. Self-injurious behavior (SIB) involves the deliberate infliction of direct physical harm to one's own body, without the intent to die as a result of the behavior itself (Simeon and Hollander 2001). However, it appears that the subgroup of eating disorder clients who self-injure (e.g., cut, burn, or scratch themselves) may be different from those who do not. The prevalence and seriousness of this behavior makes this another area that clinicians who treat eating disorders should be aware of and trained in. For more information on this topic, readers are referred to *Self Harm Behavior and Eating Disorders* (Levitt et al. 2004) and *Cutting* (Levenkron 1998).

An important note: Most of our knowledge and understanding of eating disorders comes from information gathered on young, white females diagnosed with these illnesses. Anytime that data are collected on a small subsample of the general population, even if that is the group in which it is assumed to be most prevalent, we should be cautious. Furthermore, our assumption about who suffers from these disorders is changing. I am treating more clients who are younger and older than ever before. My treatment programs are serving an increasingly international and multicultural population. All ages, non-Caucasians, and both genders develop eating disorders, and in many cases, these numbers are increasing. Therefore, we must continue to expand and broaden our own scope and understanding, as we will discuss in the next chapter.

2

Young, White, and Female: Myth or Reality?

It is generally assumed that the problem of eating disorders is primarily an issue for young, white females. Appearance, weight, and dieting seem to be predominately female preoccupations, and young, white girls and women are the focus of magazine articles, television shows, movies, and books dealing with eating disorders. But things are not necessarily as they appear.

Eating disorders are on the rise in various populations. The problem is not getting better, it is getting worse. First, the more body dissatisfaction people have, the more eating disorders we will have—case closed. Second, people are more knowledgeable about eating disorders and more likely to recognize the signs and symptoms and to seek help, which is more readily available with the growing number of treatment programs. Furthermore, historically, once an illness is identified and the public is educated about it, it appears that people are more likely to develop it, though the exact reason for this is undetermined.

Considering Ethnicity

The effects of rapid globalization have made eating disorders a worldwide condition increasingly prevalent within various cultural groups. Clinical eating disorders, poor body image, severe dieting, and preoccupation with weight are no longer restricted to certain high-risk groups in limited geographic locales. The spectrum of body image and eating problems appears in every economic, racial, and ethnic stratum of American culture and in at least 40 countries worldwide, including places as unlikely as China, India, Mexico, Nigeria, South Africa, South Korea, and the former Soviet Union (Gordon 2000). Even though we now know more about the diversity of eating disorders, race, age, and gender still influence the likelihood of one being recognized and treated. In one study, college students were given a scenario of a 16-year-old girl's eating and exercise over a five-day period. "When Mary was depicted as white, 93 percent of the participants recorded that she had an eating disorder. When she was depicted as either African American or Hispanic, only 79 percent of participants recognized an eating disorder" (Keel 2005).

Some acknowledge that eating disorders are found in all ethnicities but continue to believe that such cases are rare. Many think that African American women are "protected" from getting anorexia and bulimia because their body ideal is heavier and more voluptuous. Indeed, studies show that these women have less body image dissatisfaction and disordered eating and a greater acceptance of higher weights than white women, along with fewer reported cases of anorexia and bulimia nervosa. However, binge eating disorder rates for this population seem to be close to or the same as for Caucasians, and obesity with its complications (e.g., high blood pressure, diabetes) is also a major problem.

Hispanic females, on the other hand, seem to have eating disorder rates equal to whites, and for Hispanic females, acculturation to U.S. values is associated with higher levels of eating pathology. Native American populations appear to have high rates of disordered eating and obesity and to engage in extreme measures to try to control weight. The findings on Asian females with eating disorders appear to be mixed. More research is needed in all of these areas, but clearly in the United States ethnic minorities do get eating disorders, some at the same rate as whites. Historical and cross-cultural experiences suggest that cultural change itself may be associated with increased vulnerability to eating disorders, especially when values about physical aesthetics and gender roles are involved. This may happen when an immigrant moves to a new culture or a given culture changes over time. (Westernization as an eating disorder risk factor is discussed further in Chapter 4).

Does Age Play a Factor?

I used to have mothers calling me about treatment for their daughters; now I get calls from daughters seeking treatment for their mothers. Eating disorders in midlife is a growing area of concern. According to one treatment program, in the last few years cases of women over 30 seeking treatment for an eating disorder have increased 400 percent. Most treatment programs, including mine, Monte Nido (see Chapter 15), report increasing numbers of women in their 30s, 40s, and 50s seeking treatment for eating disorders. Margo Maine and Joe Kelly discuss this phenomenon in their excellent book *The Body Myth* (2005).

Hard data on eating disorders in adult women are limited, but we have compelling information about the extent of dieting and body image concerns, both of which can be precursors to clinical eating disorders. The following are examples:

- Body image dissatisfaction in midlife has increased dramatically, more than doubling from 25 percent in 1972 to 56 percent in 1997.
- When asked what bothered them most about their bodies, a group of women aged 61 to 92 identified weight as their greatest concern.
- Sixty percent of adult women have engaged in pathogenic weight control; 40 percent are restrained eaters; 40 percent are overeaters; only 20 percent are instinctive eaters; and more than 90 percent worry about their weight.

Some issues differ for older women in treatment. Treatment providers should be attuned to the issues of menopause, empty nest syndrome, divorce, and the realities of aging in youth-oriented cultures. Also, some issues such as the following get in the way of older women seeking treatment:

- Thinking that an eating disorder is only a "young person's illness"
- Not being properly diagnosed
- Having an insurance company that does not take the condition seriously
- Having children or husbands to care for at home

Some suggest that women in midlife need their own treatment programs, but I think this is unnecessary because time and again I see younger female clients benefiting from the older ones and vice versa. At both Monte Nido and my day treatment program, the Eating Disorder Center of California, I have been able to successfully mix older teens, young adults, and mature women. As long as extensive individual therapy is provided in a treatment setting (which it should be), individual issues can be addressed.

Is Anyone Too Young for an Eating Disorder?

In December 2005, *Newsweek* devoted a cover story to the issue of children and eating disorders. Recently, I took three calls in the same week from different mothers seeking treatment for an 8-year-old, a 9-year-old, and a 12-year-old. In the last 10 years, several programs specifically geared for young children have been established in response to the growing need. Specialty programs are important for young children to avoid exposing them to a possibly sicker and more chronic population, to address their developmental needs, and because parental involvement needs to be far more intensive. Assessments have been developed specifically for children and there is an increasingly amount of literature on this subject. For an excellent book on understanding and treating eating disorders in children, readers should see *Anorexia Nervosa and Related Disorders in Childhood and Adolescence*, edited by Bryan D. Lask and Rachel Bryant-Waugh (2000).

It is not surprising that eating disorders are happening at younger and younger ages. Four-, five-, and six-year-olds are repeatedly exposed to thin idealization and fear of fat through print, television, movies, and the Internet combined with witnessing their own mothers, sisters, or friends dieting to lose weight. Young girls are indoctrinated into the cult of thinness. My own six-year-old niece, at a normal weight for her age, came home from school and complained of being too fat because her tummy stuck out too much and asked to go on a diet like her friend, who was also normal weight. In my book *Your Dieting Daughter* (1996), I discuss the problem of our dieting youth, of trying to raise or care for a child in this current cultural climate where desiring and striving for thinness is almost a required part of being female. When a six-year-old girl in my waiting room boasts about having the chicken pox because it meant she got to go to bed without dinner, thus no calories, we are all in trouble, and our youngest are not unscathed.

Examining Gender

I have treated fathers; brothers; sports figures; stockbrokers; and gay, straight, old, and young men with eating disorders. Among the first well-documented accounts of anorexia nervosa, reported in the 1600s by Dr. Richard Morton and in the 1800s by the British physician Sir William Gull, are cases of males suffering from the disorder (Keel 2005). However, eating disorders have "the most lopsided sex ratio of any disorder known to psychiatry" (Gordon 2000) and thus eating disorders in males have been overlooked, understudied, and underreported.

Binge eating disorder is found in men more often than any of the other eating disorders; some suggest that approximately 40 percent of cases are male (Keel 2005). The number of males suffering from anorexia and bulimia (5 to 10 percent of cases) is far less than that of females (90 to 95 percent of cases). Not only do females identified with anorexia and bulimia outnumber males by a large margin, but gender issues such as homosexuality or bisexuality are also prevalent in reported cases involving males. Definitive explanations for this phenomenon are not available, but sociocultural influences, such as what males find sexually appealing, appear to play a much bigger role than biological ones. In this regard, as is the case for females, body dissatisfaction is associated with increased levels of disordered eating. When there is more body dissatisfaction, there are more eating disorders. Dieting, thinness, and obsession with appearance are precursors for eating disorders, and these have tended to be predominantly feminine preoccupations. Males, however, are increasingly the targets of the media onslaught and the culture's preoccupation with appearance and weight.

In his first book, *Males With Eating Disorders* (1990), Arnold Andersen points out that articles and advertisements concerning weight loss are far more frequent in the most popular women's versus men's magazines, with a ratio of 10.5:1. It is an intriguing coincidence that this ratio closely parallels that of women to men with eating disorders.

Furthermore, in subgroups of males where there is a great emphasis on weight (wrestlers and jockeys, for example), there is an increased prevalence of eating disorders. In fact, whenever weight loss is required for a particular group, male or female (e.g., dancers, models, gymnasts), there is a greater likelihood that those individuals will develop eating disorders. This strongly suggests that as our society increasingly objectifies men's bodies and pressures men to be weight- and shape-conscious, we will see an increase in males with eating disorders. In fact, it is already happening. Men's bodies are more frequently the targets of advertising campaigns, leanness for men is increasingly being emphasized, and the number of male dieters and males reporting a spectrum of eating and shape-related disorders (e.g., body dysmorphic disorder) appears to be on the rise (Pope et al. 2000).

Identifying males with eating disorders is a challenge for several reasons. Consider that, for at least 20 years, the diagnostic criteria for anorexia nervosa has included amenorrhea. Given that males cannot have amenorrhea and the pronounced gender difference in prevalence, it is not surprising that clients, clinicians, and the public tend to believe that males do not develop eating disorders. Also true is that being overweight and/or overeating are culturally more acceptable and less noticed in males; therefore, BED also tends to be underrecognized.

In applying the criteria for anorexia to men, it has been suggested that we can use an abnormality of reproductive hormone functioning, instead of amenorrhea because just as estrogen levels lower in women, testosterone levels lower in men.

The essential diagnostic features for bulimia nervosa—compulsive binge eating, a fear of being fat, excessive influence of shape and weight on self-concept or self-esteem, and compensatory behaviors used to avoid weight gain—can also be equally applied to males and females. For binge eating disorder, both males and females binge eat and feel distress and out of control over their eating. However, until recently men with eating disorders have been so rarely acknowledged or encountered that the diagnostic possibility of anorexia nervosa, bulimia nervosa, and even BED has often been overlooked when they present with symptoms that would lead to a correct diagnosis if seen in a woman. Studies have shown that, all else being equal, physicians are more likely to recommend treatment for an eating disorder when a person is female.

Diagnostic criteria aside, the problem of identifying men with eating disorders is heightened by the fact that, while admitting to an eating disorder is difficult for anyone, it is even more difficult for men because of the widespread belief that only women suffer from these illnesses. People were shocked when actor Dennis Quaid admitted in a recent interview that he suffered from an eating disorder after he had to lose a lot of weight for a role in the film *Wyatt Earp*. In addition, heterosexual men with eating disorders and homosexual men who have not yet come out commonly report fears of being suspected of homosexuality for having what is considered a "female problem."

Differences Between Men and Women

Andersen (1990) and Keel (2005) report that eating disordered men differ from eating disordered women in a few ways that may be important for better understanding and treatment:

- Boys and men tend to have genuine histories of preillness obesity versus chronically "feeling fat or overweight."
- Males often report losing weight to avoid weight-related medical illnesses found in other family members.
- Males often have sexuality and gender-identity issues, and the prevalence of eating disorders is higher among homosexual compared to heterosexual men. This does not appear to be true for women.
- Males are often intensely athletic and thus are more likely to have begun dieting to attain greater sports performance or alleviate the fear of gaining weight because of a sports injury. In fact, many eating disordered men may fit another proposed but not yet accepted diagnostic category, referred to as compulsive exercise, or a term coined by Alayne Yates (1991), *activity disorder.* This syndrome is similar to but separate from eating disorders and is discussed in Chapter 3.
- About as many men want to gain weight as lose it. Men may present with a different type of eating disorder because they want to achieve both less fat and increased muscle mass in accordance with the media's masculine ideal. This disorder of body image and eating has been described as *reverse anorexia* or *muscle dysmorphia* (Pope et al. 2000).

Reverse Anorexia or Body Dysmorphia

Instead of overshooting the mark for the thin ideal and developing a disorder, some males try to decrease body fat while increasing lean muscle and overall body size; thus, they strive intently for an "ideal" male body by taking extreme measures. They have an altered body image, seeing themselves as "weak," "puny," or "flabby" (without muscle definition) even when they are not. Excessive exercise, diuretics, dieting, extremely high protein intake, and anabolic steroids are all used to excess and to the detriment of health and well-being. The obsession with weight and shape as central components of self-concept, the body image dissatisfaction, and the use of extreme and even dangerous methods to alter the body constitute a definite parallel with eating disorders in women.

Treatment and Prognosis for Males

Although more research is needed on the specific psychology of men with eating disorders, the basic principles for treatment are similar to those for treating women.

Short-term studies suggest that the prognosis for males in treatment is comparable to that for females, at least in the short term. Long-term studies are not available. Empathic, informed professionals are necessary, because males with eating disorders feel misunderstood and out of place in a society that still doesn't understand these disorders. Although it may turn out to be true, it is often mistakenly assumed that men, most particularly those with anorexia nervosa, are more severely disturbed and have a poorer prognosis than women with these disorders. This appears to be the case because first, since males often go undetected, the most severe cases are probably those who enter treatment and thus come under scrutiny. Second, along the same lines, there seems to be a contingent of males with other serious psychological disorders, most notably obsessive-compulsive disorder, in which food rituals, food phobias, food restriction, and food rejection are prominent features. These individuals end up in treatment mostly because of their underlying psychological illnesses, not for their eating behavior, and they tend to be complex, difficult-to-treat cases.

The field continues to search for an understanding of the biological, psychological, social, and cultural factors that contribute to a spectrum of body image, eating, and weight management disorders in boys and men. As we gain more knowledge and as the problems gain more recognition, it is hoped that optimal prevention and treatment protocols will be revealed.

3

Activity Disorder: When a Good Thing Goes Bad

IF DIETING TAKEN to the extreme becomes an eating disorder, exercise taken to the extreme may become an "activity disorder" (Yates 1991). Exercise, like dieting, can be a good thing, but much like dieting, it can take on a life of its own when the exercise itself becomes the goal and is pursued beyond reason. Health and fitness go by the wayside, and exercise becomes all-important—even if the person is exhausted or injured, or when exercising means missing or losing something else. What starts out as a good thing can go very, very bad.

Accompanying the steady increase in the number of people with eating disorders has been a rise in the number with exercise disorders. These are individuals who define themselves through their overinvolvement in exercise to the point where instead of choosing to participate in their activity, they have become "addicted" to it—continuing to engage in it despite adverse consequences.

In our society, exercise is increasingly being done less in pursuit of fitness or pleasure and more in pursuit of a thinner body or a sense of control and accomplishment. Female exercisers are particularly vulnerable to problems arising when restriction of food intake is combined with intense physical activity. A woman who loses too much weight or body fat will stop menstruating and ovulating, which has a negative effect on bone density thus she will become increasingly susceptible to stress fractures, possibly even irreversible osteoporosis. The "female athlete triad" of disordered eating, amenorrhea, and osteoporosis can be devastating. I have seen several women in their 20s with bone densities of 80-year-old women. The problem with amenorrhea and bone density in female athletes has been known for more than 20 years. "As many as 66 percent of all female college athletes have irregular or nonexistent menstrual periods. . . . It is so prevalent among elite athletes that when California endocrinologist Robert Marcus began his 1984 study comparing the bone density of amenorrheic and normally menstruating athletes on the Stanford's women track team, he had to g outside the team to find a control group. Every athlete on the train was amenorrheic" (Ryan 1995). Still this problem often goes unrecognized.

Similar to individuals with eating disorders, those with activity disorder are not deterred from their behaviors by medical complications and consequences. They feel as if they can't stop. Participating in their activity has become obligatory. They have been referred to as obligatory or compulsive exercisers because they seem unable to "not exercise," even when injured, exhausted, or begged and threatened by others to stop.

The terms *pathogenic exercise* and *exercise addiction* have been used to describe the condition of people who are consumed by the need for physical activity to the exclusion of everything else and to the point of damage or danger to themselves and their relationships with others. For the rest of this chapter, the term *activity disorder* will be used to describe the overexercising syndrome because this term seems most appropriate for comparison with the more traditional eating disorders.

Signs and Symptoms of Activity Disorder

The signs and symptoms of activity disorder often, but not always, include many of those seen in anorexia nervosa and bulimia nervosa. Obsessive concerns about being fat, body dissatisfaction, binge eating, and a whole variety of dieting and purging behaviors are often present. Furthermore, it is well established that obsessive exercise is a common feature seen in individuals with anorexia and bulimia; in fact, some studies have reported that as many as 75 percent use excessive exercise as a method of purging and/or reducing anxiety. Therefore, activity disorder can be found as a component of anorexia or bulimia or—although there is currently no *DSM-IV* diagnosis for it—as a separate disorder altogether. Many individuals have the salient features of activity disorder but do not meet the diagnostic criteria for anorexia nervosa or bulimia nervosa. The overriding feature of activity disorder is the presence of excessive and purposeless physical activity that goes beyond any usual training regimen and ends up being a detriment rather than an asset to a person's health and well-being.

A Look into the Mind-Set of Someone with Activity Disorder

Activity disorder is often found in athletes but nonathletes also suffer from this problem. Activity disorder usually involves overexercising by excessive amounts of cardio workouts and/or weight training. However, this problem can also involve constant random activity, such as moving one's legs while sitting, standing while eating, or walking while reading. The individual often feels compelled to move in order to maximize caloric expenditure. In the following excerpt, I have taken a few poignant statements from a few therapy sessions with a young woman suffering from a very activity disorder. Combining parts of these sessions will allow readers to glimpse the mind set of this illness. Keep in mind this is not one session and the information here was gathered over a few weeks. The dotted lines demarcate a different day.

Carolyn: So what are your goals for coming here to see me?

Mira: Well, I have a problem with exercise, I think. Well at least everyone else seems to think so. I have tried to cut down but it makes me feel miserable and depressed. Besides exercise is a good thing. It is not like I am doing anything bad.

Carolyn: How many hours a day are you exercising?

Mira: You mean as formal exercise like running or weight training?

Carolyn: Yes, let's start there. But are there other things?

Mira: I do all kinds of stuff. I feel like I need to move all the time.

Carolyn: OK, I know what you mean, and we will talk about that too, but let's start with the exercise stuff.

Mira: Hmm, I . . . probably . . . it varies, but probably about four hours. In the morning, I do some kind of cardio for about two hours, like running, Stairmaster, or bike all combined. Then I go to the gym in the afternoon or evening and do another 45 minutes or so of cardio then about one to two hours of weight training or a kickboxing class or something else. I mix it up but I always feel like I need to get in about four hours. [When I asked her to keep track it actually turned out to be more like five hours.]

. . . .

Carolyn: OK. [Looking at her activity journal] Wow, I am so sorry for you that you feel you have to do all of that. . . . Are there other things you feel compelled to do that you haven't told me? Are there rules that you follow, like exercising when you watch TV?

Mira: Well, I always walk rather than stand; stand rather than sit; and if I have to sit, like for a class, I have to go run stairs in between classes, or I ask to be excused to the bathroom during class and I go run the bleachers, stuff like that.

Carolyn: You must live with a pretty harsh task master inside that head of yours. Is this difficult for you?

Mira: I guess you could say that. It is hard for me to even come and sit in here.

Carolyn: Wow . . . well, I am glad you came back. You mentioned that there are other kinds of stuff. What else do you do? How does your day start?

Mira: Well, I set my alarm to go off at 4:30 A.M. so I can do crunches in my room and jumping jacks before I even go out for my run. And when I walk around in my house when no one is home, I walk doing squats.

Carolyn: That sounds kind of crazy, like a tic, like being driven by some internal mechanism; it sounds like you feel that it is out of your control.

....

Mira: What do you mean?

Carolyn: Would you like to have a choice in whether or not you exercise? You do not seem to choose to do all these things but seem driven or obligated to do them. You can't *not* do it. Do you see the difference?

Mira: Yes, but I am not sure. If I think about not doing it, I can't even stand it. I can't even go out to a movie or to dinner with people because I cannot sit that long. And I cannot imagine not doing everything I do. It freaks me out to think about it.

Carolyn: But if you could, would you like to have the choice? To be free to choose to exercise or not, to sit through a movie or go out to dinner?

Mira: I think so. I don't really know. I have tried and I feel worse not doing it.

Features of Activity Disorder

Not all people with activity disorder are as severe as Mira (who was introduced in the sidebar), but you can see from her responses that activity disorder is not always limited to traditional exercise. Mira is an exceptional case but often people with this condition need to move in whatever way they can. At Monte Nido, my treatment center, we often see these people tapping their feet or doing isometric exercises even while sitting in group or at the dinner table. They do jumping jacks in the bathroom stall and try to stand all day rather then sit. I often assign a staff member to be with them one-on-one to prevent their endless, restless activity and to help them during this difficult time which they experience much like a drug withdrawal. Just like with eating disorders, people with activity disorder vary a great deal. Some do not engage in the kind of activities described by Mira but overexercise and are not OK without doing so.

In *Compulsive Exercise and the Eating Disorders*, Alayne Yates (1991) proposes the features of someone with activity disorder:

- The person maintains a high level of activity and is uncomfortable with states of rest or relaxation.
- The person depends on the activity for self-definition and mood stabilization.
- There is an intense, driven quality to the activity that becomes self-perpetuating and resistant to change,

compelling the person to continue while feeling the lack of ability to control or stop the behavior.

- Only the overuse of the body can produce the physiological effects of deprivation (secondary to exposure to the elements, extreme exertion, and rigid dietary restriction) that are an important component to perpetuating the disorder.
- Although someone may have coexisting personality disorders, there is no particular personality profile or disorder that underlies activity disorder. Sufferers are apt to be physically healthy, high-functioning individuals.
- People use rationalizations and other defense mechanisms to protect their involvement in the activity. This may represent a preexisting personality disorder and/or be secondary to the physical deprivation.
- Their achievement orientation, independence, self-control, perfectionism, persistence, and well-developed mental strategies can foster significant academic and vocational accomplishments in such a way that they appear as healthy, high-functioning people.

Those afflicted with an activity disorder are extremely committed individuals and pride themselves on putting mind over matter, valuing self-discipline, self-sacrifice, and the ability to persevere. They are generally hard-working, task-oriented, high-achieving individuals who have a tendency to be dissatisfied with themselves as if nothing is ever good enough. Those with anorexia and bulimia and those with activity disorder are similar to one another in many respects. Like eating disorders, even though we may find some sort of genetic predisposition, activity disorders are expressions of and defenses against feelings and emotions and are used to soothe, control, and maintain self-esteem. Both groups attempt to control the body through exercise and/or diet and are overly conscious of calories taken in versus calories expended. The emotional investment both groups place on exercise and/or diet becomes more intense and significant than work, family, relationships, and ironically even health. Those with activity disorder lose control over exercise just as those with eating disorders lose control over eating and dieting, and both experience withdrawal when prevented from engaging in their behaviors.

Cognitive Distortions in Activity Disorder

People with activity disorder usually score high on the Eating Disorder Inventory subscales of perfectionism and asceticism (EDI; see Chapter 7) and have similar distortions in their cognitive (thinking) styles. The following list includes examples of the thinking patterns of people with activity disorder that are similar to the mental distortions in those with eating disorders:

- **Dichotomous, black-and-white thinking.** If I don't run, I can't eat. If I am not moving, I am doing nothing.
- **Overgeneralization.** Like my mom, people who don't exercise are fat. Sitting down means you are lazy.
- **Magnification.** If I can't exercise, my life will be over. If I don't work out today, I'll gain weight.
- **Selective abstraction.** If I am winning races, I must be fine. I feel great when I exercise, so if I exercise, I'll never be depressed.
- **Superstitious thinking.** I must run every morning or something bad will happen. I must do 205 sit-ups every night.
- **Personalization.** People are looking at me because I'm out of shape. People admire people who exercise.
- **Arbitrary inference.** People who exercise get better jobs, relationships, and so on. People who exercise don't get sick as much.
- **Discounting.** My doctor tells me not to run, but she is flabby so I don't listen to her. My stress fracture is not that bad. No pain, no gain.

Physical Symptoms of Activity Disorder

A key determinant of whether a person is developing activity disorder is if he or she has the symptoms of overtraining (seen in the following list) yet persists with exercise anyway. *Overtrain-*

ing syndrome is a state of exhaustion in which individuals will continue to exercise while their performance and health diminish. This syndrome is caused by a prolonged period of energy output that depletes energy stores without sufficient replenishment and includes the following symptoms:

- Fatigue
- Reduction in performance
- Decreased concentration
- Inhibited lactic acid response
- Loss of emotional vigor
- Increased compulsivity
- Soreness and/or stiffness
- Decreased maximum oxygen uptake
- Decreased blood lactate
- Adrenal exhaustion
- Decreased heart rate response to exercise
- Hypothalamic dysfunction
- Decreased anabolic (testosterone) response
- Increased catabolic (cortisol) response (muscle wasting)

Sometimes the only cure for these symptoms is complete rest, which may take a few weeks to a few months. To a person with activity disorder, resting is like giving up or giving in. This is similar to an individual with anorexia who feels like eating is giving in. While giving up their exercise behaviors, those with activity disorder will go through psychological and physical withdrawal, often crying, yelling, begging, and pleading with statements such as the following:

- I can't stand not exercising. It's driving me crazy. I'd rather die.
- I don't care about the consequences, you have to let me work out or I'll turn into a fat blob, hate myself, and fall apart.
- This is worse torture than any effects of the exercise. I feel like I'm dying inside.

These feelings diminish over time but need to be attended to carefully. Clients will do anything to get their fix: leg lifts in the shower, running in place when no one is watching, holding themselves off of a chair when they are supposed to be sitting, and anything else they can think of. They will also lie about how much they are doing and therefore cannot be trusted, at least not in the beginning stages of treatment.

Approaching Someone with Activity Disorder

In January 1986, the article "Pathogenic Weight-Control Behavior in Female Athletes" in the *Physician and Sports Medicine Journal* (L. W. Rosen 1988) discussed excessive exercise (referred to as "pathogenic exercise") in athletes and listed recommendations for approaching athletes who have this problem. The recommendations can be adapted for use in approaching those with activity disorder who are not necessarily considered athletes:

Summary of Guidelines

- Someone who has good rapport with the person, such as a coach, should arrange a private meeting to discuss the problem in a supportive style.
- Without judgment, specific examples of the behaviors that arouse concern should be given.
- Let the person respond, but do not argue.
- Reassure the person that the point is not to take away exercise but that if he or she does not cut back or stop, at least for a while, participation in exercise will ultimately be curtailed through an injury or compromised health.
- Try to determine if the person feels beyond the point of being able to abstain voluntarily from the problem behavior.
- Be persistent. These individuals resist admitting that they have a problem, and it may take repeated attempts to get them to acknowledge their behaviors and/or seek help.

- If the person continues to refuse to admit that a problem exists in the face of compelling evidence, consult a clinician with expertise in treating these disorders and/or find others who may be able to help. Remember that individuals with activity disorder are usually very independent and success oriented. Admitting they have a problem they are unable to control is very difficult for them.
- Be sensitive to the factors that may have played a part in the development of this problem. These individuals are often unduly influenced by significant others and/or coaches who suggest that they lose weight or who unwittingly praise them for excessive activity.

Examining Risk Factors

In a society that places a high value on independence and achievement combined with being athletic and thin, involvement in exercise provides a perfect means for fitting in or gaining approval. Exercise serves to enhance self-worth when that self-worth is based on appearance, endurance, strength, and capability.

Child-rearing practices and family values contribute to an individual choosing exercise as a means of self-development and recognition. If parents or other caregivers endorse excessive behaviors and they themselves diet or exercise obsessively, children will often adopt these values and expectations at an early age. Children who learn not only from society but also from their parents that to be acceptable is to be fit and thin may be left with a narrow focus for self-development and self-esteem. A child reared with attitudes such as "no pain, no gain," may endorse this attitude wholeheartedly without the maturity or common sense to balance this notion with proper self-nurturing and self-care.

As with eating disorders, researchers are exploring what biological factors may contribute to activity disorder. Certain people seem predisposed to need a high level of activity. Perfectionists, overachievers, and those who have the capacity for self-deprivation will be more likely to seek out exercise and become addicted to the feelings or other perceived benefits that exercise provides. We know that in animals the combination of food restriction and stress causes an increase in activity level and that food restriction with increased activity can cause the activity to become senseless and driven (W. F. Epling 1983). Furthermore, parallel changes have been detected in the brain chemicals and hormones of women with eating disorders and long-distance runners that may explain how they tolerate starvation and pain/exhaustion, respectively. People with activity disorder may be different biochemically and more easily led and trapped into a cycle of activity that is resistant to intervention.

Treatment for Activity Disorder

The principles of treatment for individuals with activity disorder are similar to those for people with eating disorders. Medical issues must be handled, and residential or inpatient treatment may be necessary to curtail the exercise and deal with any depression or suicidality that results. Many cases, if they have not progressed too far, should be able to be treated on an outpatient basis, unless the activity disorder and an eating disorder coexist. This combination can quickly present a serious situation. When a lack of nutrition is combined with hours of exercise, the body gets broken down at a rapid pace, and residential or inpatient treatment is usually required. Sometimes 24-hour care is encouraged and used as a way to relieve this vicious cycle before a breakdown occurs.

Eating disorder treatment programs are currently the best choice for those with activity disorder. An eating disorder facility with a special program for athletes or compulsive exercisers is ideal. I have found that it is important to understand, assess, and treat the particular aspects presented by those with activity disorder present. Staff members with training and experience in this area are a key to successful treatment. Very few programs in the country specialize in treating this disorder. (See the description of the Monte Nido residential treatment facility in Chapter 15.)

Therapy for Activity Disorder

People with activity disorder tend to be intelligent, internally driven, independent individuals. They will most likely resist showing any kind of weakness, such as the need for help or treatment, unless they are injured, face some kind of ultimatum, or experience a significant loss due to their excessive exercising.

I always say that when treating someone with activity disorder, look for intimacy issues. Excessive activity protects these individuals against the desire to and/or fear of getting close. They have a hard time taking in something from another person or depending on anyone. They have a very hard time with what I call the *V* word—*vulnerability*. Therapists have to maintain a calm, caring stance with the goal of helping this kind of client define what he or she needs, rather than focusing on taking things away. A therapeutic task is to help the client receive and internalize the soothing functions relationships can provide, thus promoting connection with others over activity just as with eating disorders. Therapeutic issues to discuss include intimacy, vulnerability, communication, tension tolerance, body image, body and self care, physiology of exercise, rest, and mindfulness.

Specific interventions for activity disorder include but are not limited to the following:

- Decreasing the length of time spent exercising (This might take starting in small increments.)
- Changing the type of exercise (adding yoga or weight training), for example, walking instead of running
- Decreasing the number of days the person exercises
- Setting a weight goal that is necessary in order to continue exercising
- Possibly stopping exercise altogether for a period of time (Sometimes this is necessary for health reasons or to break the addictive cycle.)
- Getting a bone density test to check for bone loss (Even if the problem has not been going on for very long, a baseline test is important for comparison at a later date.)

The treatment of activity disorder is a lengthy process. The techniques used in the treatment of eating disorders, as described in this book, can be applied. It is important to look for exercise issues and activity disorder when treating people with eating disorders and to keep in mind that activity disorder can also exist by itself. Similar causes contribute to the development of eating and activity disorders, and the next two chapters are devoted to a discussion of these causal factors.

4

Genes or Jeans: What Causes Eating Disorders?

WHEN I TELL people what I do for a living, they always ask, "What causes eating disorders?" I never really know how to begin. There are so many variables, so many risk factors, so many different ways people develop their eating disorder, and so many variations of eating disorders.

A growing body of research has caused a number of people in the field to surmise that genetics play a role in eating disorder etiology. There is evidence that one has a higher risk of developing an eating disorder if a relative has one and an even higher risk if it is a first-degree relative. However, it is hard to separate out genetic and environmental factors when it comes to causality since they are always in a pattern of interacting. Evidence that genetic differences explain a portion of the presence or absence of an eating disorder does *not* mean that all eating disorders are genetic or that environments are irrelevant. The belief held by several researchers in the field is that an accumulation of various genes—each with a small, additive influence—together with certain environmental factors increases one's risk of developing an eating disorder. Prominent genetic researcher Cynthia Bulik once stated, "Genes load the gun and environment pulls the trigger."

We know that dieting is linked to disordered eating attitudes and behaviors (Keel 2005). Studies have found that girls who dieted were seven to eight times as likely to develop an eating disorder as those who did not diet (Keel 2005 and Gordon 2000). Most clients with anorexia, bulimia, or binge eating disorder admit to dieting before the onset of their disorder, and several studies have confirmed this. Furthermore, cross-cultural studies reveal an increase in eating disorders with an increase of urbanization. In Fiji, before television, dieting did not exist and there were no eating disorders; after television was introduced, Fijian girls were, for the first time, dieting, reportedly, as a way to improve their status and by three years 11 percent were even vomiting to lose weight! Certainly their genes did not change. This type of evidence has caused Richard Gordon and others like him to assert that "without our cultural preoccupation with dieting, there would be no epidemic of eating disorders" (Gordon 2000, 158). So the question is, are individuals with eating disorders trying to fit into their jeans, their genes, or both?

Genes: Loading the Gun

Serious questions remain regarding the relationship between those with severe eating disorders and those in the general population who fall somewhere else on the continuum of weight and shape preoccupation. Are some people more prone to develop an eating disorder and/or body image and eating issues because of a genetic predisposition? Do eating disorders run in families and, if so, does this mean they are genetic? If they are genetic, can we find the genes that contribute and ultimately develop new treatments such as new medications to help treat or prevent these disorders? This is where the researchers are headed today.

Despite varying methodologies, studies have consistently demonstrated "a strong familial component." This is due to elevated rates of anorexia and bulimia in families of individuals with these disorders compared to control populations. However, there is a difference between "running in families" and genetic heritability. First-degree relatives share both genes and environment, so in the absence of adoption studies, teasing out what contributes to what is a difficult task. This makes studies of twins particularly interesting and important. Research has indicated that if one identical twin suffers from anorexia nervosa or bulimia nervosa, the second twin is at a higher risk to have the same condition than if they were nonidentical twins or nontwin siblings. This points to genetics as making the difference. But, others ask, couldn't this be because identical twins are more often treated the same and exposed to environments that are more similar than are nonidentical twins?

Researchers tell us that these factors are not the explanation. They call this the "equal environment assumption," which means they assume that the identical twins share the same or equal environment as nonidentical twins. Many question this conclusion (Colbert 2001), in part, because people often treat identical twins more similarly than fraternal twins. Identical twins also often claim to have more influence over each other than fraternal twins and nontwin siblings. For example, if identical twin sisters look alike and one goes on a diet, this might be more persuasive in influencing her sister to diet than would be the case with a fraternal twin sister. The equal environment assumption in eating disorders has not been validated. Adoption studies would be the most valid means of sorting out genetic influence, especially when involving identical twins, but no such research has been conducted. Twin studies, particularly of anorexia nervosa, are difficult to conduct because of the low rate of the disorder in the general population, much less in adopted twins.

A detailed summary of the genetic contribution to eating disorders can be found in Cynthia Bulik's chapter in the *Clinical Handbook of Eating Disorders* (Brewerton 2004). A brief summary of her findings are presented in the sidebar.

Proceeding with Caution

It has been reported that for anorexia nervosa, twin studies suggest that the contribution of additive genetic effects to individual differences in liability across large groups of people is somewhere

Summary of Family Studies

- Eating disorders are familial.
- First-degree female relatives of patients with an eating disorder are at a substantially increased risk for developing an eating disorder. Relatives of individuals with anorexia nervosa are 11.3 times more likely to have anorexia nervosa than relatives of controls. Relatives of bulimia nervosa are 4.4 times more likely to develop the illness.
- There is a shared liability between anorexia nervosa and bulimia nervosa and EDNOS. Several studies showed an increase in rates of anorexia, bulimia, and EDNOS in relatives of individuals with anorexia or bulimia compared to rates of relatives of controls.
- Preliminary findings suggest that binge eating disorder is more commonly found in family members of individuals with BED than in family members of individuals without BED.

between 58 and 88 percent. For bulimia nervosa, heritability estimates vary between 28 and 83 percent (a huge variation), with environments unique to one twin versus the other contributing to the rest of the variance. These are interpretations based on formulas and statistics. Researchers have to extrapolate, or what some describe as "play with," the numbers to arrive at these figures. I have looked at the actual studies and still cannot quite grasp how these percentages determine, or what they mean, so the average reader will probably not fully understand either. However, many people have jumped on the bandwagon proclaiming that anorexia and bulimia are "genetic illnesses." We must be cautious in regard to this conclusion. First, even if genes play a role, there must be an environmental trigger. In fact, one twin study showed a higher concordance rate for anorexia nervosa in fraternal rather than identical twins.

What are we to understand from all this? The lay public sees the figures that are reported and mistakenly assumes eating disorders are genetic illnesses and that if you have the genes for anorexia, you have up to an 88 percent chance of developing the illness. In fact, these figures only mean that in *some way* genes seem to play a role in determining the *extent* to which some individuals are *likely* to develop an eating disorder.

To actually prove a genetic etiology, molecular studies have to be done in which researchers look for the actual genes (more properly called gene alleles) that increase the risk of developing an eating disorder. Only a small number of these studies have been conducted, and they reported mixed results. In one of the most promising areas, called the 5HT2A receptor, five studies reported an association with anorexia nervosa. However, six other studies showed no association! Those who are skeptical cite the fact that to date no genes have ever been found as the cause of any mental illness. For a detailed critique of the genetic etiology of mental illness, the reader is referred to Ty Colbert's *Blaming Our Genes.*

More evidence is needed as to the extent, nature, and significance of genetic and biological liability (or liabilities) in anorexia, bulimia, and BED. Examination of the nature of these illnesses suggests a number of possibilities of genetically transmitted "tendencies" or "vulnerabilities" that might affect the development of an eating disorder, for example, some variant of a genetic propensity for anxiety, depression, or obsessive-compulsive behavior. It makes sense that the most anxious and compulsive among us would be more susceptible to cultural influences and possess the temperament to follow through with extreme dieting. It stands to reason that the most perfectionistic among us would be the best at pursuing and obtaining the culture's idealization of thinness. This is a good explanation of why when I went on a diet in high school with several friends, only I developed anorexia nervosa.

I believe there is a genetic predisposition that makes certain people, like myself, more vulnerable to developing an eating disorder, particularly anorexia nervosa. I am sure I have those genes. However, my genetic predisposition wasn't a problem when it helped me make straight As, skip sixth grade, go off to college when I was only 16, and achieve two master's degrees by the time I was 21. It was only when I applied it to dieting that I got into trouble. Had I lived in a different culture where there was no emphasis on thinness and where all my friends were not on diets, I believe I would not have developed anorexia. However, given the cultural climate I grew up in (Twiggy was very popular) combined with psychological stressors in my own life history, fitting into Twiggy's jeans was a reasonable desire and tenaciously restricting my food, at least initially, was a reasonable response.

Core personality characteristics, such as harm avoidance or obsession with perfection and exactness, that predispose one to an eating disorder may be related to some kind of biological factors such as alterations of serotonin neurotransmission. Walter Kaye (1998), an award-winning researcher in the field of eating disorders, has reported widely on abnormal serotonin activity that persists during recovery in eating disorder patients. However, we don't know if the alteration existed before the illness. In addition, preillness and postrecovery studies find an association between eating disorders and traits of anxiety/harm avoidance and obsession with perfection, symmetry, and exactness. Serotonin may contribute to the development of eating disorders through its effect on such traits and on satiety. Additionally, newer research indicates that disturbances in dopamine function appear to contribute to alterations in weight, feeding, motor activity, and reward in anorexia nervosa. We have yet to determine what any of this actually means, but there is one major fact that cannot be ignored. For the most part, all the biological abnormalities found during an eating disorder—whether in neurotransmitters, hormone levels, temperature, even brain shrinkage—return to normal upon weight and nutritional restoration. There is some new emerging research that might indicate alterations in certain neurotransmitters, for example dopamine, after recovery. These alterations may have existed prior to the eating disorder. More research is required. There are also some exceptions to this in the area of bone density loss and amenorrhea, but these are thought to be the direct result of the illness not the cause.

The Implications of Studying Possible Genetic Causes

Progress in the fields of genetics and neurobiology has helped the field of medicine in numerous ways. Results have implications for developing new medications and specific psychological treatments to compensate for possible genetic predispositions. This is the most promising result that could come from discovering a genetic etiology. Furthermore, it is hoped that biological information will help convince insurance companies that eating disorders are legitimate illnesses and not voluntary lifestyle choices.

However, one hopes that if we do find genetic and/or biological markers of risk, insurance companies will not require tests for these markers. Could a positive test result disqualify individuals who are seeking to obtain insurance? Furthermore, could individuals who develop eating disorders, but test negative, be denied coverage for treatment even if they do have insurance, because they are not legitimate cases of the illness? Although I have disturbed some of my colleagues for bringing up these issues, I believe they are important questions to ponder as we head down this path.

Another important consideration regarding genetic etiology concerns the fact that there has been a huge increase in reported cases of anorexia and bulimia over the last 40 years, even if (as some have indicated) this increase slowed or perhaps even halted for anorexia nervosa in the 1990s. Our species has not developed new genes, so how can we explain this? The same goes for cross cultural studies; what has changed in other cultures and countries that makes their inhabitants more vulnerable to eating disorders is certainly not their genes. Since we know that in any event causality must be a combination of genetics and environment, it makes sense to look at what kinds of environments would set a predisposition off. After all, we can change environments, whereas changing large numbers of addictive genes would, shall we say, present major problems. Furthermore, despite decades of research showing that alcoholism and chemical dependency may be influenced by genetic vulnerability, we have yet to find any such genes or medication to successfully treat or prevent these illnesses. Even top researcher Cynthia Bulik (Brewerton 2004), when discussing the implications of family and twin studies, said,

> By emphasizing the fact that they have the ability to influence the environment and that environment can serve a protective function as well as an evocative function, parents can begin to see that although there is nothing they can do to alter the passing down of DNA, they can alter environments that influence the likelihood of genes being expressed.

This is my kind of thinking! We need to work on altering the environment. Bulik further suggests that preventive interventions might focus on prenatal and postnatal care for women with a current or past history of an eating disorder. But this begs the question, shouldn't we be doing that now? We know eating disorders run in families, so do we have to know that the illness is genetically transmitted in order to intervene? Prevention efforts should be made in these families and in fact in all families.

One last recommendation made by Bulik discusses the children of women with anorexia and bulimia who are considered at high risk for developing eating disorders. She says, "In much the same manner that children of alcoholics are encouraged to delay the onset of alcohol consumption, offspring of individuals with eating disorders could be provided with assistance to avoid the pitfalls of dieting, for developing non-body-centered self-esteem, and other ways to prevent the development of eating disorders." This is sound advice that we can follow right now even without discovering causal genes—and should do for all girls and boys not just those with a family history of eating disorder. Genetically based or not, to prevent eating disorders we need to alter the environment that triggers and perpetuates them.

Environment: Pulling the Trigger

How does one avoid the pitfalls of dieting or develop non–body-centered self-esteem in a society where what you weigh is more important than who you are? For more and more young girls, to be female is to be on a diet. Studies show that the vast majority of American girls and women, perhaps more than 90 percent, report disgust or disappointment with their bodies. One study revealed that 80 percent of fourth-grade girls reported dieting, with 10 percent of them admitting to self-induced vomiting. Many adolescent girls are smoking cigarettes, and some are snorting cocaine—not to get high, but to lose weight. Some girls claim they would rather be dead than fat. With the plethora of evidence showing that a drive for thinness, an irrational fear of being overweight, body image disturbance, and episodes of dieting and weight preoccupation are found in the histories of those with eating disorders, we cannot downplay cultural, social, and psychological phenomena as significant risk factors in their development.

Fijian Islands: How Television Changed the Cultural Landscape

The study performed by Anne Becker and colleagues (2002) in the Fijian islands is a profound example of the influence of environment. I was at a conference when I first heard Anne describe how shocked she was at the impact of the introduction of television to Fiji. She had spent time in the islands when she was younger and had witnessed that "the prevailing 'pressure to be slim' thought to be associated with dieting and disordered eating in many industrialized societies was distinctly absent in traditional Fiji." In fact, traditional Fijian values and practices encouraged robust appetites and body size. Individual efforts to reshape the body by dieting or exercise were not part of the culture; there is even a culture-specific illness known as "macake," which means "going thin." When someone lost weight, neighbors would try to fatten them up. Anne Becker and her colleagues from Harvard set out to study the impact of the introduction of television on Fiji's 2,000-year-old culture. Would western television have any effect on disordered eating attitudes and behaviors among ethnic Fijian adolescent girls?

Television was introduced to Nadroga, Fiji, in 1995, just one month prior to collecting the first set of data. The second set of data was collected in 1998, after Fijian girls had been exposed to television for just over three years. Becker's group found that key indicators of disordered eating were significantly more prevalent in 1998. Narrative data revealed that approximately 80 percent of Fijian girls were now interested in weight loss as a means of modeling themselves after Western television characters. Many associated weight loss with enhancing their prospects of securing a job or improving their career prospects. A disturbing finding was that "the percentage of subjects reporting self-induced vomiting to control weight was 0 percent in 1995 but had reached 11.3 percent by 1998." Fijian girls did not develop new genes during this study. They developed a desire to fit into new jeans and engaged in behaviors to help themselves do so.

The Media's Influence

The Fiji study is just one indication that in our global, media-based world, thinness increasingly represents not only attractiveness, but also self-sacrifice, virtue, success, control, and status. The pervasive attitude seems to be that the more fat one has, the more unattractive, self-indulgent, lazy, out of control, and old-fashioned one is.

Culturally dictated biases toward weight and shape are conveyed in various ways through media other than television. In a print advertisement featuring an extremely thin model and the slogan "Just the right shape," one wonders whether it is the body or the outfit being sold. Media advertisements like this reflect and shape our perceptions and standards of beauty. Advertisements for taking off weight and keeping it off are found in every magazine and newspaper, and on billboards, television commercials, and bumper stickers with messages such as "Lose Weight Now, Ask Me How." It is alarming to recall that when writing this book 10 years ago ads in magazines showed females saying something like, "I went from a size 16 to a size 10 in 12 weeks," or "I lost 10 pounds in 4 weeks." Today I see ads with women saying, "I went from a size 6 to a size 2 in two weeks," and "Lose 10 pounds by tomorrow." Worst of all is the magazine ad I saw for a restaurant in New York. It is a picture of a fork set against a black background with white type; it reads, "Supermodels love our pasta. It comes up as easy as it goes down." If you are as outraged as I am at this, you can join one or more of the eating disorder organizations who work on prevention listed in the appendix and help fight back.

Weight-loss programs, diet books, and media advertisements for diet products have been increasing steadily, resulting in a multibillion-dollar industry. As diet commercials have increased, the body size of *Playboy* centerfolds, Miss America contestants, and fashion models decreased to the point where many of these individuals have ended up with eating disorders. Is it any wonder that there has been a significant increase in the prevalence of disordered eating and eating disorders? Since the culturally prescribed body weight is so unrealistically low, fear of fat is so high, body dissatisfaction is so widespread, and mountains of evidence show that diets don't work (approximately 98 percent of those who lose weight gain it back), it follows that some individuals will resort to extreme measures such as starving or purging to deal with their frustration over their figure or size, striving to obtain "just the right shape."

Most ads and diet products are directed toward females, but males are no longer spared. Males are increasingly portrayed as ornamental objects in advertisements and targeted for the purchase of beauty and weight-loss products, as women have been since advertising began. Still, eating disorders remain a predominantly female problem, with women accounting for approximately 90 to 95 percent of all known cases. In this regard, it is worth remembering that men are still judged more for what they do and women for how they look. Out of 50 years of *Life* magazine covers, only 19 featured women who were not actresses or models (or wives of someone else who was famous) that is, women who were not on the cover because of their beauty (Wolf 1991). In our culture, women have been taught that their value is associated with their appearance and their bodies.

Females are disturbed by their perceptions of their body weight or shape based on society's view of what is acceptable and what is not. Current cultural standards actually promote body image disturbance, one of the diagnostic features of anorexia and bulimia. After all, it is body image disturbance that distinguishes these illnesses from other psychological conditions that involve weight loss and eating abnormalities. There have been cases of these illnesses in which individuals do not report body image disturbance or weight loss as a motivator for their symptoms (for example, in other cultures such as China), but such cases need more study before the body image criteria will be changed.

Body image disturbance is defined in the eating disorder section of *DSM-IV-TR* as follows:

- **For anorexia nervosa.** Disturbance in the way in which one's body weight or shape is experienced, undue influence of body weight or shape on self-evaluation, or denial of the seriousness of the current low body weight.

- **For bulimia nervosa.** Self-evaluation is unduly influenced by body shape and weight.

After almost three decades of working with eating disorder clients, I continue to be persuaded that our society, not any particular combination of genes, has brought about and reinforced the undue influence of weight and shape on self-concept and self-esteem. Technological progress has fostered and extended the obsession with women's bodies and overall appearance with the invention of items such as the compact mirror (so you can always know what you look like) and cosmetics (so you can always improve what you look like). Technology has also given us the power to flash images across a screen in our homes and on billboards outside that constantly remind us of what we are supposed to look like. Now our wonderful technology can "cosmetically" remove fat from our thighs and add it to our breasts. Plastic surgery for cosmetic reasons is being performed on children as young as 12. Is it any wonder that younger and younger children develop eating disorders?

Consistent with the Fiji study, research has shown that, although eating disorders are increasingly appearing in a variety of cultures around the world, Westernized women (non-Western women who come into contact with Western values and ideals) are at greater risk, and the degree of Westernization seems to increase the risk (Dolan 1991). An extensive and historical cross-cultural review by Miller and Pumariega (2001) indicates "cultural change itself may be associated with increased vulnerability to eating disorders, especially when values about physical aesthetics are involved."

The requirement to be thin is just the latest version of torture used to mold women's bodies into a set standard of beauty, one that changes over time and from culture to culture. In the United States, Canada, Europe, Australia, and a growing number of countries, women have gone through fundamental changes in their place in society, both economically and politically, and thinness has come to symbolize status, virtue, and control. A young woman growing up and searching for her identity takes on these messages from her culture and her female role models. At the same time she is developing breasts and body fat to prepare for menstruation, pregnancy, and eventually childbirth and breast-feeding, she is compelled to be accepted and to fit in, which means being thin. Eating disorders need to be understood within the context of the current culture, where the idea that extreme thinness is attractive and desirable for females is so commonly accepted that it is rarely even questioned.

Here is what some women have to say about these cultural dictates:

- You can't trust your body. It defies you and shows all your faults. I always thought I could do anything, but I can't look like the models on Madison Avenue. But I can certainly try.
- When no one else is there, food is there; food . . . exactly what I want, when I want. I need no one's approval and no one's involvement which might disappoint me. Why do I choose food to act out this need? . . . Because I'm not supposed to have it.
- I will never allow myself to be fat. I saw what that did to my mother and my sister, and if I have to die trying, I will stay thin.
- I have accomplished something by being thin. Everyone tells me so. Even those who want me to gain weight reinforce the idea that I have achieved an extreme that few people ever equal.

These women are all expressing a struggle deeper than thin versus fat. In essence, they are also describing a struggle for power, success, and control—for being special and accepted. The issue seems deceptively clear: mind over matter. We tend to look up to people who can lose weight and keep it off even if they are unhealthy and unhappy. The ultimate power felt by individuals with anorexia is that they do without, punish their bodies, and will them to obey. The increased prevalence of anorexia and bulimia in certain subgroups, such as dancers, models, gymnasts, and jockeys, lends even further credence to cultural factors as causal in eating disorders.

The Bigger Picture

Although it would be easy to blame the current eating disorder epidemic solely on our society's standards of thinness, this is a far too simplistic and naive view. Eating disorders are highly complex manifestations of both our culture and various underlying struggles in the core of relationships, personality, and most likely the biochemistry and genes of the individual afflicted. After all, not every woman in our "thin-is-in," image-conscious society develops an eating disorder. Not all of the fourth-graders who report dieting become eating disordered. Two young girls can grow up in the same household with the same parents and the same basic cultural influences, yet one develops an eating disorder while the other maintains a normal relationship with food and weight throughout her lifetime.

As discussed in Chapter 1, there were cases of anorexia nervosa and bulimia nervosa even back when society's standards of thinness were very different. In his book, *Holy Anorexia*, Rudolf Bell (1985) makes a compelling and thought-provoking analogy between certain medieval Italian saints, to whom he refers as having "holy anorexia," and individuals who fit the diagnostic criteria for anorexia nervosa today. Bell describes how, in the service of purity and the search for perfect holiness, the saints starved themselves, were hyperactive and perfectionistic, and lost an excess of 25 percent of their normal body weight.

Bell's view is that today's cultural ideals are physical health, thinness, and self-control; in medieval Christendom, they were spiritual health, fasting, and self-denial. In both instances, only truly rare individuals become champions of self-sacrifice and mind over matter in the quest for the ideal (perhaps those with the right genetic temperament). For both the "medieval holy anorexic" (word choice of Bell) and today's sufferer, the behaviors and compulsive devotion that are initially rewarded and praised by their elders and their peers become self-destructive and turn into a life-threatening loss of control that eventually requires intervention.

Nevertheless, even today, people with anorexia often report starving for purposes other than thinness, such as feelings of cleanliness, purity, control, and accomplishment that are hard to give up. In other words, in the search for both holiness and thinness, the pursuit becomes the goal. Self-sacrifice and control, an independence from physical needs, and the act of nurturing others while abstaining oneself are all sought-after characteristics.

Our real task and our true battle in the fight against eating disorders is to disconnect the cultural ideal of thinness from feminine beauty, acceptance, and esteem, so that self-starvation is again without a purpose.

Although it is important to understand eating disorders as being culturally mediated, we cannot blame them solely on the cultural pressure to be thin. The current body image standards and the war on obesity, along with the sheer abundance of food in the lives of many people, provide a perfect setting for a struggling will to do battle, for an insecure feeling to have power, and for a sense of despair to gain control. The next chapter deals with the last area of eating disorder etiology, the emotional arena and each person's underlying psychological issues that contribute to the development of an eating disorder.

5

Eating Disorder Behaviors As Adaptive Functions

A STRUGGLING WILL, an insecure feeling, and despair may manifest themselves in problems with the care and feeding of the body, but they are fundamental problems with the care and feeding of the soul. In her aptly titled book *The Obsession* (1994), Kim Chernin writes, "The body holds meaning . . . when we probe beneath the surface of our obsession with weight, we will find that a woman obsessed with her body is also obsessed with the limitations of her emotional life. Through her concern with her body she is expressing a serious concern about the state of her soul." What are the emotional limitations commonly seen in individuals with eating disorders? What is the state of their souls?

Common States of Being in Eating Disorders

How and why a particular person uses starving, bingeing, or purging as a way to cope is an individual issue but it is easy to understand how a person in one or more of the following emotional states will naturally seek comfort for, alleviation of, or distraction from his or her feelings.

- Low self-esteem
- Diminished self-worth

- Belief in the thinness myth
- Need for distraction
- Dichotomous (black-or-white) thinking
- Feelings of emptiness
- Quest for perfection
- Desire to be special or unique
- Need to be in control
- Need for power
- Desire for respect and admiration
- Difficulty expressing feelings
- Need for escape or a safe place to go
- Lack of coping skills
- Lack of trust in self and others
- Terror of not measuring up

In her splendid book, *Appetites* (2003), Caroline Knapp, who recovered from her own eating disorder, describes starving as follows:

> . . . a solution to a wide variety of conflicts and fears, or at least it starts out resembling a solution: Something feels perversely good, or right, or gratifying about it, some key seems to slide into place, some distress assuaged, and the benefits of this are strong enough to outweigh whatever negative or painful feelings are aroused, such as shame, confusion, or physical hunger.

And in describing bingeing she writes,

> . . . the endlessly daunting business of defining a self—naming one's needs, speaking up for oneself, tolerating pain and frustration and disappointment—simply ground to a halt in the narcotizing stupor of a binge, all anxiety focused on the procuring of food, then eased, briefly, but powerfully in its consumption.

Knapp is talking about the last category of causation in eating disorder etiology: each person's individual, underlying emotional and psychological issues that come into play, contributing to or perpetuating eating disorder behavior. Not everyone who is exposed to the culture's idealization of thinness and goes on a diet develops an eating disorder. Some may even have the genetic predisposition, in other words the gun is loaded, and be in a trigger-pulling environment but no eating disorder. Why? These are people who, for whatever reason, are strong enough, together enough, stable enough, resilient enough, or protected enough as to be inoculated against developing an eating disorder. Some might develop subclinical eating disorders and escape serious consequences or even recognition. Others might develop an anxiety disorder or a phobia but not have eating problems. Others go unscathed.

For the most part, people who develop eating disorders have some psychological vulnerability or sensitivity; or there is an event, trauma, or family dysfunction in their lives that occurs at the right time, or is of the right duration or severity, to set them up for being the one person out of all their dieting friends who goes from diet to disorder. If, as the research shows, people can recover from this illness, what do they recover from? What have we treated when people get better? So far, not their genes and not (unfortunately) the culture. What unique features or events in a person's life (aside from dieting) contribute to eating disorder susceptibility that can be dealt with to help him or her heal? My answer to this question relies in large part on my experience of treating eating disorder clients and their families for almost 30 years. I am not a researcher, but I have gathered countless hours of data on this subject and have collaborated with my colleagues and my clients, who have indeed been my best teachers.

Disordered Eating Behaviors: Serving a Purpose

Even if they started out as dieting techniques, eating disorder symptoms end up serving some kind of purpose that goes well beyond weight loss as a goal. Certain people begin to use disordered eating behaviors as substitutes for psychological functions that have not been developed: "If I don't purge, I'm anxious and distracted.

After I purge, I can calm down and get things done," or "Not eating makes me feel safe and in control."

In trying to understand the meaning behind someone's behavior, it is helpful to think of the behavior as serving a function or "doing a job." Once the function is discovered, it becomes easier to understand why it is so difficult to give the behavior up and what might have to be done to replace it with something else. When exploring deep within the psyche of eating disordered individuals, one can find explanations for many of their behaviors that substitute for missing functions they do not have. Perhaps they were not developed in childhood. Paradoxically then, an eating disorder, for all of the problems it creates, is an effort to cope, communicate, defend against, and even solve other problems. This concept is critical in understanding and treating these disorders. For some, starving may be in part an attempt to establish a sense of power or control, self-worth, strength, and containment. Bingeing may be used to numb pain because of a developmental deficit in the ability to express grief or sadness or self-soothe. Purging may become an acceptable physiological and psychological release of anger or anxiety if the expression of one's feelings in childhood was not fostered or was met with misattunement in the form of neglect, criticism, or abuse.

Whether consciously or not, when people cannot cope in a healthy way, they often develop adaptive measures, the purpose of which is to make them feel whole, safe, secure, and in control. Some individuals use food, weight loss, and eating rituals to cope with other problems and to either avoid or meet emotional needs. Obsessively counting calories can alleviate anxiety and starving can serve as an unconscious cry for help. Bingeing and purging can be a reenactment of sexual abuse. Some individuals use dieting and weight loss as a means to gain acceptance and social status. In other eras, different means might have been sought, but today, dieting to gain a sense of success and validation is understandable in the context of the sociocultural factors described in the previous chapter. Praise and admiration come easily to anyone who loses weight, whether they needed to or not. When dieting fails, vulnerable individuals turn to excessive measures such as purging. When dieting results in deprivation, others will resort to bingeing. For still others, dieting is extremely successful and at first they receive praise and reinforcement, but eventually they take it too far. However it happens, behaviors that start out as dieting often end up serving several other goals or "adaptive functions."

The following is a list of adaptive functions that eating disorder behaviors commonly serve:

- Comfort, soothing, nurturance
- Numbing, sedation, distraction
- Attention, a cry for help
- Discharge of tension, anger, rebellion
- Predictability, structure, identity
- Self-punishment or punishment of "the body"
- Self-cleansing or self-purification
- Protection or safety (through creation of a small or large body)
- Avoidance of intimacy
- Proof for self-blame instead of blaming others (for example, abusers)

As an eating disorder therapist, I help my clients discover the adaptive function(s) their eating disorder symptoms serve and what their specific manifestation of behaviors means. The behaviors often express inner conflict and can be paradoxical:

- An expression of and defense against early childhood needs and feelings: "It's too scary to need anything, I try not to even need food."
- Self-destructive and self-affirming attitudes: "I will be the thinnest girl at my school, even if it kills me."
- An assertion and a punishment of self: "I insist on eating whatever and whenever I want, even though being fat is making me miserable. I deserve it."
- Cohesive functions that psychologically hold the person together: "If I don't purge, I'm anxious and distracted. After I purge, I can calm down and get things done."

The Eating Disorder Self

Eating disorder symptoms are the behavioral component of a separate, split-off self, or what I have come to call the "eating disorder self." This self has a special set of needs, behaviors, feelings, and perceptions, all of which are dissociated from the individual's core or what I call "healthy self." The eating disorder self functions to express, mitigate, or in some way meet underlying needs and make up for the developmental deficits.

The problem is that the eating disorder behaviors are only a temporary Band-Aid, and the person needs to keep going back for more; that is, he or she needs to continue the behaviors to meet the need. The person becomes dependent on these "external agents" and an addictive cycle is set up—not an addiction to food, but an addiction to whatever function the eating disorder behavior is serving. There is no self-growth, and the underlying deficit in the self remains. To get beyond this, the adaptive functions that the eating and weight-related behaviors serve must be "put out of a job" and replaced with healthier alternatives. To accomplish this, the eating disorder self must be recognized and understood in terms of why it exists. In addition, the person's healthy self has to be strengthened in order to take over the job. Eventually healing takes place when the two selves are integrated and no longer functioning as separate entities. (This may seem confusing but details are explained in Chapter 9.)

Treatment involves helping clients get in touch with their unconscious, unresolved needs and providing or helping to provide in the present what was missing in the past. One cannot do this without dealing directly with the eating disorder behaviors themselves, because they are the manifestation of and windows into the unconscious or hidden needs. For example, when a young woman with bulimia reveals that she binged and purged after a visit with her mother, it would be a mistake just to focus on how she feels about her mother. The therapist needs to explore the meaning of the bingeing and purging. How did the client feel before the binge? How did she feel before the purge? How did she feel during and after each? When did she know she was going to binge? When did she know she was going to purge? What might have happened if she didn't binge or purge? Probing these feelings will provide valuable information concerning the function the behaviors served.

When working with someone who has been sexually abused, the therapist may have to explore the meaning of food behaviors in detail, such as examining food-restricting behaviors to discover what the rejection or acceptance of food means to the client. How much is too much food? When does a food become fattening? How does it feel when you take food into your body? How does it feel to reject it? What would happen if you were forced to eat? Is there a part of you that would like to be able to eat and another part that won't allow it? What do they say to each other? Discussing how acceptance or rejection of food may be symbolic of controlling what goes in and out of the body may be an important component of the therapeutic work. Since sexual abuse is frequently encountered when dealing with eating disordered individuals, especially those in treatment settings who purge, therapists should be trained and confident in dealing with these issues.

Parents of children with eating disorders are not bad, nor did they all do terrible things, but somehow a problem existed—even though it may have been subtle or gone unnoticed—that became fertile ground for the development of an eating disorder. Sometimes it is simply a misattunement due to very different temperaments of parents and child. Sometimes it is an over focus on appearance and dieting. (See Chapter 11 for more on this subject.) Other times it is a more overt offense such as abuse or neglect. We do know that parent and child relationships matter, and we must pay attention to our clients' early development and attachment issues.

Eating Disorder Behaviors and Attachment

Research data and literature on attachment and eating disorders suggest that eating disorder symptoms may be substitutes for a secure attachment to help the patient overcome a real or perceived sense of inadequacy, insecurity, or fear. Data suggest that the frequency and intensity of anxious attachment in eating disorder individuals is greater than in control subjects. It seems that those with eating disorders are capable individuals who can use their intelligence and skill to manage major life issues but are highly sensitive and overreact to life's daily stresses and complexities. This fits with the typical story of someone who, although at the top of her senior class or vice president of a bank, comes to therapy because of her sensitivity to comments that were made about her weight, which sent her into a dieting spiral. (It is worth noting that individual biology, for example anxious temperament, may come into play.)

In a summary of their research on eating disorders and attachment, Ainsworth and Roth (1989) reported that the development of a sense of secure attachment and the ability to respond to situations with self-reliance may have been derailed in some way for all kinds of eating disorder individuals, resulting in self-blame, anger, and rejection as well as denial of these emotions. These people feel inadequate and essentially unworthy even in the face of many accomplishments. They are unable to validate themselves internally and look for external means to do so, making them more susceptible to an exaggerated focus on appearance.

Most eating disorder clients (at least those suffering from anorexia and bulimia) are not suffering from low self-esteem but rather from low self-worth. For example, imagine a client pressuring herself to make straight As. She has a healthy amount of self-esteem because she believes she should make straight As and is capable of it. However, once she achieves the desired grades, this is still not good enough. Now she will want an A plus or to take advanced classes and obtain all As. She never feels worthy enough. If she accomplishes a goal, another one is set. The bar is always raised. The same is true regarding weight. This kind of client sets a goal of losing five pounds, but once she has accomplished that, she still feels unworthy; there is always more to accomplish. The goal of finding self-worth is never accomplished. Individuals from all kinds of backgrounds develop eating disorders, so it may be that different child-rearing experiences are similar in their effects on attachment and the development of core beliefs regarding self and relationships. Uncovering and repairing any attachment issues can be an integral part of recovery.

The scope of this book does not allow a detailed analysis of every possible underlying emotional or psychological cause for eating disorders. Only an overview has been presented here. Additional details on emotional and psychological issues can be found in the chapters on therapy, Chapters 9, 10, and 11. Furthermore, a whole book could be written on spirituality and eating disorders, or what I call "tending the soul." For more information on how I use spirituality and soul work with eating disorder clients, see my book *100 Questions About Eating Disorders* and "Soul Lessons," an article I wrote for *Eating Disorders: The Journal of Treatment and Prevention.*

6

To Those Who Love Them: Guidelines for Family and Significant Others

IF YOU LOVE or care about someone who has an eating disorder, it is difficult to know what to do for him or her—or yourself. No matter what efforts you might make, such as helping find a therapist, sitting up all night talking, taking away laxatives, and so on, ultimately you have no power over another person's behavior. You do have power over what you choose to do about the situation and how you take care of yourself. The more knowledgeable and prepared you are, the better chance you have for success.

How to Approach Someone You Suspect Has an Eating Disorder

If you suspect that a friend, relative, student, or colleague has an eating disorder and you want to help, organizations like the National Eating Disorder Association (and others listed in the appendix) can help with information and brochures. Even though you don't know how your friend or loved one will react to your concern, it is important that you express it and offer to help. Even if your concern or help isn't well received, don't give up.

It is difficult but important for friends and family members to keep reaching out to facilitate a person with an eating disorder

Checklist of Observable and Nonobservable Signs of an Eating Disorder

Use the checklist here as a guide to substantiate your concerns.

- Does anything to avoid hunger and eating and feels guilty after eating
- Is obsessive and preoccupied with food
- Eats large quantities of food secretly and/or eats when upset
- Counts calories obsessively
- Disappears into the bathroom after eating (probably to vomit food)
- To lose weight takes diuretics, diet pills, laxatives, enemas, ipecac, and so forth
- Must earn food through exercising or exercises as punishment for overeating
- Is preoccupied with fat in food and on the body
- Increasingly eliminates food groups and/or eats only nonfat or "diet" foods
- Becomes a vegetarian but also avoids nuts, cheese, pasta, and many other foods
- Displays rigid control around food (e.g., type, quantity, and timing of food eaten)
- Complains of being pressured by others to eat more or less
- Weighs obsessively, panics without a scale, is terrified of gaining weight
- Isolates himself or herself socially

- Substitutes sweets or alcohol for other nutritious foods
- Constantly needs reassurance regarding appearance, self-denigrating
- Constantly checks the fit of a belt, a bracelet, a ring, or "thin" clothes
- Checks size of thighs when sitting and space between thighs when standing
- Uses large amounts of coffee, diet drinks, caffeine pills, or other stimulants

getting help and to support and encourage her during the struggle. People who have recovered from eating disorders often cite (and research backs this up) that having someone who loves, believes in, and did not give up on them were crucial factors in their seeking treatment and getting well. If you have observed behaviors in friends or loved ones and are concerned that they have a problem with food or weight, that is enough reason to say something. You do not need to wait until you have signs or proof of a full-blown eating disorder. The sooner you discuss things the better, for your sake and theirs. Pick a time and place where there will be no interruptions, allowing for privacy and time for everyone to say all that needs to be said.

Be Empathic and Understanding

The first step and most important thing to remember is to have empathy. Empathy is like standing in someone else's shoes. It is an effort to understand another person's experience as she experiences it and to convey that understanding. The only way to do this is to not be invested in changing the person; that can come later. Before a loved one can see another perspective, she will need to know that someone recognizes the legitimacy and importance of her own experience. Don't worry that empathizing is not enough and that you need to do something or get your loved one to take action. It is true that if all you do is empathize, you can love and understand someone with an eating disorder to death, but empathy is a necessary first step and must be maintained continually.

Coming on too strong and demanding change may simply cause the person to shut down and offer no information at all. Once someone knows you understand and are not going to try and take over or take the eating disorder away, then you can begin helping in other ways, such as getting information, finding specialists, making appointments, reassuring, and even confronting. Just remember that all of this needs to take place *after* she first feels understood and accepted.

Asking for help is usually one of the hardest things for those suffering from eating disorders to do. They need to learn that asking for and receiving help is not a weakness, and they do not need to handle everything alone. Even if there are limits to what you can do, she needs to know you can help, even if that means simply being there and listening. Ultimately, this helps her learn that she can reach out to people instead of her eating disorder behaviors to escape from her pain, deal with problems, or simply interrupt what may have become an addictive process.

Express Concern About Your Observations: Speak from Your Own Experience

It is important to stay calm and keep to specific personal examples. It is best to use "I" statements rather than "you" statements. Using "I" statements reflects your opinion or that you are speaking only from your own perspective. "You" statements sound judgmental and are apt to create a defensive reaction. Here are some examples:

- Instead of saying, "You're too thin," say, "I see you getting thin, and I'm scared."

- Instead of saying, "You have to stop throwing up," say, "I heard you throwing up and I'm worried about your health."
- Instead of saying, "You are ruining our relationship," say, "I'm concerned for you and felt like I had to say something and be honest in order to save our relationship."

Be careful not to use "you" statements that are disguised as "I" statements, for example, "I think you are just trying to get attention." Talking about specifics is important, but don't focus all of your discussion on food, weight, exercise, or other behaviors. It is easy to get caught up and stuck in discussing weight or behaviors such as bingeing or purging. These are valid concerns and worthy of comment, but focusing on behaviors alone can be counterproductive. For example, a person with anorexia may be pleased rather than alarmed to hear that she is painfully thin. Remember, the underlying issues, not just the behaviors, are important. She may be less defensive when approached with the idea that she seems sad, "not herself," or unhappy. She is likely to be less threatened by discussing these problems rather than issues of food and weight.

Provide Information About Resources for Treatment

It is wise to be prepared with helpful information and suggestions in case your friend or loved one is ready and willing to receive them. Try to have the name of a doctor and/or therapist, the fees they charge, and how to make an appointment. If a treatment program is needed, have that information as well. Ask her to consider going to at least one appointment and offer to go with her. Of course, if you are a parent of a minor, you need to go to the appointment too, and you should be included in the treatment. The person with the disorder must feel safe and confident with the therapist. Check out your resources to be sure you are dealing with a professional who is trained in treating eating disorders.

Do Not Argue but Do Not Give Up

Expect to be rejected in the beginning. It is very likely that the individual will deny the problem, become angry, or refuse to get help. It does no good to argue. Stick to your feelings, how you experience the situation, and your hope that she will get help. Parents may eventually have to use their authority over a child and force him or her to go to treatment. Let a therapist help negotiate power struggles, but do not give up and do not let yourself be left out of the treatment process.

Do not give up if rebuffed initially. Several conversations are often necessary to get people to realize or admit they have a problem. However, if you believe someone's life is in danger, you must get immediate help from a professional. Go to the appointment yourself even if she refuses. A professional can help you deal with a person who is in denial or resisting treatment. If all else fails, ask eating disorder professionals in your area if they can, or know of someone who can, help perform an intervention. An intervention is a carefully orchestrated event planned with the help of a professional in order to confront a loved one, discuss concerns, and compel her to get help. Interventions are well known in the field of drug and alcohol abuse, but not used as frequently for eating disorders.

You must think of an eating disorder as a serious illness. I often ask family members to imagine what they would do if this same person were shooting up heroin.

Accept Your Limitations

There is a limit to what you can do for another person. It is easy to fall into the trap of believing that if you could say or do the right thing, then your friend or loved one would be helped and you would not feel powerless. There is a lot you can do, but ultimately you alone cannot change the problem or make it go away. You must learn to accept your own limitations as to what you can and cannot do. Keep in mind that people often need to hear something several times before they act on it. Remember that everyone has a right to refuse treatment. Even minors, when forced to go to treatment sessions, can sit silently and refuse to talk or otherwise accept help.

Living with Someone with an Eating Disorder

Individuals with eating disorders directly or indirectly affect those with whom they live or who love and care about them. Family patterns of socializing, preparing food, going out to restaurants, and just talking to each other are all disrupted. Everything from finances to vacations seems jeopardized, and the person with the eating disorder is often resented for an illness she feels unable to control.

Someone with an eating disorder may not be the only member of the family with problems. It is common to find mood or behavior control difficulties in other family members. In the case of a child or adolescent, the level of functioning and boundary setting among parents and siblings should be evaluated. In many families, there is a history of excessive reliance on external achievement as an indicator of self-worth, which ultimately or repeatedly fails. Fluctuations between parental overinvolvement and abandonment may have occurred for some time, leaving clients feeling lost, isolated, insecure, rebellious, and without a sense of self. Parents—who have their own past and present issues—are often frustrated, fighting between themselves, and unhappy. Overinvolvement with an eating disordered child is often a first reaction in trying to gain control of an out-of-control situation. Futile attempts at control are exerted at a time when understanding and supportive direction would be more helpful.

In a marriage where one partner has an eating disorder, the spouse's concerns are often overshadowed by anger and feelings of helplessness. Spouses often report a decrease in intimacy, sometimes describing their loved ones as preferring or choosing the eating disorder over them. Spouses should be involved in the therapy process (see Van Den Broucke and Vandereycken 1997). Children, whether siblings or offspring of the client, should always be considered by the treatment team. They too will have feelings that need to be discussed and attended to and information to add. Whether to bring children in for a family session or talk to them individually or at all should be the decision of the therapist and/or treatment team. (See Chapter 11 for details on family therapy.)

When a Loved One Is in Treatment

The following are a few guidelines to help family members and significant others when a loved one is in treatment for an eating disorder. Each case is unique and warrants individualized attention, so use these with the assistance of a professional.

Be Patient—There Are No Quick Solutions

Recovery from an eating disorder takes a long time. Even if you are aware of this, you may still be inclined to think that the person should be improving faster and that more progress should be made. Long-term thinking and endless patience are necessary. Research suggests that full recovery will most likely take several years.

Avoid Power Struggles

Just as with approaching someone to get help, as much as possible find alternatives to power struggles, especially when it comes to eating and weight. Don't make mealtimes or eating a battle of wills. Don't try to force or overly control eating. Leave these issues to the therapist, dietitian, or other treating clinician unless your involvement is discussed, requested, and worked out with help from a professional. Family involvement is necessary in the treatment of adolescents, and parents may be instructed that it is necessary to "out will" their child in order to get him or her to eat. Parents will need help in this difficult process because it can be very hard on them. Family-based treatment is achieving a high degree of success with adolescents. Originally known as the Maudsley method, this approach is described in the book *Help Your Teen Beat an Eating Disorder* (Lock and Le Grange 2005) and discussed in Chapter 11.

Avoid Blaming or Demanding

Don't try to find causes or someone to blame for the eating disorder, and don't plead or demand that your loved one stop her behavior. Neither of these actions will help; they will only serve to oversimplify the situation and may cause shame and guilt. It is easy for her to feel responsible for your or someone else's feelings. Go to therapy together.

Don't Ask How You Can Help—Ask a Professional

Your loved one will not know how you can help and may feel worse if you ask. Another possibility is that she thinks she knows what will help but is wrong, and this will make matters worse. Trying to help when you are unsure of what to do might cause more fighting and new problems. A professional is in a better position to give you advice.

Deal with the Feelings of All Family Members

Unfortunately, family members, especially siblings, are often left out of the therapy process. It doesn't help to keep feelings bottled up inside; therefore, it may be useful for all family members to be involved in the therapy. Family therapy can be an important, even critical aspect of recovery. It is especially important for adolescents. Therapists need to find a way to work with family members even if family therapy is inappropriate. Asking family members to express themselves in journals, letters, or face-to-face discussions as a way of getting their feelings out and communicating may be helpful. (See Chapter 11 on family therapy for more details.)

Show Affection and Appreciation Verbally and Physically

A little unconditional love goes a long way. There are many ways to show affection and support besides talking (e.g., hugging or spending special time together). Consider writing letters or just little notes to your loved one, even if you live together. This is a good way to express encouragement, concern, and support without expecting a response or putting the person on the spot.

Do Not Comment About Weight or Appearance

Avoid making looks a focus. Don't comment about her or other people's weight or appearance. It is a trap to answer questions like, "Do I look fat?" If you say no, you won't be believed, and if you say anything else or even hesitate for a moment, your reaction may be used as an excuse to engage in eating disorder behavior. Telling someone with anorexia that she looks too thin is a mistake. This is what she wants to hear.

Telling someone with bulimia she looks good on a particular day may reinforce her binge/purge behaviors if she believes they are responsible for the compliment. I tell parents, spouses, and all significant others that when they're asked, "Do I look fat in this?" or some similar question, to answer honestly with some version of the following:

- "You and I know that there is no answer I could give you that would really work or make things better."
- "I think it is best if we stay away from talking about your weight."
- "You know this kind of question is a dead-end street for us."

Do Not Use Bribes, Rewards, or Punishments to Control Eating Behavior

Generally speaking, trying to externally control eating disorder behavior through bribery, punishment, or enticements—if it works at all—is only temporary. It puts off the person having to deal with internal means of controlling her behaviors. If you are the parent of an adolescent, as mentioned earlier, you might be directed to act differently for a period of time but, no matter what, eventually internal control is necessary.

Don't Go Unreasonably Out of Your Way to Prepare Special Foods

It is fine to help out by buying foods she likes and feels safe eating up to a point. Don't drive all the way to the frozen yogurt store because that is all she will eat. Don't be pushed into any action by the threat "I won't eat unless . . ." If a person refuses to eat unless strict circumstances are adhered to, she may ultimately need inpatient or residential treatment. Giving in to every whim will only postpone the inevitable.

Do Not Monitor Her Behavior, Even When Asked

Do not become the food or bathroom police. Loved ones may ask you to stop them if you see them eating too much or tell them when they have gained too much weight. They may seek your praise for the amount of food they are eating. Monitoring their behaviors may work for a short time but usually ends up backfiring. Get professional help and become a monitor only when and how advised.

Don't Allow Her to Dominate the Family's Eating Patterns

While nurturing others, individuals with eating disorders will often deny their own needs for food. As much as possible, the family's normal eating patterns should be maintained unless they are also in need of altering. Don't let the person with the disorder shop, cook for, or feed the family unless she also eats the items bought, prepared, and served.

Accept Your Limitations

Accepting your feelings and limitations means learning to set rules or say no in a caring and reasonable but firm and consistent manner. You may have to discuss cleaning the bathroom, limiting the amount of food she goes through, or charging for binged food.

You may have to tell her that you can't always be available and that calling you at work is unacceptable. Establish certain rules—for example, that laxatives or ipecac syrup aren't allowed in the house. If the illness progresses, you may have to add many more rules and reevaluate your own limitations. Don't try to become a substitute for professional care. Eating disorders are very complicated and difficult to treat; getting professional help is essential.

Getting Help and Support for Yourself

If you care about someone who has an eating disorder, it can be painful, frustrating, and confusing. You need knowledge, guidance, and support in dealing with the situation. The more knowledge you have about eating disorders and what to expect in regard to assessment and treatment, the easier it will be for you. Check the appendix for reading suggestions and other resources.

You are going to experience a range of emotions: from helplessness to anger to despair. You may find yourself losing control of your feelings and actions. You may even become preoccupied with your own and other family members' eating and weight. It is important to get help for yourself. You need to talk about your own feelings as well as getting guidance about how to deal with your loved one. Good friends are important, but a therapist or support group may also be necessary. You may need to go to an individual therapist where you can discuss your particular situation, feelings, and specific needs in detail.

Whether or not your loved one gets help, let her know that you are getting help for yourself. This may help her take the situation more seriously; even if it does not, you must take care of yourself. If you do not stay healthy and strong, you will not be able to help someone else. Remember the instructions the airlines give to put on your own oxygen mask first, then put one on your child. With your own "oxygen mask" on, you can safely explore, pursue, and participate in help and support for those you care about and love.

When you suspect or know that someone has an eating disorder and are ready to get them help, the first step is to have the person evaluated by trained professionals. It is important to get a thorough assessment to determine the nature and extent of the problem and to help devise an appropriate treatment plan. The next chapter provides details on assessing the situation.

7

Assessing the Situation

A CLINICAL DIAGNOSIS is important but insufficient for a full understanding of the problem, severity, and psychological or medical complications a person with an eating disorder may experience. This chapter discusses the behavioral and psychological assessments used by health care professionals to comprehensively evaluate a client's condition.

What a Professional Assessment Entails

A thorough assessment is an important first step in the treatment process. Getting the necessary information may take time, and professionals often set up longer or additional appointments for this purpose. They may also send some materials ahead of time for the client to bring to the assessment session. The professional can follow several methods in assessing an individual with disordered eating, including face-to-face interviews, inventories, detailed history questionnaires, and mental measurement testing.

Assessment Strategies

Assessing for an eating disorder is a difficult task that takes patience, empathy, and finesse. Clients almost always minimize how bad the problem is. They are ambivalent about recovery, particularly at the beginning of treatment when they do not know what to expect. The health care professional must get necessary information while at the same time establishing rapport and creating a trusting, supportive environment. I try to stress to clients that I am not going to use the information to do anything to them but rather to make recommendations so we can formulate goals together.

In the beginning, I let adults know that they are in charge; they are hiring me and, of course, can fire me and leave treatment at any time. In the case of adolescents, I focus on how to help get their parents "off their back" and how to keep them out of more restrictive forms of treatment. In both cases, I establish eye contact and conversation rather than filling out too much paperwork or going over forms. It is far better to interact with the client and his or her family during the assessment, saving paperwork for later. It is crucial for individuals with eating disorders and their families to know that the professional is there to help and understands what they all are going through.

Assessment Information

Health care professionals follow certain guidelines for gathering information about clients. It may take a while to get information in each of the areas discussed. In some sense, assessment continues throughout treatment. It may actually take months of therapy for a client to divulge certain information and for the clinician to get a clear picture of all the issues involved and how they relate to the eating disorder and necessary treatment.

Identifying Data and Presentation

The preliminary information identifies the client—age, name, phone, address, occupation, marital status, and so on. The professional also observes how the client looks, acts, and presents herself.

Reason for Seeking Treatment and Safety

The clinician needs to hear the client's reason for seeking help in his or her own words, because seemingly obvious assumptions can be wrong. Some individuals with bulimia nervosa come in because they want to be better restrictors. Some clients want treatment for their depression or relationship problems. Others might be there because of pressure and/or threats from a parent or spouse. Still others come in because they think the clinician has a magic answer or diet to help them lose weight.

It is also critical to assess whether the client is safe or needs immediate intervention. Suicidal thoughts, plans, or ideas must be evaluated along with self-harm behaviors or ideation.

Family Dynamics and Psychological History

Next comes information about the client's parents, spouse, and/or any other important family members. This information will be elicited from the client and, if possible, the family members as well. How do they all get along? How does each of them see the problem? How have family members attempted to deal with the client and the problem? What is the family history? Is there anyone else in the family with an eating disorder, psychiatric diagnosis, or addiction?

Therapists and treatment teams often fall short in assessing family background. I am often thanked profusely for caring enough to see what these individuals have to say. With permission from the client, I send a written assessment for spouses and parents to fill out (even with adult clients). Comparing this to the client's information provides interesting insights into the dynamics of family perceptions, attitudes, secrets, and so on.

Family Patterns of Health, Food, Weight, and Exercise

I explore the issues of food, weight, and exercise through written assessment forms and face-to-face discussions, because they can have a great bearing on the cause of the eating disorder and/or the forces that sustain it. For example, clients with parents who have struggled unsuccessfully with their own weight over the years may promote early weight-loss regimens in their children. Parents who push exercise and sports or test their child's body fat (believe me, I have seen this far too often recently) may contribute to the development of compulsive and perfectionistic exercisers.

If there is poor or no nutrition or exercise knowledge in the family, the clinician may be up against unhealthy but long-held family patterns that will need to be worked through respectfully. I treated a client with anorexia whose mother had been strictly "macrobiotic" and had raised her children that way. My client was even limited in the amount of fruit she ate because fruit was "high in sugar." She remembers being scolded for eating an extra apple. This woman had years of indoctrination and ingrained guilt about eating anything outside of the macrobiotic diet or anything she had come to call "extra." Dealing with this issue was part of her recovery.

Client's Weight, Eating, and Diet History

When possible, a thorough weight, dietary, dieting, and nutrition assessment should be performed and is often done so by a dietitian trained in working with eating disorders (see Chapter 12). All this information should be shared with the therapist. However, therapists should not solely rely on reports from other professionals and need to ask questions such as the following:

- What are the client's weight and weight goals?
- How often does she weigh herself?
- What was her weight and eating like when she was a child?
- What are all the ways he tried to lose weight, and why does he think they have or haven't worked?
- What is an example of a good day of eating and a bad one?

These are just a few of the questions that will reveal healthy or unhealthy behaviors and how chronic and/or severe the problem is.

Support Systems and Personal Goals

Who does the client usually go to for help? From whom does the client get her normal support (not necessarily regarding the eating disorder)? With whom does she feel comfortable sharing things? Who does she feel really cares? Research has shown that a significant factor in recovery is having a support system, whether it's family or close friends.

In addition, what are the client's goals regarding recovery? It is important to determine these, as they may be different from those of the clinician. To the client, recovery may mean being able to stay 95 pounds, lose weight, or simply get everyone to stop nagging her. Deep down, all clients usually want to stop hurting, torturing themselves, and feeling trapped. If they don't have any goals, the therapist may suggest some, asking whether they would like to be less obsessed or, even if they want to be thin, whether they wouldn't also like to be healthy. Clinicians should not argue about goals in the assessment phase but rather be establishing understanding without judgment. The clinician should tell clients the truth but not be setting any personal agendas of his or her own.

Chief Complaint and Interference

The clinician needs to establish what's wrong from the client's perspective. This will depend on whether the person was forced into treatment or came in voluntarily, but either way, the chief complaint usually changes as the client begins to feel safer with the clinician. Some of the questions asked at this stage may include the following:

- What are you doing with food that you would like to stop doing?
- What can't you do with food that you would like to be able to do?
- What do others want you to do or stop doing?
- What thoughts, feelings, or behaviors get in the way of having the life you want?

In addition, the professional should be finding out how much the disordered eating, body image, or weight control behaviors are interfering with the client's life. For example, does she skip school because she feels sick or fat? Does she avoid people? Is she spending a lot of money on her habits? Is she having a hard time concentrating? How much time does she spend weighing herself? How much time does she spend buying food, thinking about food, exercising, purging, reading about weight loss, or worrying about her body? How has all of this affected her relationships, work, and social life?

Psychiatric History

Has the client ever had any other psychological problems or disorders? Have any family members or relatives had any psychological or mental disorders? The clinician needs to know if the client has or had any other psychiatric conditions, such as obsessive-compulsive disorder, depression, or anxiety, that would complicate treatment or indicate a different form of treatment. Several studies have shown that approximately 50 to 60 percent of individuals diagnosed with anorexia nervosa or bulimia nervosa have previously been diagnosed with an anxiety disorder. Furthermore, some studies show that as many as 70 to 80 percent have a lifetime history of being diagnosed with anxiety disorder (meaning that the anxiety diagnosis could have been prior to or after the eating disorder diagnosis).

Assessing for depression is also important. Many times clients are depressed because of the eating disorder and their unsuccessful attempts to deal with it. Clients also get depressed because their relationships often fall apart over the eating disorder. Depression can also be caused by nutritional inadequacies. However, depression may exist in the family history and in the client before the onset of the eating disorder. Sometimes it is hard to sort out which came first, creating "the-chicken-or-the-egg" scenario. The same is often true for other conditions such as obsessive-compulsive disorder.

Other comorbid conditions also require further assessments and treatment recommendations; for example, post-traumatic stress disorder is often seen in individuals with purging behavior. A psychiatrist experienced in eating disorders can provide a thorough psychiatric evaluation and recommendations regarding treatment of these issues.

Medical History

The clinician doesn't have to go into great detail for the medical history because this information should be obtained from the client's physician. However, the treating clinician should ask questions in this area for several reasons: to get an overall picture of the client's general health, to establish concern in this area and emphasize its importance, and finally because clients often don't tell their physicians everything—or in some cases, anything. It is valuable to know whether the client is often sickly or has some current or past problems that could have affected or been related to her eating behaviors; for example, is the client cold or constipated all the time? If the client is female and old enough, treating clinicians should find out if she has regular menstrual cycles even though a physician should be getting this information. At what weight did the client begin menstruating? Is she regular? Has she stopped menstruating? At what weight did she stop? How long has she been without a period? Has she taken or does she take hormone replacement medications?

It is necessary to distinguish between physical conditions that have psychological causes and those that have medical causes. For example, true anorexia, e.g., experienced by many, which is simply a loss of appetite unrelated to a desire to lose weight (many cancer patients), differs from anorexia nervosa. A person may be genetically obese with no symptoms of BED, or he may truly be a binge eater. Vomiting may be spontaneous rather than self-induced. Food refusal can also indicate problems other than a clinical eating disorder. For instance, an eight-year-old girl diagnosed by another therapist as having anorexia nervosa was brought to me for a second opinion. She had been gagging on food and thus began refusing it which then resulted in weight loss. During my assessment, I discovered that she had developed a fear of gagging as a result of oral sexual abuse. She had no fear of weight gain or body image disturbance and had been inappropriately diagnosed.

Substance Abuse

Many eating disorder clients currently abuse or have abused other substances besides food and diet-related pills or items. Sometimes they see no connection between their eating disorder and their use or abuse of alcohol, marijuana, cocaine, and so on. Other times the connection is the reason for the substance use; for example, a client will say, "I snort coke because it makes me lose my appetite and helps me lose weight."

Clinicians need to know about any kind of substance abuse that will complicate treatment and give further clues to the client's personality (e.g., whether she is a more addictive personality type, the type of person who needs some form of escape or relaxation, or self-destructive for an unconscious or subconscious reason). Research has shown that individuals with anorexia nervosa who abuse alcohol have higher death rates than those without the problem of alcohol. Alcohol, cocaine, or other substances complicate treatment, so clinicians need to address these issues when developing a treatment plan.

Any Other Physical or Mental Symptoms

Eating disorder clients often suffer from other problems, such as insomnia. They often do not connect this to their eating disorder and forget to mention it to their physician or therapist. To varying degrees, insomnia has an effect on eating disorder behavior. Some individuals with anorexia report a history of past obsessive-compulsive behavior, such as having their clothes arranged perfectly in the closet according to color, putting their socks on a certain way every day, or pulling out leg hairs one by one.

Clients may not know that these types of behaviors are important to divulge or that they can shed light on the eating disorder, but any physical or mental symptom is important. The clinician is treating the whole person, not just the eating disorder behaviors.

Sexual or Physical Abuse or Neglect

Clients are asked for specific information about their sexual history and about any kind of abuse or neglect. There are specific questions about the ways clients were disciplined as children, including whether they were ever hit to a degree that left marks or bruises. Questions about being left alone or being fed properly are also important, as is information such as their age when they first had intercourse, whether their first intercourse was consensual, and if they were ever touched inappropriately or in a way that made them uncomfortable.

Clients often do not feel comfortable revealing this kind of information, especially at the beginning of treatment. Bessel Van Der Kolk, a trauma specialist from Harvard, has reported at several conferences that rather than just asking about abuse, clinicians should inquire as to whether the client felt safe as a child, with whom she felt safe, and why. Many of the negative results of abuse are related to not having any supportive caregivers around to nurture and form healthy attachments with the child. As with other sensitive areas, the client may wait to reveal this type of information until she has developed more trust in the clinician.

Insight, Effort, and Motivation

The therapist should know how aware the client is regarding her problem. How well does she understand what is going on both symptomatically and psychologically? How aware is she of needing help and of being out of control? Does she understand the underlying causes of her disorder?

In addition, the therapist should find out what the client or any other professional has done to try to alleviate the problem and why past attempts have not worked. Does the client know what is expected from her in treatment?

Lastly, the clinician must ascertain how motivated and/or committed the client is to getting treatment and getting well. There has been a growing interest in the area of motivation and readiness to change in working with the eating disorder population. Motivation to change may be an important consideration in determining if and when treatment should begin and what kind of treatment would be best.

Psychometric Assessments

A variety of psychometric assessments have been devised to help professionals assess behaviors and underlying issues commonly involved in eating disorders. Advances in our understanding and treatment of anorexia nervosa and bulimia nervosa have resulted in improvements in standardized assessment tools and techniques for these disorders. Standard assessments for BED are still being developed because less is known about the clinical features of this condition. This section provides a brief overview of some of the assessments that professionals use, but readers can find more detailed descriptions of assessment measures in books such as the *Clinical Handbook of Eating Disorders* (Brewerton 2004).

Self-Report Instruments

Self-report instruments such as those in the following list are problematic because subjects are not always honest when answering questions. However, the information can be combined with that from other assessment procedures such as a diagnostic interview.

- **Eating Attitudes Test (EAT-26).** Designed to distinguish older adolescents and adults with anorexia nervosa from weight-preoccupied, but otherwise healthy, female college students. A child version, ChEAT, is available.
- **Eating Disorder Inventory (EDI).** One of the most widely used self-report measures that assesses the thinking patterns and behavioral characteristics of anorexia nervosa and bulimia nervosa. It measures attitudes and behaviors concerning eating, weight, and shape, as well as psychological traits such as perfectionism, impulse control, and social insecurity.
- **Eating Disorder Examination Questionnaire (EDE-Q).** A self-report version of a structured interview known as the Eating Disorder Examination (EDE). The EDE is time-consuming to administer and requires properly trained assessors, so the EDE-Q is considered a good substitute.
- **Revised Bulimia Test (BULIT_R).** Can be used as a screening instrument or to assess the severity of bulimia nervosa.

Body Image Assessments

Body image disturbance is a dominant characteristic of eating disorder individuals, a significant predictor of who might develop an eating disorder, and an indicator of who might relapse. To assess body image, a clinician can use body image sections of other larger assessment tools, such as the body dissatisfaction subscale of the EDI, or inventories designed specifically for assessing weight and shape concerns, beliefs, and attitudes.

One specific body image assessment is the Shape- and Weight-Based Self-Esteem Inventory (SAWBS). This assessment is experiential and visual and helps reveal the extent to which a client values weight and shape over other attributes. It can provide useful material for diagnostic and treatment purposes, such as tracking attitude changes over time. The visual and experiential aspects of this tool offer a welcome variation on question-and-answer verbal assessments.

Motivation Assessments

The field is looking for better ways to assess who is right for what kind of treatment at what time. Motivation to change assessments that informed the field of chemical dependency are receiving increasing attention for use with the eating disorder population. The following are two examples currently being used with eating disorder clients:

- **The Stages of Change Questionnaire.** Originally used with the substance abuse population, this tool can easily be used for eating disorder individuals. It assesses four stages of change: precontemplation, contemplation, action, and maintenance.
- **Readiness and Motivation Interview (RMI) (Geller and Drab 1999).** This semistructured interview for individuals with eating disorders assesses their experience of and attachment to their eating disorder symptoms. It is used

in conjunction with the EDE so that both diagnostic and motivational information can be obtained for each symptom.

Additional Psychological Assessments

Other psychological assessments can be done to help inform and guide treatment. Several tools are available, including the following:

- Beck Depression Inventory (BDI) to assess depression
- Beck Anxiety Inventory (BAI) to assess symptoms of stress and anxiety
- Dissociative Experiences Scale (DES) to measure a range of dissociative phenomena in adults
- Yale-Brown Obsessive Compulsive Scale (Y-BOCS) to conduct a structured interview for measuring obsessive-compulsive symptoms

As previously mentioned, other professionals will hopefully perform additional assessments as part of a treatment team approach. A dietitian should do a nutritional and eating disorder symptom assessment, and a psychiatrist should perform a psychiatric evaluation. An initial medical assessment and ongoing medical monitoring are critical in the overall treatment of a person with an eating disorder. Integrating the results of various assessments allows the clinician, client, and treatment team to develop an appropriate, individualized treatment plan.

8

Treatment Philosophy and Approaches

MANY THERAPISTS SUBSCRIBE to a certain model or approach that informs their interventions, strategies, and expectations for clients. The current trend in research and clinical training for eating disorders favors the use of models with specific applications, precise definitions, manuals, and what is referred to as "evidenced-based treatment." However, in my experience, a seasoned therapist will rely more on his or her own experience and whatever works for the client rather than being tied to any particular treatment model.

Currently, depending on how clinicians view the nature of eating disorders, they will most likely approach treatment from one or more of the general perspectives described in the treatment literature and summarized in this chapter. These approaches are used alone or in combination according to the treating professional's knowledge and preference, as well as the needs of the individual receiving care. Remember that there are gifted clinicians doing excellent work who may use approaches other than those described in this chapter.

The information presented here is meant to help promote an understanding of the most commonly used and accepted approaches and help individuals choose appropriate treatment. Medical and psychiatric treatment are discussed in other chapters; but it is important to note that stabilization of a client's medical

The Importance of the Therapeutic Relationship

An area worthy of more research, in terms of efficacy of treatment, that has not received enough attention is the therapeutic relationship and, more specifically, the alliance between the therapist and the client. In research conducted on models of psychotherapy, the aspect of *who* is providing the treatment cannot be ignored. In many research studies the therapists providing the treatment being studied are aligned with the treatment model. This positively affects the treatment outcome. Wampold (1997) in his meta analysis comparing psychotherapies found that studies that have pitted therapies against one another have, for the most part, shown no essential differences in outcome across modalities. On the other hand, there is a growing body of research that points to the therapeutic alliance as the most significant factor in treatment outcome across several different diagnoses. Thus, who a therapist is and how he or she relates to the client matters more than the treatment approach. Many people have heard about the importance of the therapeutic alliance but unfortunately don't know exactly what it means or how to learn more about it. Two excellent books on this topic are *The Heroic Client* (Duncan et al. 2004) and *The Heart and Soul of Change* (Hubble et al. 1999).

My own experience in treating eating disorder clients corroborates the importance of therapeutic alliance. No one treatment approach works for all individuals with eating disorders. I use a combination of the approaches described in this chapter with success, but without a good alliance with the client, it would be much harder for me to put the eating disorder self out of a job.

status and ongoing medical monitoring and treatment are necessary in conjunction with all approaches.

Psychodynamic Therapy

A psychodynamic view of behavior emphasizes internal conflicts, motives, and unconscious forces. Within the psychodynamic realm are many theories on the development of psychological disorders in general and on the sources and origins of eating disorders in particular. Describing each psychodynamic theory and the resulting treatment approach, such as object relations or self-psychology, is beyond the scope of this book.

The common feature of all psychodynamic theories is the belief that if the underlying causes of disordered behaviors are not addressed and resolved, they may subside for a time but will often return. The early pioneering work of Hilde Bruch on treating eating disorders made it clear that using behavior modification techniques to get people to gain weight may achieve improvements in the short term but not much in the long run. Like Bruch, therapists with a psychodynamic perspective believe that the essential treatment for full recovery involves understanding and treating the cause, adaptive function, or purpose of the eating disorder. Please note that this does not necessarily mean "analysis" or going back in time to uncover past events, although this may be useful or even necessary in some cases.

In all of the psychodynamic theories, symptoms are seen as expressions of a struggling inner self that uses the disordered eating and weight control behaviors as a way of communicating or expressing underlying issues. The symptoms are viewed as useful for the client, and direct attempts to try to take them away are avoided. In a strict psychodynamic approach, the premise is that when the underlying issues are expressed, worked through, and resolved, the disordered eating behaviors will no longer be necessary. Whatever the particular psychodynamic theory, the essential goal of this treatment approach is to help clients understand the connections between their past, their personality, and their personal relationships and how all this relates to their eating disorder.

The problem with a solely psychodynamic approach to treating eating disorders is twofold. First, many clients are in such a state of starvation, depression, or compulsivity that psychodynamic psychotherapy regarding underlying issues cannot effectively take place. Therefore, starvation, suicidal tendencies, compulsive bingeing and purging, or serious medical abnormalities may need to be addressed before psychodynamic work can be effective. Second, clients can spend years gaining insight in psychodynamic therapy while still engaging in destructive symptomatic behaviors. To continue this kind of therapy for too long without seeing changes in symptoms seems unnecessary, unfair, and inappropriate.

Psychodynamic therapy can offer a lot to eating disordered individuals and may be an important factor in treatment, but a strict psychodynamic approach alone—with no discussion of the eating- and weight-related behaviors—has received little empirical support. This is true, in part, because this method is often combined with others or there has been no control group. In any case, dealing directly with the disordered behaviors is important.

Cognitive Behavioral Therapy

The most well-known and studied technique or treatment approach currently used to challenge, manage, and transform specific food- and weight-related behaviors is known as cognitive behavioral therapy (CBT). It was originally developed in the late 1970s by Aaron Beck as a technique for treating depression. The essence of CBT is that feelings and behaviors are created by cognitions (thoughts). The clinician's job is to help individuals learn to recognize cognitive distortions and either choose not to act on them or, better still, to replace them with more realistic and positive ways of thinking and thus behaving.

Cognitive behavioral therapy uses homework, journals, and monitoring outside of the sessions. Educating clients about dieting, purging, medical complications, and so on is an important part of this model. Researchers have developed cognitive behavioral programs with treatment manuals that provide very specific interventions to be followed. Many clinicians find these too rigid to follow exactly and prefer to adapt to particular clients.

Functions That Cognitive Distortions Serve

Common cognitive distortions can be put into categories such as all-or-nothing thinking, overgeneralizing, assuming, magnifying or minimizing, magical thinking, and personalizing. Such distortions are well recognized in eating disorder clients and influence their behavior. A disturbed or distorted body image, paranoia about all food being fattening, and binges based on the belief that one cookie has already destroyed a perfect day of dieting are common unrealistic assumptions and distortions.

Cognitive distortions are held sacred by clients who rely on them as guidelines for behavior to gain a sense of identity, safety, and control. They serve a variety of functions:

- **They provide a sense of safety and control.** For example, all-or-nothing thinking provides a strict and rigid system of rules for an individual to follow when there is no self-trust in making decisions. "As long as I have blown it, I might as well go the whole way and indulge in all those foods that I never allow myself to eat."

- **They reinforce the eating disorder as a part of the individual's identity.** For example, eating, exercise, and weight become factors that make the person feel special and unique. "I don't know who I will be without this illness," or "I am the person known for not eating."

• **They enable individuals to replace reality with a system that supports their behaviors.** For example, magically thinking that being thin will solve all of their problems or minimizing the significance of weighing as little as 79 pounds are ways that clients can mentally allow themselves to continue their behavior. As long as John continues to believe that if he stops taking laxatives, he will get fat, it is very difficult to get him to discontinue his behavior.

• **They help provide an explanation or justification of behaviors to others.** For example, a client with anorexia may explain her reluctance to eat by saying, "If I eat more, I feel bloated and miserable." Or a binge eater may restrict eating sweets only to end up bingeing on them later, justifying the restriction by telling everyone, "I'm allergic to sugar." Both of these claims are more difficult to argue with than "I'm afraid to eat more food" or "I set myself up to binge because I don't allow myself to eat sugar." Clients will justify their continued starving or purging by minimizing negative lab test results, hair loss, and even poor bone density scans. They often try to convince others to believe that electrolyte problems, heart failure, and death are things that happen to other people who are worse off.

Cognitive distortions have to be challenged in an educational and empathetic way to avoid unnecessary power struggles. Clients need to know that their behaviors are ultimately their choice, but that they are currently choosing to act on false, incorrect, or misleading information and faulty assumptions. Regardless of theoretical orientation, most clinicians will eventually need to address and challenge their clients' distorted attitudes and beliefs in order to interrupt the behaviors that result from them. If not addressed, the distortions and symptomatic behaviors are likely to persist or return.

What Research Tells Us About CBT and the Treatment of Eating Disorders

Studies indicate that cognitive behavioral therapy is useful for treating bulimia and BED, but results are lacking for anorexia nervosa. (Readers can refer to Keel 2005 and other resources for more information on these studies.) For bulimia nervosa the results have been the most promising. Several studies show CBT outperforming other approaches used with this condition. Therefore, many top professionals consider cognitive behavioral therapy for bulimia as the "gold standard." "Cognitive Behavioral Therapy for Bulimia Nervosa," *Binge Eating: Nature, Assessment, and Treatment* (Fairburn et al. 1993) contains an example of a specifically researched approach.

Even though the findings are promising, researchers concede that the results show only that in these studies CBT worked better than other methods it was compared to and not that we have found a form of treatment that will help most clients. There are even studies surfacing showing that other forms of therapy are as useful as CBT. In fact, the majority of clients with bulimia do not recover with the cognitive behavioral approach, and we are not sure which clients will. (See the study mentioned in the next section on interpersonal therapy.)

Interpersonal Therapy

Interpersonal therapy (IPT) focuses on the links between eating disorder behaviors and underlying relationship issues. This approach has shown some efficacy in treating bulimia nervosa and binge eating disorder. The rationale for using IPT with eating disorder clients is that although etiology is multifactorial in nature, these clients often have a number of interpersonal problems that play an important role in the onset and continuation of the disorder. The problems most often identified and targeted in this treatment are role disputes (or not getting along with others); role transition (such as going away to college, getting married, or moving); grief (specifically related to death); and interpersonal deficits in intimate relationships (such as the inability to communicate well, be intimate, and form lasting relationships.)

Outside of the initial assessment, IPT does not discuss food, weight, or shape, but rather encourages clients to associate their symptoms with life experiences and interpersonal problems. Identifying and focusing on specific problems, discussing feelings and relationships, and using role playing and problem solving are all part of this therapy. Readers can look on the Internet for the International Society for Interpersonal Psychotherapy for more information on this approach.

In one of the best long-term, intensive studies that compared CBT to what was thought at the time to be a neutral control group, IPT, two important findings emerged. The first was that although CBT appeared more effective than IPT at the end of treatment and at a four-month follow-up, the benefits of IPT almost caught up to those of CBT at one year. Within five years there was no difference in how the two groups were doing, a very unanticipated result. The field needs to find out how a treatment that is food- and weight-focused and another that is not at all, end up with the same results. The second finding is even more important. By the time of the one-year follow-up, only 30 percent of the CBT group and 20 percent of the IPT group were symptom-free. Therefore, 70 to 80 percent of the subjects for both CBT and IPT remained symptomatic. We should not be satisfied with these treatment results.

More research needs to be done but at this time the prudent course of action would be to use CBT and IPT as part of an integrated, multidimensional approach in treating clients with bulimia and binge. I have also successfully used this combination with clients suffering from anorexia. The next approach described is one way of utilizing a combination of CBT and IPT techniques.

Dialectical Behavior Therapy

One therapeutic model that has gained attention over the last few years is dialectical behavior therapy (DBT), which combines cognitive behavioral techniques with interpersonal therapy. Because DBT was originally developed to treat individuals with poor interpersonal skills who also exhibited extreme mood fluctuations, poor impulse control, and self-destructive behaviors, it seems like a good choice for bulimia and binge eating disorder.

Developed by Marsha Linehan, DBT focuses on harmful and acting out behaviors before working on interpersonal issues, but both are ultimately addressed. A large part of this treatment focuses on skill building and can be adapted for eating disorders by targeting eating disorder behaviors when setting treatment goals and building skills in the area of nutrition and weight.

The main areas of focus in DBT are as follows:

- **Mindfulness.** Awareness training, or developing the ability to go inside and observe, quiet the chatter of the mind, and respond from an internal healthy self rather than react emotionally.
- **Distress tolerance.** Clients are helped to see that destructive behaviors are not long-term solutions for solving problems. Clients are taught to tolerate feelings and find alternative methods for coping with painful emotions.
- **Interpersonal effectiveness.** Working on successful relationships with oneself and others is considered crucial for long-term recovery.
- **Emotional regulation.** Teaching clients "affect regulation," or the ability to experience emotions without having to react to them, is key to a positive outcome.

I describe DBT as Zen Buddhism combined with the old Rational Emotive Therapy (RET) by Albert Ellis. (RET and CBT are similar behavioral approaches in their ideas that our thoughts and beliefs shape our behavior.) I have been practicing this combination of therapeutic approaches for many years with a high degree of success. There has been little research on DBT, but in one controlled study it was shown to be successful with bulimia nervosa, and in two uncontrolled studies it appeared that DBT may be useful in treating both bulimia and binge eating (Keel 2005). For more on DBT, readers can check out *Cognitive Behavioral Treatment of Borderline Personality Disorder* (Marsha Linehan 1993).

Addiction/Twelve-Step Model

The addiction model of treatment for eating disorders was originally taken from the disease model of alcoholism. Alcoholism is considered an addiction, and alcoholics are considered powerless over drinking because they have a disease that causes their bodies to react in an abnormal and addictive way to the consumption of alcohol. The Twelve-Step program of Alcoholics Anonymous (AA) was designed to treat alcoholism based on this principle. When this model was applied to eating disorders, and Overeaters Anonymous (OA) was originated, the word *food* was substituted for the word *alcohol* in the Twelve-Step OA literature and at OA meetings.

The basic OA text explains, "The OA recovery program is identical with that of Alcoholics Anonymous. We use AA's twelve steps and twelve traditions, changing only the words 'alcohol' and 'alcoholic' to 'food' and 'compulsive overeater'" (Overeaters Anonymous 1980). In this model, food is often referred to as a drug over which those with eating disorders are powerless.

The Twelve-Step program of Overeaters Anonymous was originally designed to help people who felt out of control with their overconsumption of food: "The major objective of the program is to achieve abstinence, defined as freedom from compulsive overeating" (Malenbaum et al. 1988). The original treatment approach involved abstaining from certain foods that were considered addictive or binge foods, namely sugar and white flour, and following the Twelve Steps adapted for OA.

Twelve Steps of OA

Step I: We admitted we were powerless over food—that our lives had become unmanageable.

Step II: Came to believe that a Power greater than ourselves could restore us to sanity.

Step III: Made a decision to turn our will and our lives over to the care of God as we understood Him.
Step IV: Made a searching and fearless moral inventory of ourselves.
Step V: Admitted to God, to ourselves, and to another human being the exact nature of our wrongs.
Step VI: Were entirely ready to have God remove all these defects of character.
Step VII: Humbly asked Him to remove our shortcomings.
Step VIII: Made a list of all persons we had harmed, and became willing to make amends to them all.
Step IX: Made direct amends to such people wherever possible, except when to do so would injure them or others.
Step X: Continued to take personal inventory and when we were wrong, promptly admitted it.
Step XI: Sought through prayer and meditation to improve our conscious contact with God as we understood Him, praying only for knowledge of His will for us and the power to carry that out.
Step XII: Having had a spiritual awakening as the result of these steps, we tried to carry this message to compulsive overeaters and to practice these principles in all our affairs.

The addiction analogy and abstinence approach make some sense in relation to their original application to compulsive overeating. It was reasoned that if addiction to alcohol causes binge drinking, then addiction to certain foods could cause binge eating; therefore, abstinence from those foods should be the goal. However, this analogy and supposition is debatable. To date there has been no scientific proof that being addicted to a certain food causes an eating disorder (much less masses of people being addicted to the same food). Nor has there been research demonstrating that the Twelve-Step approach is successful in treating eating disorders.

In an effort to find a way to treat the growing number and severity of eating disorder cases, the OA approach began to be applied loosely to all forms of eating disorders. The theory that compulsive overeating was fundamentally the same illness as bulimia and anorexia—and thus all were addictions—was a leap based on faith, hope, or desperation. Nevertheless, the use of the addiction model was readily adopted because of the lack of guidelines for treatment and the similarities that eating disorder symptoms seemed to have with other addictions (Hatsukami et al. 1982). Twelve-Step recovery programs sprang up everywhere as a model that could be adapted immediately for use with eating disorder "addictions." This occurred even though one of OA's own pamphlets, containing questions and answers about the program, tried to clarify that "OA publishes literature about its program and compulsive overeating, not about specific eating disorders such as bulimia and anorexia" (Overeaters Anonymous 1979).

Criticisms of the Twelve-Step Model

The American Psychiatric Association (APA) recognized a problem with Twelve-Step treatment for anorexia nervosa and bulimia nervosa in its February 1993 treatment guidelines. In summary, the APA's position stated that Twelve-Step–based programs are not recommended as the sole treatment approach for anorexia nervosa or the initial sole approach for bulimia nervosa. The guidelines suggested that for bulimia nervosa, Twelve-Step programs such as OA may be helpful as an adjunct to other treatment and for subsequent relapse prevention. In determining these guidelines, the APA expressed concerns that because of "the great variability of knowledge, attitudes, beliefs, and practices from chapter to chapter and from sponsor to sponsor regarding eating disorders and their medical and psychotherapeutic treatment and because of the great variability of patients' personality structures, clinical conditions, and susceptibility to potentially counter therapeutic practices, clinicians should carefully monitor patients' experiences with Twelve Step programs" (American Psychiatric Association 1993).

Recovered Versus Recovering

One of the criticisms of the addiction model is the idea that people can never be recovered. Eating disorders are thought to be lifelong diseases that can be controlled into a state of remission by working through the Twelve Steps and maintaining abstinence on a daily basis. According to this viewpoint, eating disorder individuals can be "in recovery" or "recovering" but never "recovered." If the symptoms go away, the person is only in abstinence or remission but still has the disease. A "recovering" bulimic (a Twelve-Step term, not mine) still refers to herself as a bulimic and continues attending Twelve-Step meetings with the goal of remaining abstinent from sugar, flour, other binge foods, as in the original OA, or is abstinent from the behavior of bingeing and/or purging. Most readers will be reminded of the man in an AA meeting who says, "Hi, I'm John, and I'm an alcoholic," even though he may not have had a drink for 10 years. He might also refer to himself as a "recovering alcoholic" but still he is an alcoholic. Labeling eating disorders as addictions, with the idea that one is never recovered but always recovering, may not only be a diagnostic trap but also a self-fulfilling prophecy.

Applying the abstinence model to individuals who have anorexia or bulimia is problematic. Even though the idea of restricting sugar and white flour is fading in OA groups and individuals are allowed to choose their own form of abstinence, OA can still present problems with its absolute standards and black-and-white thinking. Individuals with bulimia or binge eating who abstain from sugar, white flour, and other "binge foods" often end up bingeing on other foods. Additionally, labeling a food as a "binge food" can be a self-fulfilling prophecy and is counterproductive to the cognitive behavioral approach of restructuring dichotomous (black-and-white, good food–bad food) thinking.

Individuals with anorexia are already masters at abstinence. They need help knowing it's okay to eat any food, particularly "scary" foods, which often contain sugar and white flour—the very ones that were originally forbidden in OA. To resolve this issue Twelve Step proponents have argued that people with anorexia can use "abstinence from abstinence" as a goal, but this is extremely vague and seems to be an issue of forcing the individual to fit the model. All of this adjusting just tends to water down the Twelve-Step program as it was originally conceived and well utilized.

Furthermore, behavior abstinence, such as refraining from binge eating, is different from substance abstinence. When does eating become overeating and overeating become binge eating? Who decides? The line is fuzzy and unclear. One would not say to an alcoholic, "You can drink, but you must learn how to control it; in other words, you must not binge drink." Drug addicts and alcoholics don't have to learn how to control the consumption of drugs or alcohol. Abstinence from these substances *can* be a black-and-white issue and, in fact, is supposed to be. Addicts and alcoholics give up drugs and alcohol completely and forever. A person with an eating disorder has to deal with food every day. Hopefully, full recovery for a person with an eating disorder is the ability to deal with food in a normal, healthy way.

Twelve-Step Approach as a Means of Support

Many with eating disorders have found support and recovery with the Twelve-Step approach. There are clients who I encourage to attend Twelve-Step meetings, mostly those addicted to drugs or alcohol. I love that these groups are free and offered all over the world and that there is a mission for those recovering to give back. There are many incredibly useful aspects to the Twelve-Step philosophy, such as personal inventories, making amends, and the use of recovering sponsors to help those still not abstinent. I am moved by the devotion, dedication, and support that I have seen in sponsors who give so much to anyone who wants help. I am especially grateful to them when they respond to my clients' calls at 3:00 A.M. I have also been concerned on many occasions where I have seen "the blind leading the blind." If there is a therapist and a sponsor working with a client, they should communicate with each other to provide a consistent treatment philosophy.

If a Twelve-Step approach is used, it must be done with caution and adapted to the uniqueness of eating disorders. Craig Johnson has discussed this adaptation in his 1993 article "Integrating the Twelve Step Approach." The article suggests how an adapted version of the Twelve-Step approach can be useful with a certain population of clients and discusses criteria used to identify these clients.

Based on my experiences and those of my recovered clients, I urge clinicians who use the Twelve-Step approach with eating disordered clients to do the following:

- Adapt the approach for the uniqueness of eating disorders and of each individual.
- Monitor clients' experiences closely.
- Allow that every client has the potential to become "recovered."

The belief that one will not have a disease called an eating disorder for life but can be "recovered" is a very important issue. How a treating professional views the illness and the treatment will not only affect the nature of the treatment but also the actual outcome itself. Consider the message that clients get from O.A. literature "It is that first bite that gets us into trouble. The first bite may be as 'harmless' as a piece of lettuce, but when eaten between meals and not as part of our daily plan, it invariably leads to another bite, and another, and another. And we have lost control. And there is no stopping" (Overeaters Anonymous 1979). I think most clinicians will find these statements troubling. Whatever the original intention, such statements can set a person up for relapse and create a self-fulfilling prophecy of failure and doom. If clients *believe* they can be more powerful than food and *can* be recovered, they have a better chance of becoming so. I believe all clients and clinicians will benefit if they begin and involve themselves in treatment with that end in mind.

Professionals with Personal Recovery

Although not a treatment model per se, the concept of clinicians with a history of personal recovery from an eating disorder is an important topic that is receiving increased attention. In this regard, the Twelve-Step model has a lot to teach the eating disorder field. We are lagging behind in the open use of people who have previously suffered, gotten well, and want to help others. The whole Twelve-Step philosophy and concept of sponsors is based on the "been there, done that" approach.

Craig Johnson and I wrote an article titled "Been There Done That: The Use of Clinicians with Personal Recovery in the Treatment of Eating Disorders" (2002). In this article we discuss the advantages and disadvantages of clinicians who have suffered from eating disorders being in the field at all, and, if so, whether or not they should disclose their eating disorder history. Craig and I are both supportive of using what he calls "staff with personal recovery" and I insist on calling "recovered staff" for important reasons.

It has been my consistent experience that my private practice clients and those who come to my treatment programs cite their work with a recovered therapist or staff member as one of the most important parts of their treatment and recovery. In fact, clients regularly report choosing Monte Nido because we are open about utilizing recovered staff.

Over the years, I have been told how much this issue bothers other clinicians (sometimes by the clinicians and sometimes by others who have heard clinicians complaining). I have been told on numerous occasions that it was inappropriate to share with clients, discuss with other professionals, or write in my books and articles that I am recovered. I can only speculate as to why others find this problematic. It seems particularly odd since utilizing people with personal recovery is a cornerstone in alcohol and chemical dependency treatment.

Being recovered does not qualify me to be a good therapist. Neither does my license for that matter. There are good and bad therapists with or without recovery backgrounds. A well-trained eating disorder therapist who is also recovered should not be afraid of repercussions in the field for disclosing this aspect of his or her past. In fact, our field should embrace these individuals and help them learn how best to use their background and avoid the potential pitfalls that could arise.

What Clients Think About Working with Clinicians Who Have Personal Recovery

We need to listen to what clients tell us and stop making decisions for them regarding whether or not working with recovered clinicians is important or insignificant to them and their treatment outcome. I have been listening for almost 30 years, and they have a lot to say. Here is what two clients have written, but their comments are similar to those I receive on a consistent basis.

> My desire to work with recovered staff led me to Monte Nido after living in the confines of a full-blown eating disorder for over a third of my life. I began seeking help at home, but no matter how much anyone tried to help me, I never believed anyone truly understood what my life was like despite their desperate attempts. Immediately upon talking to the first recovered staff member, I realized there was a degree of understanding I felt that someone who hadn't been through the depths of this would never understand and somehow couldn't. In that moment when I was trying to commit to recovery, I knew I had made the best and hardest decision of my life. Recovery is tough. The absolute hardest; most trying; draining; physically, emotionally, and mentally painful thing I've ever had to do. What keeps me going the most is the people who themselves have battled their own eating disorders and fought for so long and made their way to the other side. In my rough moments, I look to them for a sense of reassurance, almost asking, "Is this okay?" or "Is this normal?" or "Should I be feeling this way?" Hearing recovered staff gives me hope that not only am I not completely crazy, I am definitely not alone.

One of the primary reasons I chose to go to Monte Nido was the recovered staff. I thought that if anyone could help, it would be people who figured out how to untangle themselves from their own eating disorders. I thought they might know things that professionals who had never struggled with an eating disorder could not. And it was true. I never had therapists who were wiser to anorexia's tricks, showed more compassion for my struggle, and who could counteract my eating disorder thoughts and behaviors so well. I have a very difficult time trusting people, especially with my food.

But it really helped knowing that they understood my fears because they had once felt the same way. This allowed me to be more honest, as I didn't fear judgment as much. I thought that at least one of the staff members had probably done any eating disorder thing I had. This also helps to make the eating disorder feel less mysterious and special. When other doctors saw it as an enigma, for some reason this made me want to keep it. When anorexia lost its mystique, it also lost some of its power. Since they were familiar with the slyness of the eating disorder, the staff members were not pushovers. Since they were strong enough to stand up to their own eating disorders, they were definitely strong enough to battle mine. Most importantly, I think, is that every time I lost hope that I myself could recover, I only had to look around me to remember that people who were just as sick or sicker than me, who once felt as desperate and hopeless, who never thought that they could gain weight, eat healthy, like themselves, recover, they did—fully, utterly, and completely. I cannot overemphasize how important this was to me, as I believe hope is a crucial component of recovery.

Although I recognize the unique contribution of recovered staff in the treatment of eating disorders, I do not promote the notion that they are the only, or even the best, clinicians to work with eating disorders. I have worked with countless excellent therapists who have no personal eating disorder history. By far the most important thing is to be a well-trained, empathic therapist, period. A former client expressed this eloquently, "Ultimately, it's the potential for and hopeful development of a connection between client and therapist that will provide an impetus for effective treatment, regardless of whether or not the therapist has experienced an eating disorder firsthand."

What I do promote is that clients have exposure to individuals who have *recovered* and furthermore if a well-trained therapist is recovered from an eating disorder, he or she should not have to hide it. If you have a tool, you should be able to use it. The combination of good professional training and experience combined with being recovered has been an overwhelmingly successful aspect of my career as a therapist and my treatment programs. I encourage the field to acknowledge this and help recovered professionals use this potential tool appropriately.

This chapter has reviewed the most widely used approaches to treating eating disorders. Undoubtedly, many others deserve attention and new ones need to be developed. Clinicians who treat eating disorders will have to decide on their own treatment approach based on the literature and research in the field so far and their own experience. The treating professional must always keep in mind he or she must always make the treatment fit the client rather than the other way around.

9

Individual Therapy: Putting the Eating Disorder Out of a Job

IN HER BOOK *Close to the Bone*, psychiatrist Jean Bolen writes, "When Michelangelo looked at a block of raw marble, he could see a figure imprisoned within it. With his talent and the tools of a sculptor, he brought forth the beauty, power and magnificence of the figure that he saw and made it visible to all of us. A psychotherapist needs to have a similar eye to help free what is true in a person. For there to be an alchemy in the work of therapist or sculptor, there must not only be training and experience but also an ability to see potential and beauty. I believe that the soul, not the mind, recognizes these qualities."

I resonate with Bolen's analogy. As an individual therapist I take on the task of freeing people from what I call their eating disorder self and discovering the potential power, magnificence, and beauty in their healthy or soul self, helping them to fully realize what is there. A therapist helps clients chip away what is unnecessary or not useful and carve out a new life. I believe that every experienced, effective therapist comes to his or her own understanding of how therapy cures and then works from that understanding, even if he or she does not consciously recognize it. To accurately describe both the technique and the art of individual therapy with eating disorder clients, I have drawn not only from the literature but also from the knowledge and experience I have gained and used with success for almost three decades.

How Does Therapy Cure?

Therapy for eating disorder clients involves providing education, insight, and a corrective emotional experience—allowing the client to rectify faulty thought patterns, fill in developmental deficits, and internalize missing psychological functions. A variety of approaches and modalities can be used, but as explained in Chapter 8, it is the alliance between therapist and client rather than any certain approach or technique that is the most critical factor for successful therapy.

In essence, the therapist uses his or her training and the therapeutic relationship to put clients' eating disorder selves "out of a job." Until clients can "do it on their own," the therapist lends his or her ego and self-organization as well as the capacity to anticipate; delay gratification; use sound judgment; relate to others; regulate tension and moods; and integrate feelings, thoughts, and behavior. Once clients have internalized these abilities into their self-structure, they no longer need to use substitute or self-destructive measures (eating disorder behaviors) to meet needs or provide important psychological functions.

Eating Disorder Self Versus Healthy Self

"I feel like there's a monster inside of me."

"I know that I only weigh 85 pounds, but when I look in the mirror I see that I am fat."

I view everybody who comes to me for eating disorder treatment as having a core, whole, "healthy self." I sometimes refer to this as the "soul self," the part of them they were born with, the part we all have. I also see that, to a greater or lesser degree, there is another split-off part, a separate adaptive, disordered self (the eating disorder self) with a separate set of perceptions, thoughts, and behaviors. The eating disorder self developed for a reason, and its behavioral manifestations are the eating disorder symptoms. The degree of a client's illness is the degree to which the eating disorder self is in control.

Therapists and clients alike need to learn about each of these parts of the self. Therapeutic work involves connecting with each person's healthy self and strengthening it, growing it stronger. It is a person's healthy self that will "take care of" his or her eating disorder self. When the healthy self can say everything it needs to say and do everything it needs to do, the eating disorder self is no longer needed and is out of a job. In other words, the objective is not to get rid of the eating disorder self but to learn from it why it developed and how its specific behaviors serve a function. Once the function for the symptoms is understood, we work on finding other more productive means to serve the same purpose. When this is accomplished, the eating disorder self can integrate back into the core healthy self. Holding the eating disorder self responsible for the symptoms allows the therapist to challenge this self while building a relationship with the client's healthy self.

Challenging the eating disorder self helps clients avoid feelings of shame and blame but does not take away personal responsibility. The eating disorder self is not some outside entity, but a part of self that clients need better access to and must take responsibility for. Working with the eating disorder self is similar to but different from a technique known as externalization. Narrative therapy, which is known for this technique, externalizes the problem—in this case the eating disorder—and sees it as separate from the person. For example, in the narrative approach, the therapist would talk to "anorexia" as its own separate entity from the client with the goal of exposing its tricks, devaluing, and finally getting rid of it. In its best form, externalization helps clients separate themselves from their behaviors and helps them see that they are not just an eating disorder, not just "anorexic" or "bulimic." This kind of separation also helps significant others align with the person against the eating disorder. *Biting the Hand that Starves You* (2004) and *Life Without Ed* (2004) are two excellent resources for the narrative approach.

Externalization is a useful tool and I value the work of narrative therapists, but this technique can lead to problems. Villainizing anorexia and viewing it as an entity separate from the person can lead to abdication of responsibility, such as "my anorexia made

Beth's Eating Disorder Self

Beth, a client who had anorexia, brought in her food journal. In looking at it, I got the feeling that it was not the truth and she had not been honest in recording her eating behaviors. I knew she would have gained weight if she had really eaten as much as she claimed. In the following excerpt from our session, I challenged her eating disorder self without pitting myself against her healthy self:

Carolyn: I don't think the information looks right here. I have a hard time believing this is the truth about what you really ate.

Beth: Why, don't you trust me?

Carolyn: I trust that when you were here last time you wanted to write your food down.

Beth: I did . . . I even started to . . .

Carolyn: But . . .

Beth: Well, but part of me kept not wanting to.

Carolyn: It seems to me that part of you isn't letting you tell me the truth because it's afraid of what I might do or try to make you do, is that right?

Beth: Well, maybe a little.

Carolyn: So when you left here last time your healthy self had agreed to do the food, but then when you started to do it, another part stepped in somehow.

Beth: Well, not right away. But after a couple of days, it got really strong, telling me to restrict and that I was giving in.

Carolyn: OK. I understand. It is very hard when this happens, hard to know which way is right. This is why I say that people with eating disorders have a healthy self and an eating disorder self.

Beth: Exactly. When I am here I think I can do it, then I leave and the part of me that doesn't want to eat gets stronger and eating feels like giving in.

Carolyn: But think about it. Giving in to who? This is when your healthy self has to be strong. You need your healthy self to remind you that you would like to get better, be able to attend school again, play soccer. If eating gives you those things then giving in to it is good.

Beth: But at the moment it doesn't feel like that. It feels like giving in to weakness or indulgence or something bad.

Carolyn: Yes, right, it is tricky. This is why it is good for you to practice talking back to your eating disorder self, because this part of you has been calling the shots for a long time. Do you know what you could say back when it tells you that you are giving in?

Beth: No, not really.

Carolyn: Well, then no wonder it takes over. You need some help. We need to practice discussing what your eating disorder self says and what your healthy self can say back to it. You have to get better at challenging your eating disorder self. Let's try right now.

We proceeded with a dialogue involving me role-playing her eating disorder self and her being her healthy self. I stepped in and helped her when she was stuck by switching roles and showing her ideas for how a healthy self would respond. (I never leave a client in the role of the eating disorder self.) After dialoguing like this with clients, I ask them to practice journaling from both points of view. Continued practice helps clients develop a stronger healthy so that part of them is back in control.

me do it!" I believe it is important for clients to recognize that the eating disorder self is not a separate entity but *a part of them* that developed for a reason and serves a purpose, albeit in a dysfunctional way. It is a subtle but important distinction; rather than, "Anorexia made you do that," I try to say, "Your eating disorder self made you do that" or "I'd like to talk to your anorexic self." It is always a part of them for which they have to take responsibility. Notice that in the last example, I use the identity term *anorexic* because I am describing a part of self that in fact does hold this as an identity.

Contacting, Transforming, and Integrating the Eating Disordered Self

Early in my career, I worked with dissociative identity disorder (formerly know as multiple personality disorder) clients, who have many ego states or parts. I learned that one of the cardinal rules is not to make an enemy with any of the parts or try to get rid of them. Making an enemy with a part of self will just cause it to go into hiding. The goal is to contact and empathize with all the parts and help them reintegrate into the core self. I recognized the applicability to my work with eating disorder clients. The goal is to contact and empathize with the eating disorder self and help it rejoin the healthy self.

To contact the eating disorder self, the therapist should wait for the client to present it. Clients usually will give the therapist some kind of a "window in." The following are some examples of "windows in" to the eating disorder self:

- Clients start expressing, verbally or through their actions, the ambivalence they have about getting better: "Part of me wants to get better and part of me doesn't." This allows the therapist to point out their two selves: "You say that stopping bingeing is the most important thing to you, and yet some part of you continues to do it every night. We need to hear from the part of you that does the bingeing."

- "I feel like there's this monster inside of me." This is an invitation to talk to that part of self: "Can you tell me more about this monster part. It's that monster part I want to talk to. You know, you've been coming to these sessions all these weeks, and the monster hasn't shown up. I think we need that part of you here."
- "I know I only weigh 85 pounds, but when I look in the mirror, I see that I am fat." This is a good example of a dissociative state. There's a rational, healthy person who knows she is underweight and another part that perceives herself as fat.
- "I tell myself I'm not going to binge, and then something comes over me and I feel like it's out of my control." At this point, I might say something like, "You tell your self that you're not going to binge. What's that like when you tell yourself? Do you say, 'Self, you're not going to binge tomorrow'? What does your self say back?" The important point is to get each client able to contact, transform and integrate his or her eating disorder self.

Amanda: Accessing Her Eating Disorder Self

One way to get access to the eating disorder self begins with a journaling assignment. Amanda, a client with bulimia, complained that she could not abstain from her binge/purge episodes even though she wanted to stop. The following excerpt is an example of how to help clients with bulimia and BED access their eating disorder self.

Carolyn: OK, let's try something. I want you to journal before you binge.

Amanda: Well, I can try, but usually when I am in that mode, I don't want to do anything else instead of bingeing.

Carolyn: Yeah, I know. That's why I did not say *journal instead* of bingeing; I said journal *before* bingeing, then if you still want to, you can go ahead and binge.

Amanda: I don't get it. If I go ahead and binge what's the point?

Carolyn: Clients always think I want them to journal instead of bingeing. If that worked, my job would be easy. What I want is for you to get access to the part of you that does the bingeing. You're in here telling me that you would like to stop bingeing and you don't want it in your life anymore, but there's a part of you that really wants to or you wouldn't keep doing it. So what I am asking is that you journal your thoughts and feelings prior to the binge and then bring your journal into session. If you don't want to binge after you journal, that's fine, but if you do, that's fine too. Really. So don't think if you journal and still binge that this isn't working. Right now the point is to get access to the part of you that does the bingeing and see what it has to say. [In Amanda's case, she also purged, but at this point I am not asking about that. It will probably come up as she writes about the bingeing but if not I will have her journal about this too.]

Amanda: No one ever put it like that before. This is going to be interesting. I don't think I know what I am thinking or feeling before I binge.

Carolyn: Exactly. Just begin writing and see what happens. Just let it flow.

Whatever clients write, the next step is to have them write back from their healthy self and ultimately to engage them in a dialogue with their two selves in writing, then through role play in the session. If they don't journal, I ask them what part agreed to do this and what part resisted and I will try to do a dialogue with them in session.

Dialoging with the Eating Disorder Self

Getting clients to dialogue with their two selves is key in getting the healthy self back in control. External control (such as punishments or containment in a hospital) may be necessary to contain eating disorder behaviors in the beginning, but the eating disorder self is still waiting to take charge when the external control is gone. The true battle for recovery is not between the therapist (or treatment team) and the eating disorder. It is between the client's eating disorder self and healthy self. Clients get better when their healthy self is back in control and the eating disorder self is no longer necessary. This is an internal process. Therapists have to help clients engage in it.

Maya: Writing Dialogues with Her Eating Disorder Self

Maya: I have been so trying to get my behaviors under control, trying to follow the meal plan Kim [the dietitian] gave me, but somewhere I get lost or off track and can't do it. We have a great idea for me to order this meal at a restaurant, and I leave her office and my healthy self is totally in charge, all the way to the restaurant, right up to sitting down, I am fine, until I see the menu.

Carolyn: When you sit down and look at the menu, where do the thoughts go? What starts to happen?

Maya: My eating disorder self is looking for the least amount of calories. What can I order that doesn't have any fat? You can't order that, you'll get fat. Don't be a pig.

Carolyn: So you're getting slammed by your eating disorder self. Can you answer back?

Maya: Well, not really. Sometimes I try, but I get shot down pretty fast.

Carolyn: Well, what would you say to your niece if she said all those things to you?

Maya: Oh. [Long pause] I would tell her that it was silly to try to order food without fat, that you need fat. I would tell her she will be OK if she listens to her body and eats what she wants. I would tell her that she is not fat and that she does not have to be afraid of food. I can think of all kinds of things.

Carolyn: So why can't you say these things to yourself? When your eating disorder self starts talking, you need to be prepared to talk back. What can you say back when you hear, "you'll get fat"?

Maya: I don't know. It's different when it is me.

Carolyn: But it doesn't have to be any different. You need to practice. Write down in your journal eating disorder thoughts you have this week and then try to write back from your healthy self. Bring these in for your session so we can role-play.

Having clients talk back to their eating disorder self is one of the most important interventions even if they have to start by using someone else (a relative, friend, or therapist) as a stand-in. Eating disorder clients most often can be strong in challenging someone else's disordered thinking but not their own. They usually have healthy selves for everybody but themselves. That's why it's so great to have them in group therapy (see the next chapter). Their healthy selves come out for other people, and the therapist helps them transfer this skill to use with themselves. The stronger the healthy self is, the better the chance for full recovery. The degree of a client's recovery is the degree that the client's healthy self is in control.

Using the Therapeutic Relationship

Over time, clients develop a stronger relationship to their eating disorder self than they have with other people. They reach out to their eating disorder rather than to relationships to get comfort, express anger, find solace, or otherwise get their needs met. For recovery, insight into what went wrong is not enough; clients must learn how to develop healthy attachments, reach out for help, and learn to solve problems in a different way. It is the therapist's task to help uncover what developmental arrests or deficits exist for each client and help "reparent" the client so he or she gains the ability to rely on self or others rather than the eating disorder behaviors.

A successful eating disorder therapist has to be more active and dynamic than is necessary in other kinds of therapy. Clients need to know the therapist has expertise; they need reassurance about how therapy works and can help them. Eating disorder therapists have to stretch the traditional boundaries and be more present and self-disclosing. This doesn't mean becoming friends with clients, but it certainly means being more than a neutral blank slate. The therapist has to be more verbal and directive—sometimes even talking as much as listening. There are clients who, when simply listened to with supportive or analytic techniques, spiral further into their own dysfunctional world. Empathic listening will not facilitate a client with anorexia to gain weight. An eating disorder therapist is a teacher, guide, and coach, not just an empathic listener. In essence, the therapist needs to provide a better relationship than the one the client has with her eating disorder. As strange as it may seem, a therapeutic task in treating eating disorder clients is to form a healthy attachment encouraging them to depend on the therapist instead of on their eating disorder. This would naturally be inappropriate without the next step, which is to then wean clients off the therapist and on to other relationships.

My working definition of *attachment* is "an enduring emotional bond that promotes active exploration and mastery of the environment, thereby supporting the development of autonomy." The function of attachment is "to develop a secure base, foster exploration, develop affect regulation and interoceptive awareness (ability to be aware of and express feelings), and create autonomy and a sense of self." These are all important tasks, not only of good parenting but of good therapy. Forming a healthy attachment begins to put the eating disorder out of a job.

Eating disorder symptoms may substitute for a secure attachment. Traits observed in individuals with anxious attachment (lacking or misperceiving their own resources, feeling ineffective or deficient, needing to control, lack of interoceptive awareness, sense of inadequacy or not measuring up, and insecure neediness) are all things we see in eating disorder clients (Armstrong 1989 and Chassler 1997). Exploring how eating disorder behaviors may be serving unmet attachment needs is often an important aspect of healing:

- Starving is likely to elicit a caregiving response without the individual having to ask for help or acknowledge any need. An emaciated body is screaming for help without the client having to say a thing. One client described it this way: "I was trying to not have any needs, but my body was betraying me by shouting, 'This girl needs help.'" This kind of behavior leads people to say that individuals with anorexia are just trying to get attention. It is important to reframe this negative perspective: these individuals "need something attended to."
- Bingeing provides nurturing or self-soothing needs that clients do not know how to get by other means. Clients

phrase it in many ways. "Eating is the only thing that calms me down." Or, "My mom had no idea how to help me. Whenever I was upset, she got even more upset than me, then I had to take care of *her*. I would go to the food for myself."

- Purging may serve as a physiological or psychological release of anger or anxiety. One client said, "Every time I tried to express anger or frustration, my mom ridiculed me or punished me. I got back at her by throwing up my food." Another client realized that, "After I got into a fight with my dad, I did not know what to do. I knew if I got angry, he would really take it out on me. I went home and stuffed as much food in as I could and then spewed it out in a violent rage."
- A focus on appearance can serve as a diversion, redirecting attention from attachment needs to more obtainable goals such as losing weight. "If you're in high school and you aren't getting any attention from guys, all you have to do is lose weight, then you immediately get attention. It doesn't matter if you started out at 100 pounds or 150 pounds, dieting is rewarded." Or, "I never felt close to anyone, or belonged, until I lost weight."

Through attunement and a healthy attachment relationship, the therapist assists the client in internalizing missing psychological functions, such as the ability to express feelings, the ability to self-soothe, and the ability to internally validate. Clients can begin to reach out to the therapist rather than to the eating disorder. This can be facilitated by a variety of strategies such as having the client call or even page the therapist before bingeing or purging. I often use transitional objects. A transitional object is a concrete item that clients can be given to keep with them as a way of staying connected to the therapist and the therapeutic work. I have a rock collection I use for this purpose. For example, a client told me that when she felt like purging her food, she forgot all of the things we discussed in our sessions and she wished I was there. This is a perfect time for use of a transitional object. I asked her to choose a rock from my collection and kzeep it with her to help remind her of our work together. This clever client put the rock on the back of her toilet and as she later described, "I would go into the bathroom to purge and there you were and I couldn't do it!"

Each therapist will have his or her own ideas about the therapeutic relationship as well as strategies and techniques for helping clients to reach out to people instead of their eating disorder behaviors. The therapist helps pave the way and eventually teaches clients how to do this.

Critical Strategies for Successful Treatment

The following are critical strategies, treatment approaches, and interventions I have used successfully with eating disorder clients in individual therapy, both in private practice and in treatment settings.

Alliance and Empathy

The therapist must establish an alliance and maintain consistent empathy with the client throughout the course of treatment. Therapists should always strive to know what it is like to be in their clients' shoes. Empathic failure can potentially lead to treatment failure.

Clients need to be reminded that the therapist is there to help them reach their goals in a healthy rather than a destructive way. At the beginning of treatment, I tell clients, "I cannot take this away from you. You and I both know I can't do that. I can't make you give up your eating disorder. I hope I can make you want to." It is common for clients to come to therapy with the experience of constantly being misunderstood and with the idea that they have a disease from which they will never recover. I let them know that what they are doing makes some sense and fulfills some purpose in a way that we will work together to understand. I let them know that they can get out of their vicious cycle and become recovered.

Dealing with Food and Weight

Perhaps due to my own eating disorder, I knew as a beginning therapist 30 years ago that if treatment were left to typical psychoanalysis, clients could take years to explain their childhoods, how they get along with their parents, their inability to control their anger, or any number of past experiences while continuing to exist on frozen yogurt and salad, bingeing all day, or purging every night. Clients can starve to death or have heart failure while trying to figure out "why" they are doing this to themselves. Therapists have to deal directly with the food and weight problems and not just the underlying psychological issues. In eating disorder clients, food and feelings are so intertwined that therapists will miss important opportunities and issues if they are not addressing both directly.

Dealing with food and weight means working with clients where they are, not where the therapist is. For example, when therapists say, "It's not about the food" or "Fat is not a feeling," I know what they mean but I disagree. It *is* about the food, and fat *is* a feeling—at least to the client, particularly in the beginning of treatment. Having been there, I remember feeling fat not just in a somatic way, but in a real feeling, emotional sort of way. So I know what they mean but I accept that fat is a feeling. The most important thing is empathy with what the client feels and not what the therapist thinks the client feels or should feel. This does not mean there isn't something else going on; there is.

A therapist cannot make assumptions; he or she must try to get at the meaning of things for individual clients, therefore I start from scratch with each client while at the same time relying on a body of knowledge and expertise. For example, it is important not to assume what a binge is, so when a client says, "I binged," I ask, "What do you mean by that? What does that mean to you?" New clients often look at me like, "You've got to be kidding. You're the eating disorder expert?" But this is an important point. I tell them, "I'm an expert in eating disorders, but I'm not an expert in you, so I need to know what *you* mean by this." For some people the word *binge* can mean a three-hour affair with food, for others it can mean eating one bowl of cereal or four cookies after dinner. One of my clients described a binge as "eating anything other than what a skinny anorexic eats." If clients have to explain in detail what they mean rather than using shortcuts like "I binged," therapists can often learn more about the meaning of their symptoms.

Making Behavioral Agreements

Behavior goals can be simple or complex, easy or challenging. The importance of setting behavior goals is to increase clients' ability to gain control so that eventually they can commit to and keep healthy goals they set for themselves. Sometimes clients are so out of control that what seems like a small step, such as writing in their journal one night prior to bingeing or adding a piece of fruit to their meal plan, is actually a big step and the start of regaining control.

Clients must be consistently reminded that small behavioral steps are going to help them recover. They must know that (a) it is not any one specific behavior but the ability to do it that's important, and (b) once the function of the behavior is discovered, healthy substitutes can serve the same purpose. Both *a* and *b* often take place in therapy with no conscious recognition of what is happening, only that the client is getting better. Once certain abilities are internalized and needs can be met in healthy ways, clients are no longer dependent on the therapist.

The following are examples of behavioral agreements:

- The client agrees to call the therapist's office or pager before self-inducing vomiting.
- The client agrees to write down everything eaten and feelings about eating it.
- The client agrees to do at least three other activities to relieve anxiety before purging (e.g., go for a walk, call a friend, hit a punching bag).
- The client agrees to take one day off from any exercise.
- The client agrees to reduce laxative intake by five per day.
- The client agrees to write and bring to the session a letter expressing any past or current feelings she has towards

a significant person in her life (for example, mother, husband, abuser, and so forth).

- The client agrees to spend 10 minutes meditating or listening to music (daily or at specific times such as before meals).
- The client agrees to set a timer in order to delay a binge. (Time can be increased, for example, starting at 10 minutes, progressing to 30 minutes, then to one hour or more, which helps clients get the behavior under control.)

Exploration of, execution of, or even resistance to these agreements can help lead the client and therapist to deeper psychodynamic issues and obstacles to recovery. Making written contracts of behavioral agreements is a useful tool. Therapists should coordinate contract goals with the rest of the treatment team as appropriate. In addition, I often send copies of a client's contract to other members of the treatment team to ensure everyone is on the same page.

Understanding Eating Disorders as Addictions and Phobias

When talking about the food, especially with someone who has anorexia nervosa, it may seem very similar to dealing with someone who has a phobia. When talking to someone with binge eating, it is easy to get the sense it is more like dealing with an addiction. When dealing with people who restrict their food intake and binge, there is a sense of both. In both phobias and addictions, the client uses behaviors to regulate emotions. A client with a phobia of snakes will engage in whatever behavior is necessary to avoid snakes. Similarly, clients with anorexia will engage in whatever behavior they can to avoid food. Addicts use substances, whether drugs, alcohol, or food, to numb pain, bury anger, or distract from loneliness or fear. This helps explain why the symptoms are self-perpetuating—they work. It is important to know how to work with both phobias and addictions even though eating disorders are not purely either one.

Treating the Phobic Aspect

When dealing with someone who has a snake phobia, one has to deal directly with the phobic object. It doesn't work to talk about his family problems and ignore snakes—hence, the need to talk directly about food and weight as discussed previously.

The therapist has to start slowly and progress step-by-step. A desensitization process is necessary. Each client is individual and will be different in how much she can be challenged and pushed. In a treatment program, the expected rate of weight gain for anorexia is two to three pounds a week. This may work for some people, but there are others for whom it will not. Even if they tolerate it physically, they might not be able to handle it psychologically. A client's body might gain the weight, but if her mind and emotions don't catch up with the weight gain and if the phobia is still there, she will most likely leave the program and lose everything she gained.

Treating the Addictive Aspect

The addictive component also has to be addressed. For example, clients become habituated to bingeing and vomiting, need increasing amounts of laxatives, feel withdrawal when they're unable to engage in their symptoms, lie about their symptoms, and choose their behaviors over relationships. All of these things are common to addictions.

Applying the addiction model to eating disorders was created when the Twelve Step program of Alcoholics Anonymous was adapted for use with what were then called compulsive overeaters, thus the term Overeaters Anonymous or OA. OA was based on the belief that binge eaters, like alcoholics, were addicted to a substance (food). However, there is no evidence to suggest that eating disorders are caused by an individual being addicted to a certain food or type of food. Furthermore, we can't ask clients to abstain from food. For the most part, the addiction is to a behavior like bingeing or purging, rather than a substance and the goal is abstinence from these behaviors. Understanding addictions can be helpful in dealing with eating disorders, but there are contraindications to using the Twelve-Step model. (More information on this topic is found in Chapter 8).

Nurturant/Authoritative Therapy

In his book *Treating and Overcoming Anorexia Nervosa*, Steven Levenkron described his style of treatment as nurturant/authoritative therapy. Like children, eating disorder clients need to be nurtured and supported, but they also need guidance and limits from a strong but compassionate authority figure. Clients need to learn how to appropriately express needs and ask for help. They need to learn the difference between self-care and selfishness and how to be less rigid toward and demanding of themselves.

They are also lost and confused or tormented and need to be led out of their chaos or self-imposed prison. Clients need to know that they can lean on the therapist for support and direction. This puts the therapist in an authoritative and directive stance; long silences must be avoided and interpretations and even advice must be forthcoming. Simply asking clients how they feel, waiting for them to speak, or acting like a blank slate can be frightening to eating disorder clients, who desperately need to feel that someone who cares is in charge and knows what to do.

The line between nurturing and being authoritative with a client is a constantly fluid one. In some sessions I am a passive presence while clients cry; I tell them I know how hard it is and reassure them that things will be okay. The therapy sometimes serves as a container for emotions. Other times, I'll be very directive and ask clients to take a risk that unsettles them. I'll challenge them for not trying hard enough. I'll push them to add calories to their daily food intake or to call me before purging. I'll explain what I think some of their recent behaviors have meant. A therapist has to know when to challenge and how far to push a client and then be clear that working through the client's response is the key.

Whether the client meets the challenge is not the most important issue. The meaning of the challenge for each client and the meaning of his or her responses are important. Working through why a client responded the way she did, what the challenge meant to her, and how she felt about the challenge and about accomplishing it or not are the important issues in therapy. Similar to parenting, nothing will be accomplished by pushing and challenging unless an alliance has been established and a level of trust exists.

Limiting Control Battles

While treating an eating disorder client in 1873, Leaseague said, "An excess of insistence begets an excess of resistance." From the beginning, I establish with clients that I will avoid control battles as much as possible. I explain the general idea that "the fight will not be between you and me, it will be between you and your eating disorder self. I am here to help strengthen your healthy self so that your healthy self will take care of the eating disorder self." If a client says she likes her behaviors and is not ready to give them up, I reply that I am not interested in taking anything from her but in helping her live a more happy and successful life and helping her get rid of any obstacles to that.

The issue of control is tricky. Dealing with adults will be different than dealing with adolescents. In some cases parents may even be instructed to step in and get back in control of their eating. This may have to be the case. But if there is another way, avoiding control battle is preferable.

Avoiding control battles also becomes tricky with an emaciated individual who is unwilling to gain weight. In this case, I am careful to pick and choose my battles wisely. For example, I may not take issue with a low-fat meal plan, but I will not allow the client to lose weight to a dangerous level without intervention. If necessary, I inform the client that since she has become incapable of fighting off the eating disorder self that is killing her, I now have to step in and take over since I will not allow anyone to die while under my care. What "take over" means depends on many things such as the age of the client, the strength of the therapeutic alliance, and available resources.

Along with not allowing clients to self-destruct, each therapist should have other treatment "nonnegotiables." For example, I feel strongly that the scale is a weapon that eating disorder clients use against themselves. Part of my work involves getting my clients to give up the scale as a way of evaluating their self-worth or their progress in treatment. If I weigh clients, I do it with their back to the scale and do not tell them the number (details are provided in Chapter 12). Each therapist develops his or her own "nonnegotiables" and decides on a case-by-case basis how far to hold the line.

Avoiding Attachment to Results and Managing Resistance

Forming a healthy attachment with the client is a main treatment strategy, but being attached to the results of therapy can be problematic. Following a philosophy of nonattachment helps the therapist limit control battles, deal with resistance, and avoid imposing his or her own agenda on clients. Nonattachment is one of the main spiritual principles of Buddhism. Nonattachment has contributed to my success as a therapist and has also allowed me to work consistently with eating disorder clients day in and day out for 30 years without suffering from burnout. For a better understanding of this concept, readers may want to look at books on applying Buddhist concepts to everyday life, such as *A Path with a Heart* (Cornfield 1993) or *The Power of Now* (Tolle 1999).

In general, therapists are trained not to be attached to the outcome and not to impose their own agenda. For example, if a couple comes to see a therapist for marriage counseling, the therapist is not there to tell them what to do but rather to help them find the solution that is best for them, the solution they really want. However, in eating disorder treatment, crossing the line and imposing the therapist's or treatment team's ideas on clients happens all too often. Admittedly this is a difficult area to navigate. We cannot sit back and let someone starve to death while under our care. I have done my share of insisting and taken heroic measures to save a life. All therapists know they may be called upon to assert their will, for example, if a client threatens suicide. But we also know that we cannot prevent someone intent on suicide, we can only postpone it unless we can get the person to change internally to the point where he or she longer *wants* to die.

In treating eating disorders, therapists have to keep in mind that each client has the ultimate right to decide whether or not to accept certain recovery goals—and whether or not he or she wants to recover at all. The therapeutic task is to help clients see the purpose or meaning of their symptoms and that there are choices and consequences for every action and that they can be in control of these. The therapist needs to help the client align with the goals that come from deep within the client's own healthy soul self.

Therapists need to deal with resistance like good aikido martial artists who do not resist their opponent's energy or force but, instead, go with it. If there is an important issue, the therapist can come back to it; otherwise it can be let go.

The following are examples of how resistance can be dealt with and avoided by using nonattachment:

Client: I am a vegetarian.
Attached response: Being a vegetarian is a form of food restriction that serves your eating disorder.
Nonattached response: That is your choice. I would like to help you learn to be a healthy one.

Client: I don't want to talk about my binge.
Attached response: It is important for you to talk to me about it if I am going to help you.
Nonattached response: I will accept that. Can you tell my why you don't want to talk about it?

Client: I don't want to gain weight.
Attached response: You have to gain weight to get better.
Nonattached response: I would like to understand that. What would that mean for you, gaining weight? (This can help clients discuss the purpose of the low weight and its pros and cons.)

Admittedly, if clients continue to not deal with important issues like weight gain, the therapist will have to make a decision whether to hang in there, refer to another therapist, or if necessary facilitate a higher level of care.

Patience and Long-Term Thinking

Therapy for an eating disorder is usually long term. Recovery can take two to seven or more years. I have had a small number of clients recover in a few months to a year, but this is very rare. Therapists who treat eating disorders need to have patience and

Nonattachment: The Case of Diane

When Diane first came to see me, she was six months pregnant and bingeing and purging daily. Her doctor had pressured her into the appointment. She was anxious and terrified in the first meeting. Through painstaking effort, I learned that her daily pattern was to drink a latte in the morning, have a light lunch, and binge and purge whatever she would eat for dinner. Her condition for participation in treatment was "I want you to help me with the bingeing and purging, but don't touch the restricting."

Having my own different parts of self, one part of me was silently saying, "*What?* You're pregnant! No way. Of course we're going to talk about the restricting." But another part of me was thinking, "I'd like to help her and to do so she'll need to come back next week." My nonattached self said out loud to Diane, "OK, you hired me. If dealing with the bingeing and purging is a goal we can agree on, we're going to work at that goal." Knowing she clearly needed more food and that there was little chance she was going to stop bingeing and purging if she didn't stop restricting, I hoped we would eventually get there, but I knew I could not be attached to my own agenda or she would not return. I worked with her on techniques for stopping the bingeing and purging while establishing a trusting relationship. Before too long Diane came into session and said, "Well, it's not really working. Maybe you were right and I do have to eat more during the day."

be willing and capable of hanging in for the long haul, through thick and thin, both literally and figuratively. It is important to remember that the client is in the driver's seat and the therapist has the road map; both are in for a lengthy, challenging, sometimes painful, but ultimately rewarding journey. Seeing a therapist once a week is not much time devoted to recovery. When a man once complained that his daughter was not better after four months of therapy, I responded, "I have only seen her for 16 hours, not four months!"

Furthermore, clients do not go on a straight upward climb to recovery in a step-by-step progression. They start, they stop, they progress, they slip back. They might get to a certain point and say they can do no more yet a year later take more steps or go the rest of the way. Every recovery is different, every individual is different. Full recovery is usually a difficult, long-term process, but it is not impossible to obtain.

Topics for Individual Therapy Sessions

The following are examples of topics that are often dealt with in individual therapy. Clients with eating disorders when given such a list often identify with many of these issues even though they have not been able to express or articulate this. Reading through a list of possible issues can help clients identify areas that resonate with them.

Poor Self-Esteem/Diminished Self-Worth

"Nothing I do ever seems good enough." "I don't think there is a thin enough I can get." Many clients present a self to others that seems very together and self-confident, but in therapy they admit to an emptiness inside and say they feel insignificant or unworthy. This brings up the important difference between self-esteem and self-worth. Someone can seemingly have a good measure of self-esteem, be on the debate team, go to modeling school, or perform to live audiences, yet whatever he or she does, it is not good enough.

These clients set high and unrealistic demands and requirements for themselves just to be acceptable. Hence, "five more pounds," "one more hour of exercise," and "nothing less than straight As" are common mantras. No matter how successful the individual is, his or her accomplishments are never internalized, thus they never enhance self-esteem.

Discovering and working through all the underlying reasons regarding why and how clients developed their lack of self-worth is important and often useful, but not always necessary for recovery. The important thing is to deal with these issues from a here-and-now perspective; in other words, how is the person being affected in the present? Helping clients set current realistic goals, internalize achievements, take compliments in the present, and find value and meaning are all important.

Belief in the Thinness Myth

"I will be happy and successful if I am thin." If individuals have to give up their health and betray their souls just to be thin, what do they achieve in the long run? They may lose weight, but they also lose themselves. They may feel happy or successful about their weight, but nothing else. In individual therapy, clients can explore what the struggle for thinness does for them. For some clients, being thin has brought them the most attention they have ever received. If this is true, they will need to discuss whether it's worth it and whether there is a healthy way to achieve the same thing. For others, being thin does not measure up to the myth, but they fear that letting go would mean defeat or some fate worse than the one in which they find themselves.

Feelings of Emptiness and the Need for Distraction

"Eating helps me forget my problems." Individual therapy can help clients solve problems so that the need to binge, purge, or starve is no longer necessary. They need help resolving their issues rather than trying to distract themselves. Even when distraction is called for, healthy alternatives need to be devised. For example, when sad, clients can learn to listen to music or call a friend, rather than binge. Furthermore, clients also need help filling themselves up with life: in with the good, not just out with the bad.

Dichotomous (Black-and-White) Thinking

"I am perfect or a failure. I am thin or fat. I starve or binge." A goal in individual therapy is to help clients see how and why they may have developed dichotomous thinking and how it sets them up for continued problems and pain. For example, the therapist helps uncover why a person needs to be the best at everything, why being perfect is so important. Exposing faulty thought patterns is also important. People may not even be aware of the impossibility of the perfectionist thinking, "If I work hard enough, I will not make a mistake."

Desire for Attention and to Be Special or Unique

"If I give up my eating disorder, I won't be special anymore. I have nothing else that is unique." The symptoms become the goal when clients don't know what they would have without their eating disorder and giving it up means having nothing in its place. The ability to pursue the goal, do the behaviors, and follow the self-imposed rules becomes a special way of behaving and getting needs attended to. A client who said, "If I get better, people will think I'm OK," was telling her therapist that her eating disorder was getting her the attention she needed but was unable to ask for. A 12-year-old client once asked me, "If I get better, does that mean I can't see you anymore?" I was attending to certain needs that she was afraid would go unmet. Every therapist's task is to help clients find a way to be special and unique, without having an eating disorder, and to get their needs attended to in some other healthier way.

Need for Control

"If I refused to eat over 700 calories, I knew I could keep my body under control." "I know I purged often to get back at my dad. It would be the only thing that got him really mad that he could do nothing about." If there is one consistent feature seen in all eating disorders that causes and perpetuates their existence, it is the need for control. Eating disorder behaviors create the illusion of control. Giving up the behaviors feels like losing control and becoming powerless. Therapists can help clients resolve issues and alleviate the need for behaviors such as starving or purging. However, even if the underlying issues are not resolved the therapist should help the client find a sense of control and personal power in other ways, showing the client that it is the eating disorder that eventually leaves her out of control and powerless.

Therapists need to be assertive in challenging clients to face the reality that what they think is control is not:

- Is it really control to not even be able to eat a cookie?
- Are you in control of whether or not you run, or are you compelled to do so?
- Is it control to avoid going to a party because there will be food there?
- Is purging a form of control or a means to cover up your out of control behavior with food?
- Is going in and out of treatment programs what you had in mind when wanting to be in control?

Stages of Recovery

Understanding the stages of recovery is helpful to clients, their significant others, and those who endeavor to treat them. Knowledge of how treatment progresses will prevent unrealistic expectations. It will also help clients and significant others to understand what is in store during the treatment process. Slips and even relapses during recovery will be better prepared for and handled if they are seen as a potentiality. Going over the stages of recovery can help clients and their significant others see where they are in the process and discuss this with the treatment team. Finally, knowing where they are going can help motivate clients to get there.

- **Presence of behaviors with no sense of a separate eating disorder self.** At this stage clients often do not even accept that they actually have an eating disorder, much less an eating disorder self. The behaviors are seen as being something they are either willfully or uncontrollably doing.

- **Denial of seriousness.** When clients do admit they have an eating disorder, they are almost always in denial of how serious it is or can be.

- **Beginning awareness of a split self.** Continuing their behaviors, in spite of wanting to get better and their own ambivalence about recovery, helps clients begin to see that they have both a healthy self and an eating disorder self.

- **Active engagement with the eating disorder self and the healthy self.** Client's journal from and dialogue with the two selves. This helps to discover the function of the eating disorder self.

- **Need for behaviors while developing the healthy self.** The eating disorder self will still be acting out through behaviors, while the client is strengthening the healthy self.

- **Decrease in behaviors but thoughts/desire for behaviors, strong.** The healthy self gets stronger and can fight off some of the eating disorder urges. The habitual nature of the symptoms begins to diminish, but the eating disorder self is often still in control.

- **General symptom control with reduced thoughts/desire.** The healthy self is in control most of the time, but clients still battle eating disorder thoughts and act on them occasionally.

- **Control of symptoms by healthy self but remaining thoughts/desire.** At this point the healthy self is in control of the symptoms, but clients are at risk for returning to the behaviors, because the need for the behaviors has not been resolved and eating disorder thoughts are still present. Treatment should continue until the need for the behaviors is significantly diminished. It is common for clients, significant others, and insurance companies to think that at this point clients are recovered or well enough to stop treatment. This is not the case and often leads to relapse.

- **Integration of eating disorder self and healthy self (recovered).** Clients do not have to work at abstaining from eating disorder behaviors because there is no desire to engage in them. The need for the eating disorder is gone. Clients turn to people or to their inner self to regulate emotions or otherwise get needs met. There is no separate eating disorder self; it has been integrated so there is one whole self. The person has a normal, healthy relationship with food and weight and does not need to use eating disorder behaviors to deal with problems. This is what I call "recovered."

Inside an Individual Therapy Session

The following dialogue is an excerpt from a session conducted with Jena, an extremely emaciated female in her early 20s who had been suffering from anorexia nervosa for approximately six years. Jena had been hospitalized elsewhere on at least three other occasions and had relapsed after discharge each time. Jena came to Monte Nido weighing 54 pounds at 4 foot 11 inches tall. I was very worried about Jena because she was obviously medically compromised despite the fact that the hospital she had come from insisted she was medically stable. She kept saying she wanted to die and did not want to be in treatment. This excerpt is from a session that took place a few days after her admission to Monte Nido.

I present Jena's case for several reasons. Many of the ideas discussed in this chapter are demonstrated with this client who has a very severe and chronic case of anorexia. It is often said that you cannot do therapy with someone in a starved state. I think this session proves otherwise. Admittedly, we did not talk about psychodynamic underlying issues or how she got along with her mother; we talked about exactly where she was emotionally—terrified of food and of losing control. The reader will see how easily the topic of the eating disorder self comes up and how I begin to get Jena, even in this critical state, to see she has another voice, another choice.

Furthermore, this excerpt shows me talking about numbers to a client in a way that elsewhere in the book I advise not to—a good example that sometimes you have to break your own rules. I decided to be different with Jena to give her more comfort and safety in the way she needed. Prior to this session I had made an agreement to tell her when she reached 70 pounds

I made this unusual move because I thought she might leave treatment and die if I didn't reassure her that I would not let her weight get out of control. Although I never gave her a final goal weight for discharge, giving her an initial cap of 70 pounds, at which point we would renegotiate, served its purpose. Jena stayed until she gained approximately 30 pounds. Although she did not know her weight at this point, she was adamant that she could do no more and was discharged to outpatient care. Finally, Jena's case is a perfect example of using nonattachment. Today Jena still maintains her weight gain, and although it is still low, for her height, she is working, happy, social, and living her life.

Right before the session I was told that she was very upset and wanted to leave because the treatment team was "lying" to her about her calories.

Carolyn: Well, I heard you had a bad day yesterday, so I thought we could talk about it a little bit.

Jena: I just knew that I've been eating a lot of food, and I just got really, really mad.

Carolyn: You mean you got really mad because you think that you were told one thing and it was another?

Jena: Yeah.

Carolyn: That's what I heard, but I think I ought to talk to everybody today about how the calorie plan goes here, because there is never an exact amount.

Jena: I just feel like that's the only thing anyone talks to me about around here. That's the one area where I said I would trust, and I said, "OK, I'm going to trust and stuff." So for a few days I thought, "This is ridiculous, I'm getting so much and stuff," and I'm like, "No, I'm going to trust," and finally I'm just like, "No, screw it." I feel like I'm being lied to, and I figured out my calories and I was getting a lot more than I thought (agitated energy).

Carolyn: You mean you sat down and wrote them out and they . . .

Jena: Yeah.

Carolyn: But how do you know what they come to as opposed to . . . We have a general idea, not an exact amount. For example, our chicken—what if one piece is bigger than the other? Or what if this bread is a little bit different than that bread or . . . [seeking clarification]?

Jena: I mean just generally.

Carolyn: Yeah, so I don't really know. We try not to talk calories here. You know we talk about energy units. Anyway, we don't want to give you too much food too fast. I think what you should trust is what we agreed on, and what we agreed on is that you're not going to gain weight too fast and I'll tell you when you get to 70 pounds [confirming my previous commitment]. So how do you account for the fact that you didn't gain any weight? That means you're not getting too many calories at least [not challenging but questioning].

Jena: I just think it's getting really scary for me.

Carolyn: Yeah, I think so too.

Jena: Like the food.

Carolyn: Is there anything less scary that we could do?

Jena: I don't know. I just feel like I'm going to start restricting again.

Carolyn: Well, let's talk about that, because I'm interested in that. What happens in your head when you want to start restricting? What are you afraid is going to happen [going with her resistance]?

Jena: I just feel out of control. I feel that the whole exchange system is so out of control too. Like, I dunno. I just feel out of control.

Carolyn: Well, what does that mean, "out of control"? That you're not going to be able to stop? That you are going to want more and more? Is that what you think [seeking clarification]?

Jena: No, I just feel like my body . . . It's just out of control, and the food and shakes and everything is out of control. [She looks away, far off and appears hopeless.]

Carolyn: Oh, I see. It seems like so much compared to . . . [validating]

Jena: All of a sudden. It's like all shakes. I want all shakes. I want it like . . .

Carolyn: Because shakes are a little more precise [empathizing]?

Jena: Yeah, it's precise and stuff. [She is more animated, excited that I understand.]

Carolyn: Same thing every day [calmly, empathizing].

Jena: Same thing. Yeah [shaking her head yes and using her hands].

Carolyn: And you can count on it. I understand that. I think it's a little bit regressive if you go back to shakes. It's a little bit going backward. I hope we don't have to do that, but sometimes we have to do that. Maybe we can come up with other things that are more precise. I don't know, because I don't think anyone is trying to fool you or trick you or anything because the proof is going to be what happens in your body no matter what. Do you know what I mean? And we have a deal. I have to tell you what happens. And I agreed to tell you when you reach 70.

Jena: I dunno, and 70 seems like such a huge number to me [again looking away, sad].

Carolyn: That's interesting, isn't it? Why do you think 70 sounds so huge [again going with her resistance]?

Jena: Oh, it doesn't matter [fading].

Carolyn: OK, when you weighed 107, didn't 70 seem like for really, really, skinny, anorexic people?

Jena: Oh, I don't know.

Carolyn: Can't remember?

Jena: Seventy just seems like a lot here. Oh, I don't know, just . . .

Carolyn: Here at Monte Nido? Why here?

Jena: I dunno, it just seems like a lot.

Carolyn: Hmm.

Jena: Seems like a lot.

Carolyn: Maybe because it's changing from sixes to sevens. Maybe it's going up a whole range or something, and that sounds big [not challenging, just searching for an understanding].

Jena: I dunno. It just seems like a lot of weight. I don't know. I guess ultimately I'm just trying to weasel my way out of this, and my eating disorder is really, really bad right now, I guess [getting agitated].

Carolyn: Well, what is it saying [she has now given me a window in to her eating disorder self and I ask what "it" is saying]?

Jena: "Don't eat. Don't eat. Don't eat. Don't eat. Get out of there. Get out of there. Just die."

Carolyn: Does it tell you why? Does it tell you why not to eat [very empathic]?

Jena: I dunno.

Carolyn: You don't know why? Does it give you any reasons? Does it tell you that you don't deserve to eat? Or does . . .

Jena: Yeah.

Carolyn: It does? And does it tell you why you don't deserve to eat?

Jena: No, I dunno.

Carolyn: So what do you say back to it? Do you ever say anything back to it when it says that? When it tells you not to eat, is there anything you can say back? Well, let's talk about that. Hanna, for example, hers tells her not to eat too. What would you tell her? Sometimes it's easier when you try to work on how you would help somebody else. When her eating disorder starts saying "don't eat" and "only shakes are safe," can you imagine what you might say to her to help her [trying to contact her healthy self and bring it forward]?

Jena: Hmm. [Shakes head no at first, looking down, but then begins to smile as she realizes what she would say.]

Carolyn: No?

Jena: Um. You need it . . . but . . . [She is now smiling realizing what she has just said.]

Carolyn: Well, that's a good start, I mean I really think if you were sitting with Hanna and she was struggling, I think you could say that to her. You could tell her she needs it. Like when you told me how you really cared about Hanna and how you were concerned about her leaving. I see compassion and empathy come out of you, and it looks like it's real to me.

Jena: [Not knowing how to deal with my comments, she quickly resorts to her current stress.] I dunno. I just think I should leave here, and I know I can't go home. I don't know what's going to happen to me, but I think I should leave here, because I don't want to be here and everyone says that I want to be here and that I'm getting better and I'm sick of hearing it. I don't want to be here.

Carolyn: [I cringe, wondering who told her she is getting better.] Well, let's talk about that [no resistance to her wanting to leave].

Jena: Don't you think I should leave? I mean, you want people here who want to be here [agitated].

Carolyn: Yeah, it's true. Except you know what I think? I think right now you're just not yourself. Your eating disorder is so strong that I don't know how much I'm hearing from Jena, the Jena I heard about from your therapist, or how much I'm hearing from the eating disorder part of you that's just telling you "get out," "get out," "you don't deserve."

So I'm trying to stick up for Jena, the healthy part of you. Do you know what I mean? Ultimately, you're right. I don't like to keep people here who don't want to be here. But I think I'd like to stick up for you for a little while longer while you're not able to stick up for yourself. At some point though, I'll have to give. At some point, if we can't join together and if you can't *really* feel like, "Oh yeah, I am going to get something out of here," well, then it's time. Then I'll have to give.

But in the beginning, sometimes people have come here and I have to kind of fight their eating disorder selves so they can get through this phase. And now they think they love Monte

Nido and think it saved their lives. But in the beginning they had all those feelings, like wanting to split, you know?

Jena: [Nods calmed down, looking down]

Carolyn: Sometimes I have to say, "You're not going." And I don't like being that way with people but, Jena, in recovery there's a part of us that kind of knows we have to get through this, but it's so terrifying and it's so scary. The world you created where you're just controlling your food and all that is pretty safe because you know exactly what to expect. With this, you're not sure. You feel like things are going to happen to your body that you don't know and you can't control.

Jena: Yeah [again she seems pleased that I get this].

Carolyn: If you could push a button and gain a quarter of a pound every week, and you were in control of pushing that button, maybe you could do it, but I think for me and my experience with clients, the fear is that things are going to happen and you aren't going to have control over it.

Jena: Uh huh. [She looks up, attentive, shakes her head yes as if to reinforce this.]

Carolyn: That's why I want to tell you when you reach a certain marker, so you know. So things aren't just happening and out of your control.

Jena: Have I reached 65 at least?

Carolyn: I don't want to talk numbers until you get to the one that we picked for your first weight goal, because if I do that, then you'll know how far away it is and you'll start worrying about it. But what you can know right now is that your body is not getting too much food because you are not gaining any weight.

Summarizing this therapy segment and this chapter are one and the same. Like the sculptor with a block of marble, I saw Jena as a figure imprisoned within and I took on the task of releasing her from the confinement of her eating disorder self. Therapy may not have yet cured her completely, but reatment has healed her enough so that she could leave treatment and she led a happy, productive life.

Working with Jena took a lot of compassion and nurturing but also guidance and authority. Many of the strategies discussed in this chapter were evidenced in this segment of our session. I talked about food and made behavioral agreements. I limited control battles by empathizing with her and asking for more information when she presented resistance. The concept of dialoguing with an eating disorder self is easily demonstrated as she readily tells me what this part of her is saying and how she doesn't know what to say back. I contacted her healthy self when I asked what she would say to someone she cares about, if this person were to have similar thoughts. Lastly, my work with Jena demonstrates nonattachment in many ways. She was a very sick, compromised young woman who could easily die, yet I had to be careful to avoid any kind of coercive or forceful interventions. Dealing gracefully in a nonattached way to her resistances kept her in treatment. Aside from keeping her in treatment and safe medically, I had to put aside my own agendas. In fact, Jena had insisted that she did not want to recover and therefore our first agreement was to simply see if there was a way for her to have her eating disorder and have a life, because doing it her way she was going to die. In the end, that is exactly what we did. I developed a trusting healthy attachment relationship with Jena and she depended on me until her healthy self got stronger and she could better depend on it. Jena's case is an extreme example, but it is important to note that success comes in many different ways. The philosophy and techniques discussed in this chapter and demonstrated in the session with Jena, can be used in other cases.

10

Sharing the Pain and the Promise in Group

I didn't have the language for my feelings, which, I think, contributed to my getting an eating disorder and then continued to fuel it. Group was the first time that I really met people who talked openly about their behaviors, feelings, fears, and so forth. The behaviors especially made me feel very alone and ashamed. Just being able to listen, connect, and talk with other people who shared what I thought were things only I did and thought . . . was very helpful on many levels.

I LOVE GROUP. I am always excited to facilitate a group. There are so many personalities, variables, problems, and dynamics in the room. Group therapy is an opportunity for people to sit in a circle with others and be fully present, listen attentively, practice empathy and attunement, and tell the truth without judgment.

Although it is important for group members to bring up topics to deal with in the group sessions, I start my groups with a question or topic for everyone to respond to such as, "What was your last eating disorder thought?" or "What are all the good reasons you have your eating disorder?" This is my way of doing the traditional "feeling round." I believe this builds commonality yet separateness, seeing how many different and/or similar ways people can respond to the same thing. Without the group members having to tell me how they feel, I pick up their mood by the way they

A Look Inside a Group Session

The following is a look inside a group session:

Today the opening topic is "Why does getting better feel so bad?"

Amanda, who suffers from bulimia, usually has something to say, and usually goes first, offers, "I'll go. It feels bad because it feels like things get taken away. I liked eating whatever I wanted, that part was good."

"OK, which way do you want to go, left or right?" I ask. I'm essentially asking her to choose which person will have to speak next. If that person does not speak, he or she is resisting a peer, not me. The person chosen will usually answer.

"Uh, right, I guess."

Niki, on Amanda's right, says, "Well, I think it feels bad because when you get better, I mean when your symptoms are better, like you gain weight or are eating more, then people think you are OK."

"Ah," I say. "This is a very common concern. You are afraid that it is your symptoms that speak for you, telling others you are hurting, you need help, and you are not OK. And without the symptoms, you will not get the help you need."

"Exactly," Niki replies.

"Do you all get that?" I ask. "Anyone else feel this way too?" Lots of heads nod, and I continue, "OK, next."

Elizabeth, to Niki's right, says, "Well for me, it is the identity thing. I still don't know who I will be without it. It feels like you are taking me away, not my eating disorder."

The group continues like this until everyone has a turn.

respond, such as who goes first, what tone each person uses, who passes, and whose body language gives his or her mood away.

The Importance of Asking Questions and Listening in Group

I have so much information to deal with, so many ways to go to explore all that has been said, but my first question is "Who has a question or comment to someone else about what they said?" I let the group explore further with each other. Teaching members to ask questions, to be better listeners and better helpers is an important part of the group therapy process. It also keeps the group interactive rather than allowing all the comments to be directed to the therapist. Redirecting dialogue is a necessary task of the group therapist to ensure that the group continues to deal with each other. It is one example of how the therapist will set desirable standards such as a high level of involvement between group members, nonjudgmental acceptance, a high level of self-disclosure, a desire for self-understanding, and a desire for change. After some group interchange, I go with an issue that many relate to or one that seems highly charged. I might get through several of these issues in a group or one issue might take up the entire group if everyone has something to say or a few people have a lot to say. One of the advantages of group is that not everyone has to "work" in every group to learn from every issue or interaction.

In the group quoted in the sidebar, we got into a discussion of how prevalent the fear is that giving up eating disorder symptoms may mean the person won't get the help he or she really needs. All eating disorder groups should, in part, be educational groups. In this group, we discussed how people get their needs attended to, which is a big issue with eating disorder clients and their significant others.

First, I spent time discussing that getting needs "attended to" is not the same thing as getting needs met. Just because we want them to be met and we learn how to ask, it does not mean they will always be met. Furthermore, needing something attended to is a better way of looking at things than "needing attention." Family members and significant others often say eating disorder clients just want attention. Helping clients and significant others see it more as needing things attended to takes away the negativity, blame, and judgment.

We then spent time on how the clients could ask for help (get their needs attended to) without using their symptoms. This included how to be vulnerable and how to speak up and be assertive but not angry.

I often end group with an assignment for all members or a specific member to do. At the end of this session, I asked the group members to write in their journals about the original question "Why does getting better feel so bad?" and to make a list of ways they could let people know they needed something attended to without using their eating disorder. I often suggest that a client (or clients) take something that came up in group back to their individual therapist. I might even call the therapist myself.

Topic Ideas to Start a Group Discussion

Group is often a way to begin talking about subjects, to see how others are coping with the same or similar things, and to get ideas to take back for more specific work in individual therapy. All of this comes from starting with just one topic question. The following are some starting topic ideas:

- What was your last eating disorder thought?
- What are all the good reasons you have your eating disorder?
- Say one or two words only that describe the opposite of what you are feeling. (This one is great. After everyone shares, we discuss what it is like to say the opposite of what you feel.)
- Say how or what you think the person on your right is feeling. (This is good empathy practice.)
- On a scale of 0 to 10, with 0 representing the worst you have ever been and 10 being fully recovered, what number

are you right now and why? What would you have to do to be a 10? How does this compare with what others said? Do you want to change your number after hearing others, and if so, why?

- Complete the following sentences:
  - An obstacle that is in my way, interfering with my recovery, is ________.
  - A personal trait I like about myself is ________.
  - A time I resisted my eating disorder was ________.
- What will a day in your life be like when you are fully recovered?

I also sometimes bring in a quote, song, or poem and have everyone respond to that. For example, I've used the Alanis Morisette song "That I Would Be Good" and the Mary Oliver poem "The Journey."

Examples of Group Processes

There are various types of activities and processes that take place in group. The following information discusses some important examples.

Giving Assignments to Share in Group

Group can be an effective way to work through assignments. It can be informative, therapeutic, and healing to work through issues with others who can witness, give feedback, empathize, and even challenge. When a client reads an assignment such as "My Worst Eating Disorder Day," she is being vulnerable in front of the group and telling the truth about what her eating disorder was really like, sometimes for the first time.

Having others witness this and give feedback is an important aspect in owning up to the depths of the illness and making it real. Also, when clients later forget how bad they were, others who have heard about their worst eating disorder day can remind them. Sometimes it is a client other than the one reading the assignment who gets the most out of it. I have seen listeners break down, realizing how devastating their own eating disorder was when hearing someone else's worst day.

The following are some examples of assignments I've given clients to share in group:

- Write about what brings people closer to you and what pushes them away.
- Discuss times you have lied about your eating disorder and how you can avoid this in the future.
- Write a good-bye letter to your eating disorder self. (Then have your eating disorder self write a letter back.)
- List 10 warning signs that you might be headed toward relapse.
- What client(s) in the group do you feel closest to and why?
- Pick a situation you would like to do over, describe it, and then describe how you would have liked it to happen.
- Share some of the adaptive functions of your eating disorder.
- Describe ways in which you have instilled trust and mistrust in relationships.

Asking for Time

It is useful to see what clients bring to work on with the group. Eating disorder clients (especially those with anorexia) often hold back and are not good at initiating taking time in group (or in life) for themselves. If no one is saying anything at all, I push to help facilitate this by asking something like, "Who wants time in group?" or "If you were in an individual therapy session today, what would you bring up?"

Exploring Group Dynamics

One of the most important things about group has nothing to do with the topics or the content of the material, but rather the process: who always talks, who keeps quiet, who gets angry easily, who shuts down, who rescues, who lectures, who interrupts, who listens well, who is empathic, who is discounting of their own or others' issues, who is honest, who can confront or challenge without judgment or anger, and so on. How people behave in group is how they behave in life. How people behave in life has a lot to do with what they learned growing up and how and why they developed an eating disorder.

In an eating disorder group, members could spend session after session discussing topics such as perfectionism, where clients take turns sharing their own experiences. This kind of ongoing interaction is content-oriented. It is important, if the group is to be a true therapy group, to include process interaction, discussing the here and now as well. "How do you feel about what she just said?" "You look like you don't believe Sherry." "You look nervous and unhappy about that." Unless the discussion is redirected and the therapist establishes the understanding that process is just as—and probably more—important, group members may continue solely with content interaction.

How the group members feel about and relate to each other is vital. What they are thinking and not saying is exactly what they should be saying. The therapist can simply stop periodically and ask a member or members what they are thinking at that moment, or he or she might ask what they have thought about but have not said so far during the group session. (You would be surprised what comes out.)

The therapist must encourage members to ask questions of each other. Keeping journals and writing about the group sessions is a good way to bring process interaction into the group. In their journals, members often express much more of what they were really feeling during a group session. If they are willing, participants can read what they've written at the next group session. This usually brings up important feelings and leads to a good process discussion. Group members eventually start to bring up process comments on their own during the sessions.

Role-Playing, Psychodrama, and Reenactment

Being in a group provides the opportunity to perform various role-play and reenactments that can help clients practice responding to certain situations in healthier ways. The following are examples of this process.

Role-Play of an Anticipated Event or Reenactment of a Past Event

Clients need to practice more appropriate ways of responding to circumstances and events. A client who had a fight with her parents while at a restaurant and then purged can have group members play her parents, reenact the scene, and come up with a different result. A client who is going to visit her relatives may describe how she always restricts her food because she feels out of control and out of her routine, and the food is different and scary. Group members playing her relatives can help her practice speaking up, using her healthy voice instead of her behaviors, and asking for help. Role-play is also important in issues that are not food-related.

Role reversal can also be useful. The client plays the other person in a scenario and a group member plays the client, or the client watches other group members enacting a scene from his or her life.

Dialogue Between the Eating Disorder Self and the Healthy Self

This is one of the most important and useful interventions in the treatment of eating disorders, and group therapy offers an excellent way to facilitate it. For example, if Jenny is going to have a dialogue between her healthy self and her eating disorder self, I can ask Ashley to play the eating disorder self allowing Jenny to focus on responding from her healthy self. If Jenny gets stuck and the eating disorder self is stronger and "winning," I might also ask Elizabeth to stand beside Jenny and whisper in her ear suggestions of responses from a healthy self. It is amazing how hard it is for clients to respond from their healthy selves and yet unless they can do so, eating disorder thoughts and beliefs will continue to dominate their behaviors. The more they practice opposing the eating disorder self and strengthening the healthy self, the better they get at it, which prepares them for making appropriate decisions when the time comes.

Why Does Group Therapy Work?

One of the main reasons group therapy works is that it serves as a microcosm for the world at large. It is practice for living life in relationship with others. Aside from this global concept, this section provides a summary of other benefits to group therapy.

Providing Education

Group sessions can be a good forum to educate clients on important topics that may not be addressed elsewhere, such as nutrition, medical consequences of laxative abuse, or assertiveness techniques. Educating clients in group saves individual therapy time for more personalized and deeper issues. Group members also educate each other from their varied experiences in identifying and solving problems.

Helping Clients Feel Support and Acceptance

Group therapy can help clients feel supported and accepted and know that they are not alone. For example, one client wrote to me, "Group therapy was helpful for the obvious reasons: it created a sense of camaraderie; it helped me feel less alone and more validated. But it also helped me recognize and appreciate my individuality. I saw myself through the eyes of the other women, as a beautiful, smart, strong person, with much more to her soul than anorexia. That perspective was invaluable."

Another client revealed, "I felt as if the group members provided acceptance while at the same time supporting and encouraging necessary changes. Through truth without judgment we all learned compassion and empathy for others and then for ourselves."

Building Interpersonal Relations

Often clients have lost or never acquired the necessary trust or interpersonal skills to develop quality relationships. With the help of other group members, they can learn what their feelings are and how to communicate them. Clients who otherwise have a hard time forming relationships can eventually learn to share, get close, trust, love, and be loved.

Controversy exists over whether group members should have contact with each other outside of regular sessions. The early proponents of group therapy had the philosophy that group is meant to help clients learn how to make friends, not provide friends for them. Many female therapists, notably Dr. Melanie Katzman, have spoken out in books and at national conferences to disagree with the early concept of "no outside involvement." Instead, they encourage therapists to promote clients' using each other for support outside the group. Being in a group is obviously a good way of reaching out, contacting others, and developing personal resources. Eating disorder clients need each other this way. Sometimes just a phone call can prevent a binge, bring someone out of a depressed mood, or offer an alternative to a purge. It is up to the therapist to recognize and effectively deal with any splitting or undermining effects that outside contact or friendships have on the group.

Dealing with Confrontation

If everyone in group therapy were always nice and encouraging, it would not only get boring, but very little growth would take place. Once an atmosphere of trust and caring is established, the therapist facilitates members in confronting each other about inconsistencies, self-destructive behaviors, poor or miscommunication, and issues of disagreement.

The therapist's task is to help clients learn to challenge each other in a caring manner so they learn that they can like or love someone and still disagree with or question them. Many clients don't know how to deal with anger, discuss negative feelings, or have an argument, and they need to learn that it is *how* they go about it that makes the difference. One of the most important lessons I teach is the concept of truth without judgment. It is actually very simple. Always tell the truth from your own perspective and without any energy or anger or judgment toward another person. If you are angry about an issue, it means waiting, calming down, breathing deeply, and only speaking the truth once you're calm. It sounds simple, yet it is one of the hardest things to do. When you try it, you see how easily judgment slips in. Truth without judgment is a critical life lesson, and group therapy is a perfect place to practice it.

Types of Groups

Group facilitators need to decide whether they want to have a time-limited group or an ongoing group, which adds new members at any time. Will they run a therapy group or a support group? Will the group include all types of eating disorder clients or be limited to those with certain disorders? Therapists or group leaders must decide these issues based on their own experience, skill level, desire, and other constraints. Information on making these decisions and leading groups in general is available elsewhere in texts on group psychotherapy. However, two of these subjects are worthy of further discussion.

Mixed/Heterogeneous Group

There has been some debate as to whether all types of eating disorder clients should be mixed in one group. People with anorexia and bulimia are more similar than dissimilar, so mixing them is no problem. My opinion is that with a competent therapist mixed groups, including individuals with binge eating disorder, can be highly successful.

A mixed group helps clients see that it's what's underneath that counts. In other words, I tell them, "You are all here because you have an unnatural relationship with food and with your bodies. You are here to make peace with food and your body and not let these issues control or ruin your life." Mixed groups provide experiences that break through distorted thinking in a way that the therapist or a client with a similar illness cannot. For example, Neal, a man with BED who weighed more than 300 pounds, said to Pam, who had anorexia, "How can you sit there and say you're fat? I'm fat. If you feel fat, that's one thing, but to say you are fat is wrong."

A group situation in which only one person has BED while everyone else has anorexia or bulimia—or vice versa—should be avoided. Mixed groups are more successful when there is a fairly balanced number of diagnoses.

Support Group Versus Therapy Group

A support group is usually a "drop-in" group where new people can come in at any time. An Overeaters Anonymous meeting and an ANAD group (see Appendix, "Eating Disorder Organizations and Websites"), where the participants may vary greatly from one group to the next, are examples of support groups. By its nature, this kind of group does not allow for continuity or for the same kind of intimacy and depth as a therapy group.

Support groups are usually free or accept donations and are set up to provide support and education to members, not therapy. Support groups can be extremely valuable and have their place, but they are different than a group run by a therapist. Participants shouldn't judge any group from one experience, because they vary widely, depending on the facilitator's expertise, the attending members, and the group's philosophy.

Cautions and Concerns with Group Therapy

The following are common concerns regarding possible occurrences in group therapy. The therapist must deal with these problems to have a successful group.

Sharing Negative Ideas

The group should not turn into a sharing session of eating disorder techniques or announcements of pounds lost or number of laxatives taken. The therapist should establish that specific behaviors, such as purging techniques, and specific numbers cannot be shared in group. For example, the therapist should instruct the group that if someone wants to discuss an incident in which she vomited 10 times, she is to simply say, she purged. If a person went on the Stairmaster for two hours, he should say, "I overexercised." It is counterproductive to give specifics about the means, the amount, or other details about behaviors. Clients can get help and support from the group without giving specifics that might trigger or cause competition in other group members.

Becoming a Complaint Session

Sometimes groups can become dumping grounds or gripe sessions, where members continue to share only destructive behaviors, are not getting better, complain that recovery is impossible, or state there is no hope for them. It is destructive for a group if a member continues on a litany of horrible things she is doing or can't stop doing, especially if that person is not really asking for or accepting help or support.

There should be a rule that no one is allowed to just come in and complain. If someone has a problem to share, he or she must ask for the group's advice and support. For example, instead of coming into a session and saying, "Therapy doesn't work; it doesn't help and I know I will never get better," a group member will need to learn to reframe this statement to sound something like this: "I am struggling with the idea that I may never get better; I wonder if any of you feel that way and how you get through that feeling." Such reframing changes simple complaints to requests for advice or support and automatically adds an element of hope.

Any group member who continually ignores this rule is using the group as a complaint forum, is clearly not getting better, and must be omitted from the group in a respectful way. This kind of behavior is more easily tolerated in individual therapy but is one of the biggest causes of group drop out and interferes with the success of the group.

Normalizing/Glamorizing Eating Disorder Behaviors

When everyone in the group hates their bodies or when everyone purges, it is easy for the behavior to become somewhat "normalized." It is important that the group therapist discusses this with participants and finds ways to prevent this from happening. For example, using phrases like "I got sick" instead of "I vomited my meal" can normalize and soften the harsh reality of this symptom. Furthermore, the amount and kind of attention that individuals who have eating disorders receive can glamorize these illnesses. The media's handling of these illnesses, especially in the case of celebrities, is an example of this. Overtly discussing this in group is important. Sometimes group discussions can help serve as an antidote to the culture.

Engaging in Attention-Seeking Behaviors

Competition for attention will always exist in groups on some level, but it may get out of control and become highly unproductive. Some provocative clients will engage in attention-seeking behavior. A member of one of my groups took laxatives on learning that several members had called another participant during the week after she had reported taking them in a previous group. Facilitators must be on the lookout for such behaviors and set limits for continued participation.

In another group, two members called me over the weekend. The first just left a message asking me to call her; the second left a message that she had just taken ipecac. I was busy and only got back to the caller who had taken ipecac because this was a dangerous act. When this came up in group, the first client said, "Oh, now I know what I have to do to get you to call me over the weekend. Take ipecac." To this provocative client, I said that she would only get a return call from me if she called because she had been symptom-free for four days. Some individuals might get worse in group or continue to use group inappropriately; if so, the therapist may need to ask them to leave the group.

Participants Applying Pressure

Well-meaning or not, sometimes a group member becomes an unauthorized "cotherapist" of a group. He or she may direct others, insist on change, or judge them harshly The therapist must intervene if this happens, otherwise group members may withdraw, lie, or simply not show up. The therapist might ask, "Jamie, why is it so hard for you to accept that Alex may not agree to stop using laxatives?" or "Michelle, you seem angry that Laura threw up this week. Can you help us understand what that anger is about?" It is important to remind the group that everyone has his or her own path toward recovery or reasons for maintaining the illness. This is an example of how group therapy offers a good opportunity to practice truth without judgment and acceptance.

Although group therapy offers a wonderful and powerful component to facilitate the recovery process, not all clients are ready for or will benefit from group sessions. Some individuals are too ill to participate, too self centered to be able to deal with others' problems, or too withdrawn to engage. A therapist or other treating professional can help clients decide if and when a group experience is right for them. As one of my clients put it, "Exploring all possible treatment options is the responsibility of any health-care provider and the course of action for eating disorder treatment should be mindfully evaluated on a case by case basis."

With this in mind, in addition to individual and group therapy, there is one last modality—family therapy—that also needs to be evaluated on a case by case basis. The involvement of the family members and significant others in the therapy process is the subject of the next chapter.

11

Family Therapy: Working with Families and Significant Others

DURING THE LAST 10 years, I have worked intensely with family members at my residential program, Monte Nido, where families have come from all over the world, including Canada, Costa Rica, Greece, Guatemala, Hong Kong, Japan, New Zealand, Mexico, Spain, Turkey, and Venezuela.

I try to get a family assessment for every client I treat, whether in my outpatient practice or my residential program and whether he or she is 14 or 41. What happens in the lives of parents passes down to their children, even if no one is conscious of it. I ask parents and spouses to fill out a thorough assessment about their own lives, including traumatic events, family communication, and any kind of problems and issues related to weight and appearance. This is a valuable tool, and I encourage all therapists to do the same. Even if clients resist in the beginning, I suggest that the therapist keep trying.

The Goal of Family Therapy

These days, more than ever, parents want to know whether or not their son or daughter's eating disorder is due to something they said or did or something handed down in their genes. Suffice it to say, I tell them that both nature and nurture are at work here.

What I Learned from Family Therapy and My Own Family History

My own history provided me with interesting insight into family matters. As described previously in Chapter 4, I believe I have the genetic predisposition associated with anorexia nervosa. My father would agree since he used to tell stories of my perfectionistic, control-junkie nature and how I would organize the neighborhood, telling all my friends what to do and say. My mother would agree that I am very rejection-sensitive. I was even diagnosed with an anxiety disorder as a child, which we now know is common for individuals with anorexia.

When I was in first grade and again in third grade, I developed a bad case of separation anxiety. I refused to go to school. I would panic and vomit when forced to go and would run away unless my mother stayed in the classroom. Eventually, the school told my mother that she had to take me to therapy or I couldn't come back to school. So in the early '60s, when I was eight, my mother and I went to therapy. Back then our mother-daughter therapy consisted of weekly sessions where we each went into our own rooms with our own therapists. I can only remember playing checkers or other games, and I thought it was silly. On the ride home I would tell my mom it was a waste of our money. However, at some point, after not too long, I began willingly going to school.

Years later, in college, while struggling with anorexia, I wrote to the therapist who had treated me when I was eight and asked for records about my case. I got the records and discovered that I had been diagnosed with separation anxiety and school phobia, but the therapist noted that it was what happened in my mother's therapy that cured me. I went to my mother, and for the first time, we discussed what had happened. During her therapy, my mother, whose own mother had died in childbirth, uncovered a traumatic memory (which was later substantiated by her relatives). She remembered being at home with her father when she was about five years old and hearing a loud noise. She went to see what it was, and when she opened the door to her father's room, she found that he had shot and killed himself. Unbeknownst to me, after my mother remembered this incident in therapy and was able to discuss it and work through it, I began going to school.

To summarize what happened, when it came time for me to leave home and go off to school, in the first grade when I was the same age as when my mother found her father, and again in third grade, when there were huge stressors in my mother's life, she developed an unconscious fear (based upon repressed traumatic memories) that something bad was going to happen. Neither she nor I knew this was happening. I unconsciously picked up her fear and was unable to leave her to go to school. As soon as my mother was able to "metabolize" her own traumatic experience from childhood, I was released too without us ever having said a word about it to each other. I wonder how long I would have been in therapy if my mother had not gotten the help she needed for herself. Family issues really do matter. (For more information on parents metabolizing their own childhood events, readers can refer to *Parenting from the Inside Out* by Dan Siegal.)

Another informative aspect of my own history is that neither my brother nor my sister had separation problems or problems going to school. It was the combination of my temperament or sensitivity, combined with my mother's, that made her past trauma, current stressors, and the event of my going away to school a problem. Years later, at the age of 16, I headed off for college and only then did it become a reality that my summer diet turned into an eating disorder. My genetically predetermined temperament that had resulted in a high degree of success in school contributed to a high degree of success with dieting, so much so that anorexia was the result.

Another factor at play in the development of my anorexia was that my father had divorced my mother and married a fashion model three years earlier. Back then, I thought this had nothing to do with my own starving behavior. I see now how many things came together like pieces of a jigsaw puzzle in the development of my illness. My anorexia was a combination of my genetic temperament, the culture I lived in, and all those family matters.

As discussed in Chapter 4, researchers are finding evidence of a genetic predisposition, but a definitive answer is a long way off, and even further away is a treatment or cure for any genetic abnormality. Consider what top researcher Cynthia Bulik says regarding this issue and parenting: "There is nothing they can do to alter the passing down of DNA, they can alter environments that influence the likelihood of genes being expressed." With this in mind, part of the goal in family therapy and in preventing eating disorders is the same, to find out what is protective and what is triggering.

So what can parents do to help? What do they do that is harmful or has negative consequences? How can a spouse be supportive and what is sabotaging? It is difficult to sort through all the available information. The field of eating disorders has grown in regard to information for families and family therapy. Since I wrote my own book for families, *Your Dieting Daughter*, in 1997, a number of books have been added to the resources available for families and significant others. In 2005, I included 12 of these in "Books on Families and Significant Others" a review that I and a few colleagues wrote for *Eating Disorders, The Journal of Treatment and Prevention* (Costin, Carolyn, Ali Borden, Anna Kowalski, Jeff Radant, and Norah Wynne 2005). The books in that article provide a good overview of what is happening in the field, and both parents and professionals should consult the review and the publications discussed for further information.

Very little written deals specifically with spouses. Van Den Broucke and Vandereycken wrote *Eating Disorders and Marital Relationships* in 1997. *Eating Disorders and Marriage* by Woodside, Shekter, Wolfson, Brandes, Lackstrom, was written in 1993. *Eve's Apple* is an interesting fictional story from a man's viewpoint of being in love with a woman suffering from an eating disorder. This is a haunting book in many ways with vivid descriptions of how painful it is to watch someone you love deteriorate while trying to deceive you during the process. Rather than giving this book to husbands or boyfriends, I have given it to their wives or girlfriends with eating disorders so that they can get a glimpse of what it might be like for their significant others to be in a relationship with them. A more lighthearted book, *Honey, Does This Make My Butt Look Big?* by Lydia Hanich, tries to give spouses suggestions on what to say or not to say.

Another interesting book, *This Mean Disease*, was written by a man who grew up with a mother who had anorexia nervosa. This account of Dan Becker watching anorexia take over his mother and essentially his whole family, offers another important and increasing viewpoint: that of a child whose parent suffers from an eating disorder.

Whether a parent, spouse, sibling, or friend, all significant others are affected by eating disorders and need help too; this chapter is meant to have a little something for everyone. When I use the term family or families, I most often mean all significant others, siblings, spouses, and possibly even friends fill in where necessary. Some things are geared specifically to parents, but for the most part, any significant other can find a way to personalize and utilize the information described here. Significant others might also be interested in the journal *Eating Disorders Today* geared specially to sufferers and their significant others.

Looking over all of the available information is bound to be confusing. The best advice I can give families is to find a trained professional with expertise and years of experience in treating eating disorders to guide you in figuring out what is right for you and your loved one.

What Is the Maudsley Method?

The Maudsley method, which was mentioned earlier, has been effective for a select group of adolescents who have suffered from anorexia for less than three years. Developed in London and now being used by practitioners in the United States, this approach is known for putting parents of adolescents with anorexia back in control of their child's eating, maintaining a position as "boss" with the therapist as a consultant. (See Locke and LeGrange 2005 for details.)

In a sense, the Maudsley method actually follows the ideas and protocols found in a successful, well-organized eating disorder program. The difference is that in the Maudsley approach, the home is the hospital and the parents serve as the nursing staff. Family members have to be willing and capable of doing all that is asked, including figuring out exactly what to feed their child, how to feed her, and how to spend every meal with her, even if it means quitting work to do it. Obviously it is critical that the parents are able to work together and get along.

Not all families will be able to accomplish Maudsley. The necessary factors for success are missing in many situations, such as where parents are hostile or incapable or other family problems are a factor in the etiology or perpetuation of the eating disorder behavior. However, for the right clients, this treatment approach can save money and prevent unnecessary hospitalization or residential care. Research indicates that the beneficial effects of this treatment for adolescents with anorexia were sustained at a five-year follow-up. These results are promising, but more studies need to be done. It is unclear at this point if this approach will work for other age groups and diagnoses, but research is underway. Furthermore it may be that the successful ingredient here is including the family. Other types of family therapy may be just as successful, as some research has already shown.

The results of the Maudsley method and other studies that show family therapy to be superior to individual therapy for adolescents are serving as a wake-up call for therapists who are not skilled in family therapy or who tend to keep families out of the treatment process. The task of family therapy is so complex, and at times so overwhelming, that therapists often shy away from it, preferring to work solely with individual clients. This can be a grave mistake. Eating disorder therapists should be trained in family therapy, and whenever possible, family members and/or significant others should be a part of the overall treatment. In general, treatment professionals and treatment programs around the country are taking a more active stance in working with families and significant others who in turn are becoming more educated and more interested in being included and involved.

I have always done my own version of the Maudsley method, and I see the success of this approach as having something to do with the motto I share with families: "My job is to put myself out of business. My job is to teach you what I am doing for your daughter (or son) that works, then you won't need me anymore."

What Therapists Do: Tasks of an Eating Disorder Family Therapist

The therapist helps family members learn to empathize, understand, guide without controlling, step in when necessary, foster self-esteem, and facilitate independence. If the therapist can help family and significant others provide a healing, therapeutic relationship for the person, the length of therapy will be reduced. Good parenting and good therapy require firmness and empathy, as well as guidance, advice, and collaboration. While writing this chapter, I asked my clients to share with their family members and significant others what the therapists at Monte Nido do that they find helpful. The following is what the clients came up with:

- They allow all feelings.
- They speak in the moment.

- They tell the truth without judgment.
- They ask specific questions and draw out information.
- They don't assume things.
- They acknowledge our fear and our ambivalence regarding getting better.
- They know that it takes time.
- They validate and acknowledge our experience.
- They are not emotionally connected to our behaviors.

This list is valuable and includes important concepts for the therapist to help significant others put into practice. For example, telling the truth without judgment is not only one of the most important concepts I teach my clients, but it is also important for significant others. When every person can tell his or her own truth, calmly with no anger or judgment, then spouses and family members can live together and work out problems harmoniously. We practice this in the family sessions. (It sounds easy, but as I mentioned earlier, try it.) I encourage other therapists to use this list and ask clients to come up with their own to share with their families.

The family therapist has many tasks. I start out telling everyone that I am there for the most amount of healing for the most people. The idea is for everyone to bring everyone else's best self forward. Aside from the normal responsibilities of any family therapist, which are explained in other books, there are tasks specifically related to eating disorders. For example, we should not be trying to get things back the way they used to be. The person will be changed when he or she gets better, and I tell family members, "Don't ask for things to go back to the way they used to be, because how he or she used to be led to an eating disorder." The following sections describe some of the other tasks.

Ensure Responsibility Without Blame

Family therapists must be careful that no one feels blamed for the occurrence of the eating disorder. Parents, at times, feel threatened and annoyed that they have to change when it is their daughter or son who is "sick and has the problem." At times, family members may feel abused and perhaps even victimized by the client and need someone to understand their feelings and point of view and even stick up for them. However, even though the focus stays off blame, everyone must recognize and take responsibility for his or her own actions that contribute to family problems and/or the eating disorder. Even if eating disorders have genetic predispositions and are real illnesses, clients have the responsibility of getting better. Even if parents or spouses don't cause eating disorders, they can contribute to or perpetuate them. Everyone has something to learn and something to gain from family sessions.

Understand the Eating Disorder from the Client's Point of View

One overall task is to help family members understand the eating disorder from the client's point of view and align with the healthy self. This means getting to know and understand both parts of the person: the eating disorder self and the healthy self. For example, to help parents and spouses avoid getting angry at or battling with their loved one, I tell them, "Understand all the reasons the eating disorder self is there, yet align yourselves with your daughter's (or wife's) healthy self and help her put the eating disorder self out of a job." I help by providing specific questions and statements they can use to accomplish this:

- "Is your eating disorder self giving you a hard time right now?"
- "I know part of you sees it that way, but there is another part of you also."
- "Is your eating disorder voice saying something?"
- "Maybe I can help you not listen to that part."
- "What would your healthy self say?"

(Refer back to Chapter 9 on individual therapy for more detail.)

Explore the Impact of the Illness on the Family

The family therapist must assess how much the eating disorder has interfered with the feelings and functioning of the family. For example, has everything else been put behind the eating disorder, including other children? This information helps the therapist and family begin to identify whether certain things are the cause or result of the eating disorder. Families need help learning what is appropriate behavior and how to respond. In some cases, parents and spouses need help in not being held hostage by someone with an eating disorder. This could mean anything from not being able to go out to certain restaurants to not be able to take a vacation, to not even being able to leave the person home alone. In some cases, the task will be to help everyone adjust to the concept that the person with the eating disorder might not get better.

Discover Parental Expectations/Aspirations

Unrealistic expectations for achievement or independence, consciously or unconsciously, can cause problems. If children get rewarded only for "what they do" as opposed to "who they are," these children may learn to depend solely on external rather than internal validation. Weight loss often becomes another perfectionistic pursuit, one more thing at which to be successful or "the best." Initially, spouses and parents often unwittingly praise the effort and the result.

Expectations regarding treatment and recovery should also be discussed. Significant others don't know what to expect from treatment or what they should be asking of their sons, daughters, or wives who are being treated. Therapists help families set realistic goals. For example, setting goals in a family session helps guide significant others in assisting with weight-gain goals while limiting their intrusiveness and past ineffective attempts.

For individuals with bulimia or binge eating, a first goal may be to get the focus off weight goals. Eating disorder behaviors can improve significantly without weight loss. Even in anorexia where weight gain is a must it is important not to overemphasize it and confuse it for real progress. Well-meaning family members often focus on weight loss or gain as a sign of progress, complaining that their loved ones have not lost or gained weight or praising them when they do. One father praised his daughter with anorexia for gaining weight, saying, "Whatever you're doing, honey, keep it up." Unfortunately, he did not know she had gained weight because she was bingeing and purging. A husband once praised his wife with BED for losing weight without realizing she started taking laxatives and diuretics to do so.

Establish the Role of the Client in the Family

In the case of parental disharmony, the eating disorder may serve as a mechanism to focus the parents' attention on the child with the eating disorder and away from their own problems. In this way, the parents unconsciously find a way to work together on something. Some children take on too much responsibility and become perfectionists and overachievers. A child with anorexia is often the "child who never gave us any problems. She was always so good, we never had to worry or concern ourselves about her." The child becomes independent and assumes too much control and self-reliance before being mature enough to handle it. She is given, or takes on, too much responsibility. The eating disorder occurs as an extension of her self-imposed need to try to control. Whatever the reason, some kids get lost in a family. If dieting wins approval from peers (which it almost always does) and gives her something to be good at, it will be reinforced. She might think, "Wow, I am successful at this," or "What else do I have?" On the other hand, some children binge as a way to ease loneliness or otherwise find comfort.

Awareness of the role or function that the eating disorder plays in the family can facilitate a solution or change toward finding healthier, more fulfilling ways of relating to each other and to the world.

Establish Structure and Communication Within the Family

Each family has unspoken rules by which its members live or function. These rules concern such things as, "What can and cannot be talked about in this family," "Who sides with whom in this family," "Conflicts are solved in this way," "When Mom is mad she does such-and-such," and so on. Understanding family structure helps explain what possible function or benefit is derived from the eating disorder in the family system. The disorder can be a way of expressing what the person is unable to say. Once put into words, the behavior begins to be understood:

- "My dad never really paid attention to me. He thought I was so capable, so accomplished. The only thing that got his attention was when I started to lose a lot of weight."
- "My bingeing and purging was definitely a way to get back at my mom, who tried to control everything I (and my dad) did, said, wore, and ate."
- "My mom tried so hard to be my best friend, and at first I thought that was cool. Eventually it was awful. We were competing with each other. I needed her to be more of a mom. I couldn't even keep up with her dieting. My bingeing and purging was partly because I couldn't keep up and partly just to piss her off."
- "If I did what I wanted, my dad was not happy. If I did what my dad wanted, I was not happy. I used my eating disorder to try to please us both."

Encourage Family Members to Resist the Temptation to Control

Many of the standard approaches used with other problems are inappropriate and simply don't work with the eating disordered individual. Praising a daughter for gaining weight, or even telling her she looks good, backfires. Taking your wife to the family doctor and having all the medical consequences of her behaviors explained doesn't work either; nor will planning a diet or guarding the bathroom. Parents usually have a hard time stopping their own monitoring, threatening, punishing, rewarding, and other controlling behaviors, even though those methods don't seem to be doing any good and often make things worse. The more control a mother exerts over her daughter's life, the more control the daughter exerts with her eating disorder. The more demands a man makes for his wife to gain weight, the thinner she gets. If yelling, grounding, threatening, or other punishments worked to control an eating disorder, it would be different—but they don't, so there is no use in continuing them.

One night I was in a family session with Kristi when I realized that the more her parents leveled attacks concerning what she was or wasn't eating, how much she weighed, and how she was harming the family, the worse she got. Some of these arguments at home ended up in hair-pulling or slapping sessions. My sessions with Kristi often dealt with repairing the damage. The more Kristi argued with her parents, the more entrenched she became in her disorder. It was clear that while being attacked by others, she was distracted from her real issues and had no time to go inside herself and "clean house," or deal with her problems. In the middle of a series of complaints by Kristi's father, I thought of the analogy, "While you are guarding the fort, you don't have time to clean house." I explained that as long as Kristi was being attacked, she was spending her therapy time defending herself and fighting off others instead of fighting the eating disorder.

Explain Genetic Predisposition and Temperament

Craig Johnson, a well-known specialist in the field of eating disorders, taught me a simple but useful analogy to use with clients and families in discussing temperament and eating disorders. Understanding this helps families in many ways, such as being more attuned with one another.

Clients have different genetic predispositions and thus different temperaments. Experienced clinicians would agree with what appears to be a difference in temperament between individuals with anorexia, particularly restrictor anorexia, and those with bulimia. Johnson explains through the analogy of turtles and hares.

Individuals with anorexia are more like turtles:

- Obsessive-compulsive
- Neophobic (afraid of new things)
- Highly rejection-sensitive
- Perfectionistic
- Control junkies

Individuals with bulimia nervosa are more like hares:

- Chaotic and impulsive
- Novelty-seeking
- More likely to take risks
- Extroverted

Although it is not a perfect analogy, and people can fall somewhere in between these two categories or switch back and forth, this explanation helps family members understand how their child or spouse or sibling with an eating disorder sees and relates to things in a way that may be very different than their own.

For example, look at the temperament of people with anorexia. These are the hyper-responsible kids who are good in school and praised at a young age for all their successes. They often do things like go off to college at 16. Things are said about them like, "She's going to be the first female president," or "We never had any problems with her," or "She was cooking dinner for the family when she was six." The problem is these kids are smart, but their emotional temperament can't and shouldn't have to handle this kind of responsibility or pressure. Their eating disorder behaviors are often the signals telling others, "Help me! I can't handle all of this, and I can't tell you that."

Addressing Abuse Issues

Numerous studies have documented a correlation between eating disorders and a history of physical and/or sexual abuse, but the association is not a simple cause-and-effect relationship. Abuse does not cause an eating disorder, but it can be one of many contributing factors. Both physical and sexual abuse are boundary violations of the body, so it makes sense that abused individuals manifest both psychological and physical symptoms, including problems with eating, weight, and body image.

Both individual and family therapists should explore family histories by asking specific questions regarding any abuse. Individuals who are or have been abused are reluctant to reveal it or sometimes have no recollection of the abuse. Obviously the perpetrators are also reluctant to have it found out. Therefore, therapists must be well trained and experienced in these matters, paying attention to signs and symptoms of possible abuse that need further exploration and treatment. How to deal with the myriad of issues that accompany sexual abuse is beyond the scope of this book. There are many resources on this topic. *The Trauma Model* by Colin Ross explains therapeutic techniques to use with this population. Another book that deals directly with the combination of both issues is *Sexual Abuse and Eating Disorders* edited by Mark Schwarz and Leigh Cohn.

Girls in this situation often starve as soon as they go off to school. There is a high incidence of eating disorders in girls after they enter college. They deal with their anxiety and, in some ways, stay attached to home through their illness. Often, these are girls who actually need to be held back for a year to get stronger developmentally *before* they go to college, but they are the ones going too early. It is really difficult to look at a family and say that. These are the girls who take on too much responsibility at an early age, and parents too often have let them go off and run their own lives. Their superegos grow too strong, and it becomes all about discipline and ego and trying to get everything right and perfect and controlled. They become way too strict as their own disciplinarians, like prisoners who become prison guards.

Parents need to say to these young girls, "Stop doing your homework and go outside and play," or "Unless you get a couple of Bs this semester, you're not driving the family car." We have to teach parents to be parents in a different way. Parents need to understand their child's as well as their own temperament and how to act with those differences in mind.

Types of Family Work

Therapy for dealing with family issues can be done in a number of ways. Sometimes the only family work is that which takes place in individual sessions, where the client talks about the family and family problems but others are not present. There are also educational groups run only for families and significant others that offer a way to get information and support without the client being present. The most common type of family therapy involves sessions with a therapist and family members or significant others in many different combinations. Lastly there is multifamily group, in which a number of families meet together.

Individual Sessions Without Family Present

Even if family members refuse, are unable, or it is contraindicated for them to attend sessions, family therapy can still occur without their participation. Therapists can explore all the various family issues, discover the family roles in the illness, and change family dynamics when working solely with the eating disorder client. However, when the client still lives at home, it is essential to have the family come to sessions unless they are so nonsupportive, hostile, or emotionally troubled as to be counterproductive. In some cases, arrangements can be made for the family members to get therapy elsewhere.

Education and Support Groups for Family Members and Significant Others Only (No Clients)

Family members and significant others need a place to go to talk about their fears and vent frustrations without fear of repercussions. They need to be with others who are also hurting and/or angry, to speak frankly and get advice out of the earshot of their loved ones with eating disorders, and to become educated regarding eating disorders and what they can and cannot do. I tend to vary this group, sometimes teaching, other times splitting the group up into dyads and letting them share with each other—sometimes I give them a topic, other times I do not. I often use handouts or suggest readings to be discussed. Although support groups for parents and significant others are rather hard to find, they have been extremely valuable for the participants that I encourage all therapists to try to find a way to offer this option to the loved ones of their clients.

If an education or support group is unavailable or inappropriate, the therapist can meet alone with family members to provide support and educate them about eating disorder causes, symptoms, treatment approaches, medical complications, length of treatment, and so forth. This information is important but time-consuming, so it is useful to provide reading materials or suggest books to read outside of session. This allows significant others to digest material and formulate questions without using valuable session time. Facts such as data regarding length of treatment can validate informationprovided by the therapist. It is also comforting for family members to read that other people have been through similar experiences.

Working with Family Members in Family Therapy

To help clients recover and family members understand, accept, and work through all the problems a loved one with an eating disorder has, successful treatment often warrants working with the family members—even when the client no longer lives at home or is a dependent. In some cases, it may be better if the client has her own individual therapist and another therapist does the family work, but my experience has been excellent with the same therapist doing both, and this is how I usually work unless there is a good reason to do otherwise. I have found that splitting the therapy and having the client have one therapist and the family work done by another therapist can drive the client even farther from family members.

I have not met a family with whom I didn't want to work, although some scared me, some were very difficult, and I knew others were probably not going to change. I can find the value in talking to an accused abuser and his daughter, whether there is a confession or not. Bring on screaming, out-of-control husbands; they are hurting too. Get restricting, exercise-addicted moms in; they need a better understanding and to be understood. Then there are all those parents and spouses who do not have any major psychological problems, lead pretty normal lives, and think they would have no issues to bring to therapy if it weren't for their suffering child or spouse. These people will be surprised at how much help and healing they can get from family therapy. It serves to educate people about and help them deal with the disorder (a sort of do's and don'ts list). It helps everyone learn to communicate and deal with each other in the most loving way possible.

Family therapy emphasizes responsibility, relationships, conflict resolution, individuation (each person developing an individual identity), and behavioral change among all family members. The therapist assumes an active and highly responsive role within this system, significantly altering the family rules and patterns. If the therapist appreciates the vulnerability, pain, and sense of caring within the family, he or she can provide support for all members.

Supportive, guided therapy can relieve some of the tension created by tenuous and previously disappointing family relationships.

In doing family work, the client's age and developmental status are important in outlining the course of treatment, as well as in highlighting the responsibility of family members. Adolescents who are older or developmentally more advanced require parental involvement that is more collaborative and supportive and less controlling. The younger the client is, both chronologically and developmentally, the more responsibility and control the parents will have. When the client is an adult, there is far less ability for parents to have control unless the person is still dependent on the parents. For example, adult clients are often financially dependent on parents who need help setting boundaries, such as not paying for college unless the person gains and maintains weight. For adults who are independent financially, family members will only be able to use their relationship with the person in trying to help. For example, I have seen women get treatment because a husband was going to leave or a father broke down and cried.

Multifamily Group

Multifamily group involves several clients and their families/significant others meeting in one large group. It is a valuable experience for loved ones to see how other people deal with various situations and feelings. It is good and often less threatening for parents to listen to and communicate with a child from another family. It is sometimes easier to listen, be sympathetic, and truly understand when hearing someone else's spouse, daughter, or son describe problems with eating, fear of weight gain, or what helps versus what sabotages recovery.

Clients often listen better to what other parents or significant others say because they feel too angry or threatened by their own family and many times shut out those closest to them. Furthermore, siblings can talk to siblings, parents to parents, and spouses to spouses, improving communication and understanding as well as getting support for themselves. Multifamily group needs a skilled therapist, sometimes even two, depending on the size of the group.

It's rare to find this challenging but rewarding type of group in settings other than formal treatment programs. It might prove useful if more therapists would add this component to their services.

Topics for Family Therapy and Multifamily Group

Therapists should always be prepared for and open to any significant other or client bringing up an issue they would like to work on in multifamily group. The therapist will have to decide if the group setting is the appropriate place or not. It is also useful for the therapist to bring topics for the group to explore. Topics such as the following can be the starting point for deeper conversations:

- **Why does getting better feel so bad?** This exercise discussed, in Chapter 10, can be brought to multifamily group to help significant others understand.

- **Random questions.** Significant others write questions and place them in a box. The clients pull questions out of the box and answer.

- **Why does praise backfire?** Clients often do not respond well to praise. "You look good" is translated into "You look fat." A discussion of this can help significant others understand.

- **Sentence completion.** The therapist gives clients a sentence to complete, such as "I wish my parents/spouse/sibling understood that . . ." The same is done for family members: "I wish my child/spouse/sibling understood that . . ."

- **How should I confront eating disorder behavior?** Significant others should bring up difficult situations. The therapist works directly with a client and significant other in front of the group, then has a general discussion about several behaviors that are hard to confront.

- **Avoiding "cheerleading."** Significant others often say things like, "I know you can beat this," or "You will probably get better soon," or "You are tough and won't need a treatment program." All can be experienced as not really understanding how bad the problem is. The individual might feel guilty and hide symptoms or escalate symptoms to demonstrate how had their disorder is.

- **What does my family do that sabotages me and what can they do to support me?** Clients share these feelings with families and others.

- **Talking sticks and heart talks.** The talking stick is a Native American tradition. Heart talks are an adapted version using a heart-shaped rock or other item in place of a talking stick. Only the person with the talking stick or heart is allowed to speak. When finished, the person holding the heart or stick puts it down, and another family member can pick it up and speak. No one can speak out of turn. This helps control emotions and allows each person to speak without being interrupted. (This is good for family sessions and group therapy also.)

Treatment for eating disorders, including family therapy, is not a short-term process. There are no magic cures or strategies. Termination of treatment can occur at different times for different family subsystems. When the client and the entire family are functioning effectively, follow-up sessions are often helpful to assist family members in dealing with stresses and transitions. Ultimately, the goal is to create an environment in which the eating disorder behavior is no longer necessary or desired.

Although family involvement in the treatment, particularly of young people, is considered vital, it is not always sufficient by itself to produce lasting changes in family members or a lasting cure for the client. Neither will the absence of family involvement doom the client to a lifelong illness. In some instances, loved ones may not be interested in participating in family therapy, or their involvement may cause more unnecessary or unresolvable problems than if they were not involved. It is not uncommon to find loved ones who feel that the problem belongs solely to the person with the eating disorder and that as soon as she is "fixed" and back to normal things will be fine. In some cases, the removal of a child or adolescent from her family is the indicated treatment, rather than including the family in the therapy process. In some cases, I have had clients bring in a best friend, sibling, or, in one instance, even a coach as their significant other to do "family" work. Sometimes our family members are people we choose, who have become family to us and not people who are legally defined as a family member. Older men and women often find this particularly helpful especially if they are single. Each therapist will have to assess the client and family and determine the best, most effective way to proceed. Working with clients and their families or significant others is challenging work but has provided me with some of the most rewarding experiences of my career as a therapist.

Individual, group, and family therapy are all important treatment components. These types of therapy all help people explore their psychological issues, family problems, and relationships that contribute to eating disorder symptoms. As seen in the previous three chapters, individual, group, and family therapists often deal directly with issues of food and weight. There are also a growing number of specifically trained professionals known as nutritionists or registered dietitians who deal with this aspect of eating disorder treatment. The topic of food and weight is so important and there is so much detail to consider that it warrants its own chapter.

12

Enough About Your Mother, What Did You Eat Today?

(Coauthored with Marcia Herin, Karen Kratina, Diane Keddy, Rebekah Mardis, Erin Naimi, Francie White, and Kim Wyman)

In 1973 Hilde Bruch, a pioneer in the treatment of eating disorders, warned about anorexia, "Don't commit the error of not correcting the dangerously low weight and the unrealistic hope that the weight will correct itself once the underlying problems have been identified and solved." Today it is universally accepted that we need to use direct interventions regarding food and weight when treating eating disorder clients. When the American Psychiatric Association came out with guidelines for anorexia and bulimia, nutritional rehabilitation was recommended as a first goal. However, there is no consensus regarding how this should take place.

Research on nutrition counseling for eating disorders is scarce. It is not clear who should be doing nutritional counseling or treatment interventions. Cognitive behavioral therapists often do it themselves. In the case of teenagers, some experts think parents should be coached to do the interventions. Physicians have also sometimes taken on this role. Increasingly today, many clinicians refer eating disorder clients to a nutritionist (in some states licensed as registered dietitians, or RDs). It is wise to check the credentials and experience of anyone doing this kind of work, but in certain geographical areas, it may not be possible to find a nutritionist or RD with eating disorder training. The physician or even the therapist might have to deal with the client's nutrition and weight management. When reading the word *nutritionist* in this chapter keep in mind that this refers to whoever is doing this type of work with the client. The information provided in this chapter will help both professionals and laypeople develop a better understanding of what takes place in this important aspect of treatment.

What Is Nutrition Counseling?

Nutritionists who work with individuals with eating disorders are in a unique position with their clients and "their food." This includes their food rules, food patterns, food likes and dislikes, shame associated with food, delight in food, restriction of food, indulgence in food, punishment through food, love of food, food allergies, and food fears. It also ultimately involves healing their relationship with food.

Nutritionists have the opportunity to witness a client's nurturing skills through their eating patterns or lack thereof. They are informed through the clients' food journals, writings, and personal discussions about how they nourishes the body and soul. In time, the nutritionist begins to teach clients how to listen to their internal compass and help arm them with practical, objective nutrition information they can rely on in lieu of their own less reliable and excessively distorted perspective. Eventually, once trust is established, the nutritionist has the opportunity to nurture the client into a new way of existing in the world and with food.

In the same way that clients who are fully recovered do not weigh themselves, they also do not follow meal plans. Intuitive or normal eating is the body's natural way of responding to food. Intuitive eating is the ultimate goal, yet novice clients, medically compromised clients, or those who have trauma backgrounds, such as abuse histories, may not be ready for a long time to depend on intuition and gut feelings for guidance. In fact, initially, most clients are misattuned with their body's needs, desires, and signals of hunger and satiety. Following their gut feelings may lead them to restrict, binge/purge, or use some other eating disorder behavior. If weight gain is necessary, it is almost never accomplished by intuitive eating because of the discomfort and distress gaining weight causes.

Some clients may be ready to learn intuitive eating sooner than others, after they have gotten used to and successful with the structure of three meals and two to three snacks a day. Some clients may not be ready or willing to move into the "gray area" of intuitive eating for some time and prefer to stick with meal plans. There are also clients who are unable or unwilling to move to intuitive eating and do better with some kind of meal plan but are otherwise symptom free.

Teaching clients that they can become fully self-reliant and intuitive in regard to food is a way to give back some of the control they are losing as they let go of their eating disorder behaviors. It is also a way to take food choices out of the dichotomous (black and white) thinking pattern that many clients have. In intuitive eating, there is no good or bad, right or wrong food. Every food choice is taken in context and becomes a way for clients to learn about themselves.

Throughout the treatment process, nutritionists must be aware of their own intentions and underlying motivation. If they are really going to facilitate healing, they must question how they can help clients eat for life instead of only for the here and now. They must guide their clients toward choices that will not only motivate them to eat while under supervision, but also to develop a desire to eat and take care of their bodies as autonomous beings.

The Dual Roles of Nutritionist and Therapist

Eating disorder clients often know a great deal about nutrition. What they don't realize is that much of their information has been distorted by their eating disorder thinking and is not based on reality. Both the nutritionist and the therapist can help individuals become aware of their faulty thinking or distortions. However, many therapists deal only minimally with specific food-, exercise-, and weight-related behaviors—partly because they have many other issues to discuss in their sessions and/or because they lack confidence or knowledge in this area.

Collaborating with a nutritionist helps keep the therapist from being sidetracked by countless details, such as how many calories to add this week or what new food to try, that can take up a whole session. It also avoids the pitfalls of the therapist challenging a client who has more nutrition knowledge than the therapist does. A certain level of expertise is necessary when dealing with eating disorder individuals, especially those who are "nutritionally sophisticated." Once someone has an eating disorder, knowledge is distorted but entrenched, and the faulty beliefs, magical thinking, and distortions will remain until they are successfully challenged.

Even if a nutritionist is used, the therapist cannot delegate all talk about food and weight to the nutritionist. Discussions of these issues are windows into underlying problems and to separate them out completely indicates to the client that the psychological and physical aspects of treatment can be compartmentalized. They cannot. Therapists should talk directly to clients about their weight and eating disorder behaviors because to avoid these areas allows clients to avoid dealing with all kinds of painful affect, dysfunctional thinking patterns, anxiety, and so on.

When working together, the nutritionist and therapist must communicate regularly, working as a team with mutual regard and trust. Sometimes clients contact a nutritionist before seeking therapy. Therefore nutritionists should have referral resources for therapists and physicians who are skilled in treating eating disorders.

Guidelines for Nutritionists

For this book, a few of the top registered dietitians in the field (my coauthors) were asked to come up with guidelines for working with eating disorder clients. The following list is compiled from the information they supplied.

- Get a detailed weight, diet, and nutrition history. Include current nutritional status, intake patterns, beliefs about food, all eating disorder–related behaviors, and their interference with the person's lifestyle and relationships.
- Develop goals, including weight and behavior change goals, in conjunction with the therapist and treatment team.
- Build trust and provide empathy. Meet the clients' needs where they are, not where you are. In other words, do not set your own agenda but rather collaborate, and whenever possible avoid imposing treatment strategies. This may be unavoidable in the case of medical necessity.
- Treatment must be individualized and not oversimplified. Clients need constant explanation, clarification, reiteration, repetition, reassurance, and encouragement.
- Accept that change will be made slowly in a nonlinear fashion. Help clients understand and expect resistance and potential relapse. Preparing them for these experiences will also help move away from black-and-white, perfectionistic thinking.
- Explore how the eating disorder may be interfering and limiting clients' life experiences, goals, social interactions, physiological and cognitive functioning, and so on. Have clients list the real-life repercussions of living with an eating disorder. Discuss Ancel Keyes's World War II study about the effects of starvation on behavior.
- Provide facts on the potential medical and nutritional complications of eating disorders. Discuss the consequences of amenorrhea, osteoporosis, anemia, hair loss, infertility, gastroesophageal reflux disease (GERD), constipation, gastritis, gastrointestinal disorders and complications, and so forth.
- Clients who have eating disorders or a long history of dieting usually ignore their signals of hunger, and feelings of fullness are highly subjective. Use food journals to monitor hunger and fullness and to review dietary and

behavioral patterns. Food journals can facilitate a more objective perspective on a client's intake without judgment or confusion. Provide a chart or graph and ask clients to provide the time and description of each meal and the level of their hunger and fullness.

- Work directly with the client's misconceptions regarding food, and deliver education about nutrients that demonstrates the benefits of changing behavior: "If you eat foods that have fat in them, your body will be satisfied for a longer period of time and you will have fewer food cravings," or "If you eat protein, your body will not cannibalize its own muscle mass and will help keep your metabolism high."
- Help clients eliminate food rituals and take risks with food. This may involve having meals or trying "scary foods" with them. Reintroduce scary foods in a safe and supportive manner.
- For clients who need to gain weight, negotiate incremental calorie and weight increases. Be careful with ultimatums about weight gain. If pushed too fast, clients will rebel or drop out of treatment. Work with a physician to determine a goal weight range and the weight range necessary to play sports or go away to college. As the client begins to consider weight gain, discuss the benefits versus the risks. Explore what it means to live in a smaller or a larger body. Help the client come to terms with living in a potentially new body.
- When clients with anorexia refuse to gain weight, let them know they are compromising their quality of life and it is a sacrifice to maintain a lower than natural weight. As an example, "Without weight gain you will be hungry, and you will not be able to think about many other things besides food, weight, body, calories, and fat. You may also repeatedly be in treatment centers if you try to lose weight or your weight is too low." If a client is at a dangerously low weight, refer him or her to a higher level of care. Nutritionists will have more leverage with

adolescents than with adults, but they may have to get parents involved to enforce weight gain or send their child to a treatment program.

- Educate clients that purging doesn't "wipe the slate clean." Approximately 1,200 calories are retained even after vomiting a binge, and there is only a 12 percent reduction in calorie absorption after using laxatives.
- Help clients learn to be comfortable in social eating situations. Changes in social eating habits can be directly related to eating and weight issues but can also be caused by relationship difficulties in general. (Refusing to eat may be a way of controlling the family or avoiding abuse or embarrassment.)
- Sometimes it is important to develop meal plans for clients. In other cases, they will be better off without a specific meal plan. In those cases, suggest other forms of structure. In either situation, it is best to work with a flexible plan that does not get caught up in calories or weighing and measuring food. What is important is that there are no forbidden foods. This does not mean clients have to eat all foods, but if they don't, they should explore why not and the meaning these foods have for them.
- Continue to question clients' behavior: "Is there anything you are doing that may be considered eating disordered?" Often clients will not own up to a behavior until they are ready to change it or have stopped doing it. They may also take up new behaviors. For example, a client who is not weighing himself at the beginning of treatment may buy a scale midway through recovery and not admit to it unless asked. A client who says she ate a sandwich may have eaten only half of a sandwich.
- Do not get stuck in endless conversations about weight. Know ways to turn these conversations into something more productive. Encourage clients to look beyond the issue of weight whenever it arises.
- Don't ignore parents or spouses. Unless there is a very good reason to the contrary, insist on parental

involvement if the client is under 18. Educational sessions and conversations with a parent or spouse regarding food and weight issues can be critical. The nutritionist can play a key role in helping parents and spouses handle food and weight issues at home. Many therapists have too much else to do or they are not prepared or do not desire to deal with specific day-to-day issues such as shopping, cooking, eating, and weighing that are important for successful recovery.

- Teach clients that normal eating is based on physical signals and is free from fear, guilt, anxiety, obsessional thinking and behaviors, or compensatory behaviors.
- Don't focus on specific calorie goals unless nothing else has worked.
- Educate clients about the possible complications of refeeding (the initial phase of nutritional restoration of a severely malnourished person). (Please see Chapter 13 for a discussion of the medical complications of refeeding.)
- Talk and teach with the compassionate voice of an ideal parent. Take the confident and compassionate but authoritative stance of "I know what I'm doing and can help you."
- Give some homework assignments, including articles and books to read.
- Do not give weight-loss diets, even to overweight clients, without a thorough understanding of binge eating disorder and the nondiet approach. Read the following books and give them to clients as appropriate: *Intuitive Eating* by Evelyn Tribole and Elyse Resch (2003), *Breaking Free From Compulsive Overeating Eating* by Geneen Roth (1984), and *When Women Stop Hating Their Bodies* by Jane R. Herschman and Carol H. Munter (1995).
- Don't ignore the rest of the treatment team. It is important for all members to communicate. For some clients, this may mean weekly communication with the therapist, psychiatrist, and/or medical doctor, while for others it could be less often.

- Don't have any preconceived ideas. Stay curious and open yet authoritative. Allow clients enough space and time for their recovery so that they are comfortable being honest about their behaviors. Do not become emotionally attached to their recovery.

Weighing Clients and Discussing Their Weight

Although nutritionists often deal with this area, I began treating eating disorders before there were any specifically eating disorder dietitians or nutritionists, so I dealt directly with the food and weight issues myself. The information provided here is based on my experience working directly with clients on these issues and on collaboration with other professionals as to what works.

It is important to wean clients off the scale and the need to weigh themselves or know what they weigh. An important aspect of recovery is weighing clients with their back to the scale and not telling them the number. As long as there is a professional who is setting goals and giving them feedback as to those goals, a specific number is unimportant for clients and can potentially trigger eating disorder behaviors.

I tell my clients that the scale is a weapon they use against themselves; perhaps someday when they're recovered, they will earn a license to use one, but if I have done my job right, they won't want to. After almost three decades of treating clients in all kinds of settings, my informal surveys have shown that not weighing has been a consistently strong factor in those who become fully recovered.

Most clients will react to a number on the scale. They will make food and behavior choices based on even the most minimal change in their weight. For example, they may compare their weight to that of others, want their weight to never fall below a certain number, or purge until the number on the scale returns to something they find acceptable. These are individuals who have been "brainwashed" to value themselves based solely on their weight. Their day can be great or dismal, depending on a number on the scale. Treatment gains can be sabotaged when a client sees or hears a number attached not just to her body, but in her mind, to her identity and self-worth.

Relying on the scale can fool, trick, or mislead anyone. All clients need to learn other measures to evaluate how they feel about themselves and how well they are doing with their eating disorder goals. They don't need a scale to tell them if they are bingeing, starving, or otherwise straying from a healthy eating plan. Scale weight is deceptive and cannot be trusted.

Ideally, weight should be taken in as consistent a manner as possible. Clients should go to the bathroom before weighing, wear a gown (if in a doctor's office or treatment program) or similar clothes each time, and if possible, weigh at the same time of day. Clients, particularly those with anorexia nervosa, often load up on fluids before weigh-ins to falsely elevate their weight. One indication of fluid loading is how fast they have to run to the bathroom as soon as they get off the scale. One of my clients didn't make it because she was so full of water. A physician may need to do a specific urine gravity test to see if a client is water loading. (This obviously should be a surprise test.)

I have seen any number of techniques used by people trying to elevate weight, such as rocks in jacket pockets, batteries in underwear, and fishing line weights sewn into jeans. One client's father even gave her salt pills to artificially elevate her weight so she could get out of the hospital sooner! It is important to understand how anxiety-producing and even phobic some clients are of being weighed and gaining weight. For those with bulimia or binge eating, I weigh mostly to reassure them and to wean them off of weighing themselves. I try to deemphasize the scale altogether.

It may be hard to get clients away from the scale. Many weigh themselves several times a day. The therapist and or nutritionist may have to help them cut back before they are willing to give it up completely. They will need reassurance about what is happening with their weight. Depending on the client and the goal, agreements can be made as to what information will be revealed, for example, telling the client whether he or she is maintaining, gaining, or losing weight.

Clients who come for treatment have usually begun to associate eating and food (not just certain foods, but all food) with weight gain. They need to learn not to associate eating with putting on weight or mistake normal fluid fluctuations for extra pounds of flesh or fat. Regardless of diagnosis, it is useful to show clients how much they can eat and stay the same weight. Individuals with anorexia think they will gain weight if they add an apple or, God forbid, a cookie to their meal. People who binge eat usually do not have any idea of their caloric needs. People with bulimia have so many fluctuations with their eating and weight that they have no consistency by which to establish how much food they need.

Maintenance is a good first goal. *Maintaining* does not mean weighing an exact number, but being within a range of two or three pounds of a certain weight.

The Hose Analogy

I always use the second weight I get on a client as the base weight from which I start measuring weight maintenance or other weight goals. In other words, let's suppose a young woman comes into treatment and her first weigh-in on my scale shows her at 110 pounds. She has been starving daily, so she is dehydrated and has no food in her stomach and intestines. This means her weight will be artificially low. As soon as she eats anything, she will rehydrate and food will begin traveling through her intestines again. This will automatically make the weight on the scale rise perhaps to 112 or 113 even though her body has not increased in size. I explain it to her this way:

> Imagine we have a garden hose and it is empty. We weigh the hose, and it weighs 10 pounds. Now we fill the hose with water and it weighs 13 pounds. The hose did not grow in size. The extra weight is due to the content inside. This is why so many individuals with anorexia and bulimia think eating or drinking anything causes weight gain. They see the weight go up, and they immediately want to go back to their old pattern of restricting. The initial

> change in weight is not actual weight gain. This is one of the reasons I weigh people with their back to the scale. If you see your weight go up, you will forget my words and your sense of reason and feel like you have to compensate for what the scale says. So since I will weigh you once a week, I will start your weight-gain goals from the second weight after you have food in your system and are rehydrated—in other words, after the hose is full.

Over the years, former clients have repeatedly thanked me for dealing with their weight in this manner and weaning them off of the scale.

Setting Weight Goals

When determining weight goals, one should always work with a range instead of a specific number. The target weight range should be set to allow for 18 to 25 percent body fat and be somewhere around 90 to 100 percent of ideal body weight (IBW) range. (Methods used to establish IBW are discussed at the end of this section.)

Aside from standard formulas, a number of factors must be considered. One should investigate the point at which the focus on food and/or weight began and explore the intensity of the eating disorder symptoms in relation to body weight. Information about food preoccupation, carbohydrate cravings, binge urges, food rituals, hunger and fullness signals, activity level, and menstrual status are all important. Clients need to try to recall their weight at the time they last had a normal relationship with food. The fact that they have a genetically predetermined set-point weight range must be taken into account. A detailed weight history, including information about the client's ethnic background and the body weight and dieting patterns of other family members, should be taken into consideration.

For some clients, the goal will be to maintain their weight. People with anorexia will need to gain. Many believe that in the case of females with anorexia, the weight at which menstruation resumes is a good guide. There are cases of females with anorexia who regain their menses when they are still emaciated or who reach fairly high weights without restoration of menses, so this measure cannot always be relied on. For other clients, particularly those with binge eating and some with bulimia who have gained weight to an unnatural size for their body, it is understandable that weight loss is one of their goals. This becomes extremely tricky and complicated. First, we have to be careful not to stigmatize clients in setting weight-loss goals for them, thus unwittingly participating in size discrimination. We also have to be careful not to set them up for failure.

Weight Loss

When individuals with bulimia or binge eating ask me to help them lose weight, I tell them I do not want that to be our goal even if they are clearly above their ideal body weight or have what is considered an unhealthy high body mass index (BMI). I point out to them how a weight-loss goal interferes with treatment. For example, a client might have a great week with no bingeing behavior until she weighs herself, discovers that she hasn't lost weight, becomes upset, feels that her efforts are useless, and binges as a result.

Nutritionists and therapists need to focus on health, helping clients repair their relationship to food. It is hoped that clients with bulimia and BED will then be able to achieve their natural weight. In my experience, this is almost always achieved with bulimia and often in binge eating disorder. Unfortunately, contrary to my experience, research shows that successful treatments for BED have not had much effect on weight loss. This is an area that needs further study.

When a client with BED or bulimia has weight loss as a goal, the nutritionist and therapist should be careful to avoid the pitfalls that might exacerbate her eating disorder behaviors. If a client is normalizing her eating, she should not be given a specific weight as a goal but rather be encouraged to make peace with food, restore her health, eat a variety of foods, eat for both health and pleasure, regain control of overeating, stop destructive eating disorder behaviors, and allow her body to normalize. If clients lose weight doing this it is important that they do not lose too much weight. Eventually the weight loss will have to turn into weight maintenance and clients often need help with this.

Weight Gain

Binge eating and bulimia have no diagnostic weight criteria; both can be resolved without a change in weight. On the contrary, a change in weight is necessary in anorexia. By diagnostic criteria alone, there is no recovery from anorexia without weight gain. It is important for clients with anorexia to understand that if they do not put on weight, they do not lose their fear of eating and food, especially certain foods; they cannot eat normally or socially because they are hypervigilant to avoid gaining even an ounce and they will usually retain food rituals and obsessions. Furthermore, without weight gain amenorrhea will most likely not be reversed. Recovery without weight gain in anorexia nervosa just doesn't happen.

Weight gain is extremely scary and disturbing to clients. Even if they have verbally agreed to gain weight, most do not want to, and their tendency will be to try to avoid and/or stop it. They need reassurance that they are not gaining too fast and are not "out of control." When clients are on a program of weight gain, it is best to set small, incremental goals and negotiate with them a certain amount of weight to gain rather than a goal weight they should reach. For example, instead of telling an 80-pound client her current weight and that her goal weight is between 115 and 120, I start with a small amount to be gained and continue with a series of these small gains:

> I know you are afraid of gaining weight, so don't think about all you will have to do. I don't want us to even try right now to think about what you ultimately need to weigh. We know you need to gain weight, so let's start with a small step in that direction. Let's set a first goal

> of seven pounds. I am sure even that feels scary enough. I do not want you to feel that it is out of your control, so although I will be weighing you with your back to the scale, I will tell you when you have gained seven pounds, but I will not tell you what you weigh. We will then see how you are doing, how you are handling it, and we will go from there.

Using numbers in this way works. Not only is it an important desensitization method, but it also keeps clients from identifying themselves with a certain number on the scale. Only as a last resort, when I cannot gain a client's trust and my usual way is not working, do I tell a client what she weighs or what I think her ideal body weight is. Since experience has shown me that this is detrimental to recovery, I believe it is critical to avoid this and am almost always successful in doing so. Revealing a specific weight goal happens with less than 2 percent of my clients. Almost all my clients leave treatment not knowing what they weigh.

In setting short-term weight-gain goals, I try for at least 7 pounds as a first goal, 10 is usually too high. Many clients will refuse to agree to even 7 and the first goal may have to be as low as a 5-pound gain. When they reach the first goal, we then set another, or I let them maintain for a week or two (maybe more depending on the severity of their eating disorder) and then set another goal. All of this has to be individualized and helps the client feel less overwhelmed and powerless. The goal is to get clients to the point where the weight gain can stop and they eventually learn how to maintain their weight on their own.

All of this can be done without clients ever needing to know what they actually weigh. The ultimate objective is for all clients to be able to live their lives without weighing or being weighed anywhere, ever! Outcome data for anorexia have shown that goal weights set at ranges below 90 percent of IBW have resulted in high relapse rates (Baran, et al 1995). Having said this, there are also certain clients who will relapse if made to achieve this level of weight gain before they're ready for it. I have seen countless numbers of them who were able to be successful with my approach.

Weight Maintenance

Weight maintenance is the ultimate goal for all clients. Many know how to lose or gain, but learning how to live normal lives and maintain their healthy weight is another set of skills altogether. All too often clients leave treatment before they have time to practice this important and necessary skill. This is particularly true of those in treatment programs. First, they are often discharged for financial/insurance reasons before they have time to deal emotionally with their new body weight or practice maintaining it. Second, many programs have complete control over food and exercise and are not set up to let clients shop for, cook, portion, or prepare food, all skills they will need to maintain their weight.

When I worked in hospital treatment settings, I watched too many clients leave treatment and immediately lose weight or binge and purge when they had to shop for all their food, make meals alone, and try to eat at times other than their inpatient schedule. This is one of the reasons I opened my residential program, Monte Nido. Teaching clients to live in the world, with all the day-to-day things they have to do, including buying, preparing, cooking, *and* eating food, is critical.

Learning how to accept one's weight and maintain it, while getting on with life, is the ultimate aim. Leaving treatment without practicing the skills of eating and living where they really count is like learning the skills of baseball without ever playing in a game. One might learn to hit a ball, but coming to bat with bases loaded and having to hit, run, and slide into third before being tagged out is another story and uses other skills altogether. For clients to fully recover, they not only need help to learn skills and accomplish weight goals, but to learn how to play the game of life and maintain their goals even when life throws curveballs.

Establishing a Healthy Body Weight

Various sources, such as the Metropolitan Life Insurance weight tables, the Robinson formula, and the Devine formula, have been established to provide ideal weight ranges. The best source to discover more about these formulas, their origin, and their limitations is on the Internet. The validity or all of these methods is subject to debate. What most people do not know is that these formulas or standards seem to all be derived from one created in 1871 by a French surgeon, Dr. P. P. Broca. Dr. Broca suggested that weight (in kilograms) should equal height (in centimeters) minus 100, plus or minus 15 percent for women or 10 percent for men. Someone later translated this into a commonly used formula:

"For women, allow 100 pounds for the first 5 feet and 5 pounds for each additional inch. For men, allow 110 for the first 5 feet and 5 pounds for each additional inch."

Later, different individuals worked with these formulas and they have gone through a variety of small changes. None has been based on population or health data and thus all are ultimately not valid.

Another indicator commonly used by health professionals is the body mass index (BMI), which is the individual's weight in kilograms divided by the square of his or her height in meters. For example, if an individual weighs 120 pounds and is 5′5″, his or her BMI equals 20. (54.43 kilograms [120 pounds] ÷ by 1.65 meters [5′5″] squared [2.7225] = 19.992, or essentially 20.)

Healthy ranges of BMI have been established. Guidelines suggest, for example, that if an individual is 19 or older and has a BMI equal to or greater than 27, treatment intervention is needed to deal with excess weight. A BMI between 25 and 27 may be a problem for some individuals, but a physician should be consulted. A low score may also indicate a problem; anything below 18 may even indicate a need for hospitalization due to malnutrition. Healthy BMIs have been established for children and adolescents as well as for adults, but standardized formulas should never be relied on exclusively.

There is a major controversy on using any method, standardized table, or formula for determining healthy weight. There are outspoken individuals in the field, such as health educator Dr. John Robison, coeditor of the journal *Health at Every Size*, and Glen Gaesser, author of *Big Fat Lies* (1996), who argue that people are unnecessarily being discriminated against by those determining what a "healthy" weight is and creating weight criteria without sufficient data. For example, neither of the calculation methods described here takes into account lean versus fat body mass. Body composition testing—another method of establishing goal weight—measures lean and fat weight. A healthy total body weight is established based on lean weight. At one point I used body composition in my practice, thinking this would be a healthier alternative and clients would stop obsessing about the number on the scale. Instead, clients obsessed about and used the body composition numbers against themselves just as they did with their scale weight. In fact, they now had two numbers to obsess about—scale weight and body composition. I stopped this practice. Now my goal is to get away from numbers as much as I can.

Whatever method is used, the bottom line for determining a goal weight is health and lifestyle. A healthy weight is one that facilitates a healthy, functioning system of hormones, organs, blood, muscles, menstruation, and so forth. A healthy weight should allow one to eat without severely restricting, starving, or avoiding social situations where food is involved. A healthy weight should not just be the result of fueling the body as some would ascribe, but about being able to experience joy and pleasure in food as well.

Nutritional Supplementation and Eating Disorders

It is common sense to assume that individuals who restrict or purge their food may have specific nutrient deficiencies. There has even been some research done regarding whether certain deficiencies existed before the development of the eating disorder. If it were determined that certain deficiencies predisposed, or in some way contributed to, the development of eating disorders, this would be valuable information for treatment and prevention. Regardless of which came first, nutritional deficiencies should not be overlooked or undertreated, and correcting them must be considered part of an overall treatment plan.

The area of nutrient supplementation is a controversial one even in the general population and more so for eating disorder clients. First, it is difficult to determine specific nutrient deficiencies in individuals. Second, clients should not believe that they can get better by taking supplements instead of eating the necessary food and calories. It is common for clients to take vitamins, trying to make up for their inadequate intake of food. Vitamin and mineral supplements should be recommended only in addition to an adequate amount of food. However, if clients take supplements, clinicians may at least be able to prevent certain medical complications by being well informed and suggesting their appropriate use, such as calcium to help prevent bone loss.

A multivitamin supplement, calcium, essential fatty acids, and trace minerals may be useful for eating disordered individuals. Protein drinks that also contain vitamins and minerals (not to mention calories) can be used as supplements when adequate amounts of food and nutrients are not being consumed. A physician, nutritionist, or other health practitioner with specific education in vitamin, mineral, and other nutritional supplementation should be consulted regarding these matters. Chapter 16 provides more information about specific nutrients used in the treatment of eating disorders.

13

Medical Assessment and Management

(Coauthored with Richard Levine, M.D., and Philip Mehler, M.D.)

ASIDE FROM THE social stigma and psychological turmoil that an eating disorder causes in an individual's life, the medical complications can be numerous, ranging from dry skin to cardiac arrest. In the past decade, there has been good news and bad news in the area of medical management of eating disorders. The bad news is that little has changed in this area. For the most part, the same assessments and treatments are being used. There is ongoing research in the area of amenorrhea, bone density, and osteoporosis, but nothing stands out as a definitive plan of treatment.

The good news is that physicians are more familiar with eating disorders, and there are more physicians who specialize in the medical management of these conditions. However, we have a long way to go. Physicians get little or no training in nutrition, much less in identifying and treating eating disorders. This is unfortunate because a physician treating a patient with an eating disorder needs to know what to look for and what tests to perform. He or she has to anticipate what is to come and discuss what is not revealed by laboratory or other medical data.

The Role of the Physician: Continued Monitoring and Treatment

The physician must have some empathy for and understanding of the overall picture of an eating disorder to avoid minimizing symptoms, misunderstanding, or giving conflicting advice. Physicians who have not been trained in eating disorders may overlook or disregard certain findings to the detriment of the patient. In fact, eating disorders often go undetected for a long time, even when the individual has been to a physician. Weight loss of unknown origin, failure to grow at a normal rate, unexplained amenorrhea, hypothyroidism, or high cholesterol can all be signs of undiagnosed anorexia nervosa; physicians too often fail to act on these signs or attribute them to other causes. Patients have been known to have a loss of dental enamel, parotid gland enlargement, damaged esophagi, high serum amylase levels, and scars on the backs of their hands from self-induced vomiting, yet they are still not diagnosed with bulimia nervosa.

I am consistently frustrated when dealing with insensitive or uninformed comments by physicians—such as "You look fine; you don't look like you have an eating disorder," or "Your cholesterol is too high; you need to cut down on your fat"—to a patient with anorexia nervosa. (In anorexia, elevated cholesterol is caused by the body not properly eliminating its own cholesterol and is not caused by eating too much fat.) There is a growing movement by several eating disorder organizations to provide information to medical schools and to doctors already in practice. The National Eating Disorder Association (nationaleatingdisorders.org) has written brochures, handouts, and letters to physicians to help facilitate this process. The Academy for Eating Disorders website (http://aedweb.org) also maintains a list of physicians who have knowledge and experience in treating patients with these disorders.

Physicians carry a lot of power and are relied on by both patients and significant others. I have worked with many good physicians and highly value their expertise. A good physician is a necessary component of a good treatment team and a good prognosis. If you are not a physician, the information in this chapter will help you understand the medical complications and monitoring involved in an eating disorder and will help ensure that you (or a loved one) get a proper medical evaluation and care. If you are a physician, I hope this information helps guide and inform you in your treatment of these perplexing and life-threatening disorders.

Guidelines for Medical Evaluation

Aside from a thorough assessment, the physician must treat any medical or biochemical conditions that contribute to the eating disorder as well as any symptoms that arise as a result of it. He or she must also rule out any other possible explanations for symptoms, such as malabsorption, primary thyroid disease, or an illness like cancer or severe depression that results in a loss of appetite.

Additionally, medical complications may arise as the eating disorder progresses or as a consequence of the treatment itself; for example, patients may experience refeeding edema (swelling that results from the starved body's reaction to eating again) or complications from prescribed medications. Ongoing, periodic assessment and treatment are necessary as part of an overall treatment strategy, and physicians should work closely with other members of the treatment team.

Of the entire gamut of psychological disorders treated by clinicians, eating disorders are those most frequently punctuated by accompanying medical difficulties. Although many of these are more annoying than serious, a distinct number of them are potentially life-threatening. The mortality rate for these disorders exceeds that found in any other psychiatric illness and may approach 20 percent in the advanced stages of anorexia nervosa. Physical complaints must be investigated judiciously and organic disease systematically excluded by appropriate tests. Conversely, from a treatment point of view, the physician has to avoid subjecting the patient to expensive, unnecessary, and potentially invasive tests.

Physicians are often the professionals called upon to do their best to assess dietary practices, nutrition intake and status, and medical complications from inadequate nutrition. If there is no psychiatrist involved, the general practitioner might be also called upon to perform this function as well.

The medical complications that arise vary with each individual. Two people with the same behaviors may develop completely different physical symptoms or the same symptoms within different time frames. Some patients who self-induce vomiting have low electrolytes and bleeding esophagi; others can vomit for years without ever developing these symptoms. People have died from ingesting ipecac or from placing excessive pressure on their diaphragms during a binge, while others have performed these same behaviors with no evidence of medical difficulties. A woman who binges and vomits 18 times a day and one who weighs only 79 pounds can both have normal lab results.

General Signs and Symptoms

Aside from an emaciated look in those with anorexia nervosa, it may be difficult to detect health problems in people with eating disorders—especially in the early stages of the illness. Over time, however, individuals who are starving, purging, or taxing their bodies through excessive exercise take on a generally lackluster appearance.

On close inspection, especially in individuals with anorexia nervosa, one can notice things such as dry skin or blotchy red marks on the skin, dry or thinning hair, or a general loss of hair. However, the growth of downy hair (lanugo) on the arms or stomach can be detected in extremely thin patients as the body tries to protect itself from the cold when it lacks body fat as insulation. Sometimes even eyelashes get fuller. One should look for broken blood vessels in the eyes and swelling of the parotid gland (in the neck below the ear and behind the cheekbone), both of which are caused by vomiting. Swollen parotid glands are often visible, but they can also be discovered by palpating the neck in this area to check for enlargement.

All patients should be questioned about and examined for hair loss, cold intolerance, dizziness, fatigue, cracked lips, sleep disturbance, constipation, diarrhea, abdominal bloating, vomiting blood, abdominal pain or distension, esophageal reflux, dental erosion, poor concentration, and headaches. Women should be evaluated for oligomenorrhea (irregular menstruation) and amenorrhea (lack of menstruation). Most of these symptoms should revert to normal with weight restoration and cessation of purging.

Many people with anorexia can be treated as outpatients. Hospitalization is indicated for patients with cardiac arrhythmias (irregular heart rhythms) or symptoms of inadequate pulse and/or blood pressure, those who are unable to sustain core body temperature and those whose weight loss is rapidly progressive or severe. Physicians used to be guided by criteria that indicated hospitalization for weight loss greater than 25 percent of ideal body weight, but this is arbitrary and many need hospitalization, or at least 24-hour care, prior to losing this much weight. The new revision of the APA guidelines, will address this issue.

People with bulimia can usually be treated on an outpatient basis unless the binge/purge episodes are so frequent that they are medically debilitating or destabilizing. Patients with an electrolyte imbalance, poor regulation of insulin, or blood in their vomit may need to be hospitalized to get these problems under control. Sometimes the bulimia is such that the person has lost their job or relationship, cannot keep down their medication, or cannot even make it to their outpatient therapy appointments. These individuals will most likely need a treatment program as well.

Managing binge eating disorder patients usually involves the same medical considerations as those involved in treating obese individuals. These considerations include heart or gallbladder disease, diabetes, high blood pressure, and so on. Most symptoms observed with BED are the result of the accompanying weight gain associated with this disorder. Occasionally people have binged to the point of becoming breathless when their distended stomachs press up on their diaphragms. In extremely rare cases, a medical emergency may occur if the stomach wall becomes so stretched that it is damaged or even tears. Readers may refer to other sources on obesity and binge eating disorder for further information on this topic.

Questions to Ask During Examination

A thorough physical should include questions about the patient's general diet, as well as his or her preoccupation with food, food fears, carbohydrate craving, and nighttime eating. Asking about these things helps indicate to the patient that all of these issues may directly affect his or her health.

The physician should also inquire about symptoms related to anxiety (e.g., racing heartbeat, sweaty palms, nail-biting); depression (e.g., hypersomnia, frequent crying spells, thoughts of suicide), and obsessive-compulsive disorder (e.g., constantly weighing oneself or food, having to have clothes or other things in a perfect order, obsessing about germs or cleanliness, and having to do things in a certain order or only at certain times). Knowing about these conditions is essential if the physician and treatment team are to fully understand the clinical status of the individual and develop a thorough treatment plan.

Medical Tests

The physician must not only check for any medical issues or complications that must be addressed, but also establish a baseline for future comparisons. For example, thyroid or bone density tests taken several months apart may indicate results that, while still in the normal range, also show a downward trend.

Vital Signs

Vital signs such as temperature, heart rate, and blood pressure should all be taken, along with weight, and monitored throughout treatment as necessary. Common signs that should be investigated and monitored closely include hypothermia (low body temperature), bradycardia (a pulse rate lower than 60 beats per minute in an adult, with lower than 40 possibly requiring inpatient care), or tachycardia (a resting heart rate higher than 100 beats per minute in an adult, with higher than 110 possibly requiring inpatient care). Blood pressure changes, such as marked orthostatic hypotension with an increase in pulse of 20 beats per minute or a drop in pressure of 20 mm Hg upon standing, may also necessitate inpatient care.

Weight

The topic of weight and weighing is extremely critical and sensitive. A detailed description of this issue is given in Chapter 12.

Laboratory Tests

An "eating disorder laboratory panel" should be part of the medical assessment. This panel of tests includes some not normally performed in a routine physical exam but helpful for a complete evaluation of an eating disordered patient. When patients have lab results that are out of the normal range, I often show them so they can see in black and white terms evidence of their body struggling to deal with their behaviors. The tests commonly used and recommended include the following:

- **Complete blood count (CBC).** This will give an analysis of the health of the red and white blood cells.

- **Erythrocyte sedimentation rate (ESR).** The ESR is a good screen for inflammation and infection. It is dependent on the patient's protein level. Usually patients with malnutrition due to anorexia nervosa have low protein levels and a very low ESR. If the ESR is elevated, other diagnoses should be explored.

- **Chem-20.** There are several different test panels, but the Chem-20 is a common one that includes a variety of tests to measure electrolytes, liver, kidney, and pancreatic function. Total protein and albumin, calcium, and ESR (see previous point) should also be included. Albumin is important to pay attention to because eating disorder patients should have normal levels. If albumin is low in these patients it is indicative of some other medical problem such as an inflammatory disease.

- **Sma7, or electrolytes often called "Chem. 7."** This panel includes sodium, potassium, chloride, bicarbonate, blood urea nitrogen (BUN), creatitine, and glucose. These are usually included in a Chem-20 panel but this test can be ordered separately.

- **Magnesium level.** Magnesium is not regularly tested with the electrolytes, but low levels can be dangerous for heart function. Magnesium levels should be tested, especially if potassium is low.

- **Phosphorous level.** Levels are usually normal in the early stages of an eating disorder. Abnormal levels of phosphorous are more likely to be found in anorexia nervosa, particularly during refeeding, because it is removed from the serum and incorporated into the new proteins being synthesized. If phosphorous is too low, patients may suffer breathing difficulties as well as red blood cell and brain dysfunction. This should be checked a few times per week during refeeding.

- **Serum amylase.** This test is an indicator of pancreatic function and is a useful indication of purging, although an abnormal result could mean other complications such as pancreatitis.

- **Thyroid.** A thyroid panel measures the thyroid and pituitary glands and indicates the level of metabolic function. T3, T4, T7, and thyroid-stimulating hormone (TSH) should be included.

- **Other hormones.** Estrogen, progesterone, testosterone, estradiol, luteinizing hormone, and follicle-stimulating hormone are all affected by eating disorder behaviors. Which of these tests to run and when to run them are the subject of much debate and should be worked out between the physician, the patient, and the rest of the treatment team.

Other tests also should be performed selectively, including the following:

- **Electrocardiogram (EKG).** The EKG measures heart function and is a useful indicator of overall heart health.

- **Chest x-ray.** This is indicated for any severe or persistent chest pain.

- **Abdominal x-ray.** This is indicated to detect any possible blockage when the patient has severe bloating that does not subside.

- **Lower esophageal sphincter pressure studies for reflux.** This test should be performed for spontaneous vomiting or severe indigestion in which food comes back up into the mouth with no forced effort on the patient's part. A gastroenterologist may be needed and may recommend other tests as well.

- **Lactose deficiency tests for dairy intolerance.** Patients often complain about the inability to digest dairy products. Some may develop intolerance, and some may have had a preexisting problem. If the symptoms become too distressing (e.g., excess indigestion, gas, burping, rashes) or if it is suspected that the patient is using this excuse to avoid eating, a lactose test may help indicate the best way to move forward.

- **Total bowel transit time for severe constipation.** Constipation usually corrects itself with proper diet. If it is unremitting and goes on for more than two weeks or is accompanied by severe cramping and pain, a bowel transit test (as well as others) may be necessary.

- **C3 complement level, serum ferritin, serum iron, and transferrin saturation level.** These four tests are not routinely performed but can be useful when treating eating disorder patients. They are among the most sensitive tests for protein and iron deficiency and, unlike the CBC and Chem-20, are frequently below normal in eating disordered patients. C3 complement is a protein that indicates immune system response; serum ferritin measures stored iron; and serum iron measures iron status. Transferrin is a carrier protein for iron; the transferrin saturation level helps identify the many patients who are in the early stages of bone marrow suppression yet have normal hemoglobin and hematocrit levels.

- **Bone mineral density test.** Patients with anorexia or bulimia may suffer a loss of bone or bone density. This is discussed later in this chapter.

Most eating disorder complaints, such as headaches, stomachaches, insomnia, fatigue, weakness, dizzy spells, and fainting are not detectable on laboratory tests and causes for them are often not found. Family members, therapists, and doctors often make the mistake of trying to scare patients into improving their behaviors by having them submit to a physical exam to discover what damage has been done. Unfortunately, patients are rarely motivated by medical test results and often have the attitude that being thin is more important than being healthy, nothing bad is really going to happen to them, or they don't care if it does. Furthermore, patients can appear healthy and receive normal lab results even though they have been starving, bingeing, or vomiting for months or even years. Medical tests often don't reveal problems until the more advanced stages of the illness. A normal lab report is not a guarantee of good health, and physicians need to explain this to their patients. At the discretion of the physician, more invasive tests may need to be performed.

If test results are even slightly abnormal, the physician should express concern. Physicians are unaccustomed to discussing abnormal lab values if they are only slightly out of range, but with eating disorder patients, this is necessary and may be a useful treatment tool. Patients who engage in dangerous behaviors and whose laboratory tests come back normal may get the wrong message. It must be explained to them that the body is wise and finds ways to try to compensate for starvation and other destructive behaviors, for example, decreasing the metabolic rate to conserve energy. It usually takes a long time for the body to break down to the point of serious, life-threatening danger. Once there are visible signs a lot of unseen damage has already been done.

A thorough medical assessment and continued monitoring are necessary components of a good overall treatment strategy and are most beneficial if the physician has developed a trusting relationship with the patient and can convince him or her to be honest.

Physicians need to know the nuances of what to look for and how to treat eating disorder patients; therapists need some understanding of the medical consequences and complications of their clients' condition; and both need to know when to refer and defer to the other. Team members working together can consult on important issues such as goal weight, ability to exercise or attend school, or criteria for a higher level of care.

Common Medical Complications

There is clearly a continuum of physical complications encountered in the different eating disorders. For this reason, we do not list the medical complications for each specific diagnosis but instead, for the most part, describe various systems affected like the gastrointestinal system or various eating disorder behaviors and their associated medical symptoms. However, some behaviors, such as self-induced vomiting, can involve a variety of systems and are hard to place in any one category. Likewise some minor conditions such as dry skin don't neatly fit in any category. Suffice it to say here that dry skin can be treated by having patients apply warm wet wash cloths on the skin prior to applying lotion. Lotion put directly onto dry skin will not serve to keep in moisture. With advice like this, physicians can help patients be more comfortable while waiting for nutritional rehabilitation to do the real repair job.

Gastrointestinal System

Complaints of constipation, fullness, bloating, diarrhea, gas, and irritable bowel are common in eating disorder patients. Usually these problems subside with treatment and cessation of behaviors, but occasionally there are lasting effects, such as with laxative abuse. The following are the most commonly reported problems.

Early Satiety and Abdominal Pain

The transit time of food out of the stomach and through the digestive tract is significantly slowed in individuals who have been restricting their food intake. Complaints of early satiety (fullness), abdominal pain, and gas are common and may be exaggerated, because of fear of weight gain, but they should be monitored. Calorie increases can be slowed down and digestive enzymes may remedy or at least mitigate this problem. If problems persist with increased pain and distention, patients may need to be sent for a two-way abdominal x-ray to determine if there is a physiological problem such as a delayed gastric emptying or a blockage. With delayed gastric emptying, often seen in anorexia, an agent that speeds emptying of the stomach should be tried.

Constipation

Slowed transit time and poor functioning of the colon secondary to inadequate food intake contribute to constipation. Patients should be forewarned that it may take three to six days for food to pass through the digestive system. They also should be educated regarding adequate intake of liquids and fiber as well as walking, because the bowel becomes sluggish when an individual is sedentary. An abdominal x-ray or even a more extensive workup may be indicated with severe pain, distention, and fever. Laxative abuse is often a cause of constipation.

Laxative Abuse

Laxatives are an ineffective method to induce weight loss because caloric absorption occurs in the small bowel and laxatives affect the large bowel by promoting loss of large volumes of watery diarrhea and electrolytes. Stimulant laxatives, if used in excess, cause the colon to become dependent causing significant problems with fecal retention, constipation, and abdominal discomfort.

It may take weeks to accomplish laxative withdrawal and restoration of normal bowel habits. If constipation persists, a glycerin suppository or a nonstimulating laxative may be useful. Most patients are successfully detoxed with this type of program, but patience is necessary to endure the transient bloating that will resolve in one to two weeks with salt restriction and leg elevation. Progressive abdominal pain, constipation, or distention warrants an abdominal x-ray and further evaluation. Loss of colonic function can become so severe that a colectomy (surgery) is needed.

Self-Induced Vomiting

A severe electrolyte disorder involving hypokalemia (low potassium), hypochloremia (low chloride), and alkalosis (high blood alkaline level) is caused by self-induced vomiting. If severe enough, vomiting can result in serious cardiac arrhythmia, seizures, and muscle spasms. Supplemental potassium can be helpful but given without restoration of the volume status, with either intravenous saline or oral rehydration solutions such as Pedialite or Gatorade, will not correct the deficiency. To induce vomiting some individuals use ipecac (a poison sold over the counter that in emergencies is used to help children vomit if they have ingested a harmful substance). This is dangerous because it is toxic to heart and skeletal muscle tissue. Ipecac's toxicity is cumulative; repeated ingestion can result in arrhythmia heart failure. Karen Carpenter died of ipecac-induced cardiomyopathy.

An early complication resulting from self-induced vomiting is parotid gland enlargement. This condition, referred to as sialadenosis, causes a round swelling in the neck below both ears and behind the cheekbones. If swelling is only on one side, physicians should look for other causes. In severe cases this condition gives rise to the chipmunk-type faces seen in individuals who chronically vomit. The reason for parotid swelling has not been definitively ascertained. Clinically, it usually develops three to six days after a binge/purge episode has stopped.

Generally, abstinence from vomiting reverses the swelling. Standard treatments include heat applications to the swollen glands, salivary substitutes, and the use of agents that promote salivation such as having the patient suck on tart candies. In the majority of cases, these are effective interventions. For stubborn cases, an agent such as pilocarpine may promote shrinking of the glands. In rare cases, removal of the glands may be necessary.

Vomiting may also cause erosion of tooth enamel (particularly on the back side of the teeth where there is the most acid exposure) and an increased incidence of dental cavities, inflammation of the gums, and other periodontal diseases. A frequent complaint of extreme sensitivity to cold or hot food is a result of exposed tooth dentin. Patients should be encouraged to get regular checkups and treatment from a dentist who has knowledge and experience in treating eating disorder individuals.

A sore throat and sores on the sides of the mouth are also caused by vomiting. Patients are advised to wipe the corners of their mouth with warm water after purging and dry the area to prevent ulcerous sores.

A potentially more serious complication of self-induced vomiting is the damage it causes to the esophagus due to damage to the one way valve leading to the stomach. Heartburn due to the stomach acid's irritant effect on the esophageal lining can cause a condition known as esophagitis. Similarly, repeated exposure of the esophageal lining to the acidic stomach contents can result in the development of a precancerous lesion referred to as Barrett's esophagus, which is very serious but if caught early is treatable. This is not common but patients whose heartburn persists with normal treatments or who have difficulty swallowing should be checked for this. Another complication presents as a history of vomiting bright-red blood. This condition is known as Mallory-Weiss syndrome or tear and is caused by a tear in the mucosal lining of the esophagus caused by forceful vomiting. This condition is not dangerous but any bleeding should be checked out immediately to rule out other causes.

Aside from encouraging the cessation of vomiting, the approach to complaints that involve dyspepsia (heartburn with a sour taste in the mouth) or dysplagia (difficulty swallowing) is comparable to that used for these complaints in the general population. Initially, the simple use of antacids, together with the cessation of vomiting, is recommended. Physicians may also prescribe other agents such as Zantac or Reglan. Resistant cases may be more serious and need a referral to a gastroenterologist.

One other important condition with regard to the esophagus is Boerhaave's syndrome, which refers to a traumatic rupture of the esophagus due to forceful vomiting. It is a true medical emergency.

Patients will complain of an acute onset of severe chest pain that is worsened by yawning, breathing, and swallowing. If this condition is suspected, a prompt trip to an emergency department of a hospital is indicated.

Starvation, Refeeding, and Refeeding Syndrome

All malnourished patients are at risk for refeeding syndrome when nutritional repletion is initiated. Refeeding syndrome was first described in survivors of concentration camps after World War II who developed complications and several died as a result of refeeding at a too rapid pace. This syndrome has multiple causes. After starvation, an intake of foods that are high in calories or glucose cause low blood levels of phosphorus, which is one of the main causes of this dangerous syndrome. Phosphorous depletion produces widespread, potentially fatal abnormalities in the cardiorespiratory system.

In addition to low phosphorous, refeeding syndrome also evolves thanks to changes in potassium and magnesium levels. Further, abrupt blood volume expansion and inappropriately aggressive nutritional intake may place excessive strain on a shrunken heart, interfering with its ability to maintain adequate circulation.

Generally speaking, it is the severely emaciated, malnourished patient with prolonged starvation who is at risk for refeeding syndrome. However, in some cases, even patients who have been deprived of nutrition for 7 to 10 days may be in this category. There are general guidelines for avoiding refeeding syndrome. The overall general rule in adding calories is "Start low, go slow." It is extremely important to address any electrolyte imbalances prior to beginning refeeding and to monitor electrolytes during the refeeding period. In severe cases requiring hospitalization or tube feeding, checking electrolytes daily for four to five days and then approximately twice a week for the first two weeks seems wise; if the level stabilizes, the frequency may be decreased. A supplement may be indicated to help avoid phosphorous and or magnesium depletion. Checking the pulse and respiratory rates for unexpected increases from the baseline as well as checking for fluid retention are crucial in avoiding refeeding syndrome. If the pulse rate becomes elevated (a physician must determine what rate would be of concern for each patient) the caloric intake should be lowered and then raised again in a few days.

Edema (fluid retention) is a common complication with refeeding and seen in refeeding syndrome. It is a common myth that this is due to low protein levels. The likely cause is that with an increased caloric intake, insulin is increased and insulin causes the body to retain sodium. A low-sodium diet (1 gram) will help this condition as well as elevating of the legs whenever possible.

A comment must be made regarding refeeding patients in general. There may be a role in some cases for Naso Gastric (NG) or Total Parenteral Nutrition (TPN). These are methods for getting adequate calories when a person is unable to consume them by eating. NG feeding takes place by a tube being inserted down through the nose into the stomach. TPN is an intravenous infusion using an IV line that bypasses the stomach and goes through a vein directly to the heart. TPN helps patients who have a hard time with the feeling of fullness in the stomach. There is a debate over whether to use these methods and if so when, but there are patients with anorexia who might otherwise die if these methods are not utilized. As the patient consumes an increased amount of food the amount of calories supplied by the NG tube or by TPN can be decreased. This of course is extremely individualized. Many factors have to be considered and of course this must be done under the care of a physician trained in these methods.

Diuretics

The main complication associated with diuretic abuse is fluid and electrolyte imbalance. In fact, the electrolyte pattern is basically the same as that seen with self-induced vomiting.

There is a reflexive development of lower leg edema (swelling) with abrupt cessation of diuretic abuse. Generally this can be controlled and treated with salt restriction and leg elevation. Physicians should explain to patients with edema that the condition is self-limited (runs a limited course) and caused by the body's initial reaction to withdrawal from diuretics. Patients who get edema will often want to take more diuretics to "fix" the problem and must be encouraged and supported not to do so. Warm baths and leg elevation when possible are helpful.

Cardiovascular System

One third of the deaths in anorexia are caused by cardiac complications. Severe weight loss causes atrophy of the heart muscle and diminished cardiac volume. As a result of this process, there is a reduction in the heart's ability to perform and function at its full maximal work capacity. Thin patients commonly present with a slowed heart rate (40 to 60 beats per minute) as their bodies are trying to conserve energy. They also commonly have low blood pressure (systolics of 70 to 90 mm Hg). It will be much harder for these patients to exercise. If patients with anorexia present with high heart rates this should be of concern as usually they are low. Refeeding syndrome might be the cause, but if that gets ruled out then these patients might be highly anxious either because of a psychological or medical condition. These patients often benefit from a medication such as a beta blocker commonly used to slow down heart rates.

Patients can also demonstrate significant orthostatic changes (upon standing) in pulse and blood pressure, with increased heart rate and decreased blood pressure. These are autonomic nervous system adaptations to starvation and can be dangerous, leading to dizziness and fainting. There is also an increased prevalence (about 30 percent of patients with anorexia) of a heart valve abnormality known as mitral valve prolapse, which can produce palpitations, chest pain, and even arrhythmias. There are medications that can help with these symptoms, but the condition is generally benign and reversible with weight gain.

EKG Abnormalities

EKG abnormalities such as brachycardia are commonly seen, particularly in anorexia. In addition, patients often demonstrate abnormal heart rhythms and other EKG abnormalities, some of which can be dangerous. For example, the electrical impulses of the heart occur at certain normal intervals, and one such interval, referred to as the QT interval, is of particular interest. It has been thought for many years that prolongation of the QT intervals was the cause of cardiac arrest in patients with anorexia. According to new research conducted by Dr. Mehler and M. J. Krantz it is not prolongation but dispersions of QT intervals that cause the cardiac problems (Mehler and Krantz 2005). In studying EKGs in patients with anorexia they found normal QT prolongation but an increased QT dispersion. These patients QT segment varies from lead to lead. In fact, the inter-lead variability in the QT segment of patients with anorexia was three times greater than in the control population. According to Mehler this means that these patients have an unusual depolarization and repolarization of the heart that leads to arrhythmias and even cardiac arrest. This is an important finding and will lead physicians to increased detection of those who are susceptible to cardiac arrest and need to be monitored closely.

Diet Pills/Appetite Suppressants

Diet pills are used as a way to restrict food intake and often as a compensatory reaction to binge eating. Most diet pills stimulate the sympathetic nervous system and are amphetamine-type derivatives. Their adverse effects include hypertension (high blood pressure), palpitations, cardiac ischemia (insufficient blood flow to the heart), seizures, and anxiety attacks. Eating disorder patients often present with high levels of anxiety and histories of anxiety disorders, which may be caused or exacerbated by diet pills. Abrupt cessation is medically safe.

Hematological System

Approximately one-third of individuals with anorexia nervosa have anemia and leukopenia (low white blood cell count). The relevance of low white cells to the function of the patient's immune system is controversial. Some studies have indeed found an increased risk of infection due to impaired cellular immune function.

Individuals with anorexia also typically have low body temperature, so the two traditional markers of infection—fever and a high white cell count—are often lacking in these patients. Therefore, there has to be heightened vigilance toward the possibility of infection when these patients report an unusual symptom. Nutritional rehabilitation, if done in a timely and well-planned fashion in concert with competent medical supervision, promotes a return to normal.

Neurological System

In severe anorexia, computed tomography (CT) scans have demonstrated cortical atrophy and ventricular dilatation. Cortical atrophy could be called reduced brain mass. Ventricular dilatation is an increase in the fluid in the ventricles that drain cerebral spinal fluid from the brain. This would be a consequence of the reduced brain matter. These changes have been shown to be reversible on CT scans with refeeding and improved nutrition. However, in some cases, abnormalities have been shown to persist on magnetic resonance imaging (MRI) scans even after treatment and weight recovery.

In studies, patients with anorexia nervosa, while malnourished, demonstrated greater cerebral spinal fluid (CSF) volumes and reduced volumes of white and gray (brain) matter on MRI. This signifies the same thing already described—reduced brain mass and a subsequent increase in fluid in the brain. Cross-sectional and longitudinal studies have shown that even weight-recovered patients had greater CSF volumes and smaller gray matter volumes than control subjects. Further studies need to be performed to determine the implications of these findings and to see if they are reversible several years after nutritional recovery.

In addition, studies are ongoing using newer functional neuroimaging techniques such as electroencephalograms (EEGs) measuring brain wave function (described further in Chapter 16), positron emission tomography (PET) scans, regional blood flow scans and functional MRI scans to further explore the neurobiological causes and effects of eating disorders.

Endocrine System

Eating disorders can have profound negative effects on all aspects of the endocrine system.

Growth Disturbance

Studies demonstrate disturbances in the secretion and action of growth hormone in patients with anorexia. Patients who develop malnutrition during their adolescent growth spurt may risk a disturbance in growth and irreversible short stature.

Thyroid Function

Generally, problems are caused by a hypothyroid (low thyroid) condition. Symptoms include hair loss, dry skin, hypothermia, and bradycardia. Lab values demonstrate a low normal T4 and TSH, below normal T3, elevated reverse T3, and blunting of TSH response to thyrotropin-releasing hormone (TRH). This is reversible with refeeding, and thus thyroid medication is contraindicated. On some occasions thyroid function does not return to normal and medication is necessary, but replacement is rarely indicated.

Amenorrhea

While the exact cause of amenorrhea (lack of menstruation) is not known, low levels of the hormones involved in menstruation and ovulation are present with weight loss, inadequate body fat content, or insufficient weight. The current theory is called the energy drain hypothesis in which the body's "energy thermostat" senses the lack of energy from food, slows down the body's metabolism, and shuts down the reproductive system to conserve energy. The exact mechanism for these changes is not known, although it is being investigated.

Clearly, there is also an important contribution from the tenuous emotional state of these patients. Reversion to the age-appropriate secretion of reproductive hormones requires both weight gain and remission of the disorder. Resumption of menses is often used as a marker of nutritional and medical recovery, but this is not always a true indicator.

Because of the increased risk of osteoporosis seen in eating disordered patients who have amenorrhea and the fact that some studies suggest that the lost bone density may be irreversible, hormone replacement therapy (HRT) has often been suggested for these individuals. It has often been advocated that if amenorrhea persists for longer than six months, HRT should be used empirically if there are no contraindications for such treatment. However, the results of research over the last decade are still unclear as to whether (and when) HRT should take place; consequently, there has been much controversy over this issue.

Bone Density

Bone loss or insufficient bone density is an important and possibly irreversible medical consequence of anorexia nervosa and sometimes of bulimia nervosa as well. Since the first edition of this book was published, there has been continued research in the area of bone mineral density and hormone replacement therapy, but results still conflict.

Postmenopausal Versus Anorexia-Caused Bone Deficiency

Results of studies from London, Harvard, and other teaching centers show that the bone deficiency caused by anorexia is not identical to that of postmenopausal women. The major deficiency in postmenopausal osteoporosis is of estrogen and, to some extent, calcium. In contrast, in anorexia nervosa, chronic low weight and malnutrition often make estrogen ineffective, even when it is present through oral contraceptives (Anderson and Holman 1997). Other factors that likely contribute to bone density problems include inadequate dietary calcium; diminished body fat, which is necessary for the metabolism of estrogen; and elevated serum cortisol levels from weight loss, other hormonal abnormalities, and comorbid depression.

There is increasing evidence that males with eating disorders are likely to have similar problems. Low body weight, low body fat, low testosterone levels, and elevated cortisol levels may play a role in bone density deficiencies.

There are three phases to bone mineral development: growth, consolidation, and senescence (aging). Adolescence represents a critical window of opportunity for the development of peak bone mass. This means that a teenager who suffers anorexia nervosa for as little as six months to one year may develop a long-lasting bone deficiency. Bone density tests have shown that many 20- to 25-year-olds with anorexia nervosa have the bone densities of 70- to 80-year-olds. Whether bone density deficiency is permanent or whether it can be restored remains unknown, and there are significant concerns about the lasting impact and possible irreversibility of osteoporosis in these young patients. Several studies have suggested that bone mass may not normalize even following nutritional recovery. Consider a bone density evaluation with a dual energy x-ray absorptiometry (DEXA) scan, a computerized x-ray to measure bone density six months to one year after development of amenorrhea. It is currently recommended that a central DEXA scan of the lumbar spine and femoral neck be performed. Some patients actually take their eating disorder more seriously when they are shown objective evidence of its consequences, such as mineral-deficient bones.

Treatment Options for Bone Density Problems

Numerous therapeutic interventions are possible, even though there is not yet enough evidence to prove that bone density deficiency from anorexia nervosa is prevented or reversed by them.

- One easy intervention is for patients to take 1,500 milligrams of calcium per day. (The current recommended daily allowance is 1,200 millgrams per day.)

- Weight-bearing exercises are helpful, but patients should avoid high-impact cardio exercise, which burns too many calories (interfering with weight gain) and may lead to fractures.

- The administration of oral contraceptives or HRT is controversial. The evidence on their efficacy is mixed. Some physicians prescribe HRT anyway but many prefer to wait until the individual gains enough weight for menses to return naturally, particularly for young teens with amenorrhea. Giving HRT at too early an age can result in improper bone development. If patients are taking HRT it is also important to prevent them from becoming complacent about their condition and their need for nutritional rehabilitation and/or weight gain. Since resumption of menses is often used as a marker of recovery, the pharmacological resumption of menses can give the patients a false sense of security that they have improved and their bones are not in jeopardy. Finally, in considering whether or not to prescribe HRT, it must be taken into consideration that even without menstruating, individuals can become pregnant. Therefore, some patients may chose to take oral contraceptives for birth control purposes.

• Physicians may also consider prescribing alendronate (Fosamax), a recently approved form of bisphosphonate. Different from estrogen, alendronate has been shown to bind to bone and positively affect postmenopausal osteoporosis by inhibiting bone resorption. This leads to increased bone mass and mineralization. Alendronate can be used either in addition to estrogen or in cases where estrogen treatment is not clinically appropriate. However, alendronate often causes severe gastrointestinal side effects that can be distressing to patients with eating disorders. It can also lead to severe esophageal irritation and cannot be used in patients who purge by vomiting. Two studies of this class of medicine have shown some improvement in bone loss but the use of bisphophanates in patients with anorexia nervosa and osteoporosis is still under investigation and is not standard treatment.

• Other proposed treatments may be effective for treating bone deficiency, but more research is needed to demonstrate their effectiveness. These other treatment options include dehydroepiandrosterone (DHEA), an adrenal androgen that increases bone formation; short-term injections of recombinant human insulin-like growth factor–1; and recombinant human parathyroid hormone.

- Clearly, the treatment protocol for eating disorder patients with amenorrhea and bone density problems has not been established. At this point, it would be wise to vigorously treat patients whose bone density deficiencies have been long-lasting or severe using a variety of methods, which may include HRT and alendronate. Those with less severe deficiencies may be treated by the more moderate methods with the addition of an estrogen-progestin combination.

- People with eating disorders may be troubled with many medical complications. With proper identification and interventions, most of these are reversible. Medical management is a building block of a successful treatment program.

Occasionally medical practitioners will be called upon to prescribe medication for psychiatric disturbances in eating disorder patients. Prescribing and managing medication to treat coexisting psychological conditions that cause or contribute to eating disorders is sometimes undertaken by the family physician or internist. Hopefully this task can be relegated to a psychiatrist who has special training in psychopharmacology and eating disorders. Information regarding the psychiatrist and psychiatric medication for use with eating disorders is presented in the next chapter.

14

The Psychiatrist's Role and Psychotropic Medication

(Coauthored with Tim Brewerton, M.D.)

A PSYCHIATRIST WHO is knowledgeable about eating disorders is an integral part of the treatment team. Psychiatrists are medical doctors who are trained to perform various types of psychotherapy and prescribe psychotropic (mind-altering) medication. A psychiatrist can be brought in as part of a treatment team at any time but is usually consulted in the beginning as part of assessment, diagnosis, and treatment. A clinician working with a patient may decide that additional help is needed and a referral for medication that affects mental function is warranted. As with all professionals, the psychiatrist should have experience in treating eating disorders and understand the complexity and special needs of this population. Patients and/or therapists should choose a psychiatrist who does the following:

- Avoids suggesting or relying on medication alone, particularly when other methods have not been tried and nutritional rehabilitation has not been started
- Educates patients and their families about the known medical complications of eating disorders

- Explains the expected benefits of any medication prescribed and its side effects
- Is empathic and understanding toward the patient
- Is board certified or board eligible
- Discusses the current research and trends in eating disorder treatment
- Communicates regularly with family members when appropriate
- Clearly spells out all policies regarding fees, emergencies, paging, cancellations, what to do in case of problematic medication reactions, and other issues

The Psychiatrist as Part of a Treatment Team

The psychiatrist is a valuable treatment team member, if not the leader of the team. Whether or not medication is being prescribed, the psychiatrist can add another dimension and perspective to evaluation and treatment, ideally one that is integrative in nature. Psychiatrists should have an understanding of the biological aspects of eating disorders and other medical or psychological disorders that go along with them. They should also keep current in the field of assessment and treatment with psychotropic medications for eating and related disorders.

The psychiatrist must work with the rest of the team on the treatment approach, including what is expected from the patient, the kind of diet and exercise advice to be given, the need for supplements, recommendations to parents or significant others, and criteria for necessary level of care. If the therapist and psychiatrist are not working together with the same goals, the patient hears different messages and uses this as an excuse not to listen to anyone, because "no one really knows what is best." Patients may think, "They can't even agree on what to do, so why should I listen to them?" To avoid undermining each other, clinicians must remain in constant contact regarding the patient. The physician, therapist, and all members of a treatment team should communicate and work together closely to avoid adding unnecessary confusion, difficulties, delays, or doubts to the already complex problems patients have.

Prescribing Medication

Eating disorder specialist and author Dr. Arnold Anderson said at a lecture on medication and eating disorders, "To every complex problem there is a simple answer . . . and it's wrong." People would like to find a simple answer to the complex problem of eating disorders, and many have gone down the "isn't there a medication that can fix this?" path. The use of psychotropic medication, otherwise known as *psychopharmacology*, may indeed play a significant role in the treatment of some cases of eating disorders, but it has not proven to be a cure. Medication solutions continue to be sought for a variety of clinical challenges such as those in the following list.

- Weight restoration, loss, or maintenance
- Normalization of thinking processes
- Normalization of mood
- Hunger inducement/reduction, increase/decrease in satiety
- Reduction in sensitivity to stress
- Reduction in anxiety, including obsessions and compulsions
- Reduction in/cessation of purging behaviors
- Reduction in impulsivity
- Relapse prevention
- Coexisting psychiatric conditions (e.g., depression or bipolar disorder)

Comorbid Conditions and Their Relationship to the Eating Disorder

Many other psychiatric disorders and conditions (called psychiatric comorbidities) exist in people with eating disorders. Individuals with anorexia or bulimia are commonly diagnosed with anxiety disorders, including social anxiety disorder, panic disorder, obsessive-compulsive disorder (OCD), post-traumatic stress disorder (PTSD), generalized anxiety disorder, simple phobias, separation anxiety disorder, and/or overanxious disorder of childhood. Other common diagnoses include major depression, substance abuse, and borderline personality disorder. These coexisting diagnoses would seem to suggest pharmacotherapy as a feasible treatment option.

The crucial question, however, is which came first. In some cases, nutritional rehabilitation and weight restoration alone have been enough to eliminate obsessive-compulsive behavior and depression, whereas in others they have not. Ideally, the use of medication should be tried only after some level of nutrition and/or weight has been restored. However, when nutritional rehabilitation cannot be accomplished readily, such as in a recalcitrant patient with anorexia, treating professionals often search for an appropriate and effective medication to help accomplish that goal. Under these circumstances, trial and error seems to be the order of the day when prescribing for anorexia nervosa.

Frustrated researchers became excited when studies on bulimia nervosa indicated that it may be closely related to mood disorders, particularly depression. Some studies reported that as many as 80 percent of the patients with bulimia had clinically significant mood disorders at some point during their lives. There was also a high incidence of the disorder in their family histories. This led to the argument that heredity and genetics play a major role in depression and bulimia, especially since a high percentage of patients with bulimia responded positively to antidepressant medication even when they weren't depressed. However, more recent research indicates that bulimia and depression are not the result of the same biological disorder.

A medication's effectiveness, as well as *comparative* effectiveness with other drugs or techniques and side effects, must all be considered. For example, studies using fluoxetine (Prozac) with bulimia nervosa have shown what is considered to be a high degree of efficacy; however, cognitive behavioral therapy (CBT) shows a greater degree of efficacy with fewer side effects and longer-lasting results.

Many experts and treatment programs use a combination of CBT and Prozac, particularly when there is the co-occurrence of mood and/or anxiety disorders. Additionally, medications that can cause weight gain, such as clomipramine (Anafranil), which is often used for OCD, or lithium, which is used for manic-depressive illness, may backfire when the individual becomes even more restrictive with eating, loses trust in the treatment, and becomes noncompliant with the medication. Other medications such as naltrexone (ReVia)—an opiate antagonist that eliminates the euphoric effects of opioids—are used with addicts and alcoholics to curb cravings and reduce the beneficial "high" they get from their drugs. These drugs have shown some promise in the treatment of eating disorders. Medications used to influence hunger and satiety have been ineffective overall in treating anorexia and bulimia, partly due to side effects.

When treating cognitive disturbances, certain drugs can help improve thought processes and clear thinking. These include antianxiety agents such as lorazepam (Ativan); medicines for attention deficit hyperactivity disorder such as methylphenidate (Ritalin); antipsychotic (also known as neuroleptic) medications for hallucinations or delusional thinking such as olanzapine (Zyprexa), risperidone (Risperdal), or haloperidol (Haldol). These are all medications with serious side effects or addictive properties and should be prescribed only with careful consideration.

Various medications such as neuroleptics or antianxiety agents are used to reduce sensitivity to stress and resultant anxiety. These drugs can work well in the short term for general anxiety, provide immediate relief, and may have some usefulness as premeal agents to alleviate the distress associated with eating. However, they do not successfully treat the core issues of an eating disorder and are usually best used in conjunction with antidepressants, which also reduce anxiety and sensitivity to stress and are generally the preferred drug treatment (unless the patient presents with starvation and/or is underweight).

What Does Taking Medication Really Mean?

Aside from the possible direct beneficial and adverse effects of medication of any kind, there is the important issue of what taking medication means or symbolizes to any given individual. The act of taking mind-altering drugs symbolizes different things to different people, but commonly it means "I'm sick/defective/imperfect/bad/crazy/out of control." Since issues of control and self-worth are already predominant in people with eating disorders, this often becomes an obstacle to effective treatment, particularly in those with significant coexisting problems and even when medications have clearly been effective.

When patients with eating disorders begin to feel better, they frequently want to stop taking the medicine(s), although it may be an important reason for the improvement. This ends up contributing to the already high relapse rate in eating and related disorders. Patients need help in understanding that medication is best thought of as a powerful tool that a person with an eating disorder can choose to use in the struggle for full recovery.

Psychotropic Medications Commonly Used in Eating Disorders

Psychotropic medications are drugs that primarily affect the brain and in turn some aspect of the psyche or mind. The most common types of psychotropic medications used in the treatment of eating disorders include antidepressants, mood stabilizers, antiobesity agents, antianxiety agents, and antipsychotic agents. The information presented here is a brief guide. It is not intended to be a sole source of information nor is it intended to replace the informed consent process between a patient and psychiatrist.

Anorexia Nervosa and Medication

No controlled trials have ever shown that psychotropic medications significantly impact anorexia nervosa when given outside a structured, hospital program. Quite simply, food remains the best "drug" for individuals with anorexia, although accomplishing the task of getting patients to eat is a profound challenge given the extreme resistance typical of the illness. After all, food refusal is the illness.

A few drugs have been found to perform statistically better than placebo in controlled trials, but the clinical significance of these findings is negligible. Lithium was shown in one study to be superior to placebo in a small group of patients treated on a highly structured, specialized treatment unit. However, the clinical effect was small and the potential risks of using lithium in a population with anorexia exceed any potential benefits, so this agent cannot be recommended. There is a serious risk of lithium toxicity, which can cause brain damage and is increased in the presence of dehydration and metabolic imbalances from purging, excessive exercising, and/or starvation. In another study, the antihistamine cyproheptadine was statistically better than placebo for restricting anorexia, while the tricyclic antidepressant (TCA) amitriptyline was better for patients with binge/purge type anorexia nervosa, but other studies had mixed results.

Although using antidepressants in anorexia seems to make sense, the results from controlled trials have been disappointing. In addition, the effects of TCAs on the heart include inducing an abnormal EKG and is a risk factor for arrhythmia and death. Selective serotonin reuptake inhibitor antidepressants might seem suitable given their usefulness in mood and anxiety disorders, their safety record, and scientific reports of serotonin-related abnormalities in anorexia.

However, in one well-controlled trial, fluoxetine (Prozac) was reported to have no therapeutic effect on weight, body image distortion, or ratings of anxiety and mood in low-weight patients with anorexia. This is due to the well-documented fact that measures of serotonin function in the brains of patients with anorexia are markedly decreased as a direct result of starvation and weight loss. The effectiveness of SSRIs depends on having sufficient amounts of brain serotonin available which, in turn, depends on having a normal body weight. In general, if weight is not enough to sustain menstrual or hormonal function, then it is also not enough to sustain normal brain function. It is essential for the psychiatrist, as well as all involved in the care of patients with anorexia, to understand that Prozac or any SSRI antidepressant will not work in low-weight patients. A few years ago, there was much excitement over a controlled trial of Prozac in weight-recovered patients with anorexia. The study indicated that relapse (which is common) was significantly reduced following treatment with Prozac in comparison to placebo but additional larger studies revealed this *not* to be the case.

One potential drug for use in patients with anorexia is olanzapine (Zyprexa) and possibly other atypical antipsychotic agents in the restricting subtype of anorexia nervosa. Zyprexa does not require a certain amount of brain serotonin or normal eating to work, so it has a great advantage over antidepressants in this population. Zyprexa 's effects are exactly what one would want in an ideal medicine for anorexia, including enhancing appetite; promoting weight gain, and reducing anxiety, obsessions, compulsions, depression, mood instability, and restless calorie-burning activity. Although no controlled drug trials of Zyprexa in anorexia have been completed as of this writing, open (not placebo-controlled) trials and case reports are somewhat encouraging. One study comparing it to the older antipsychotic drug chlorpromazine (Thorazine) showed it to be superior in reducing obsessive ruminations about weight and body image in patients with anorexia. Adult patients may resist or refuse to take olanzapine because of its weight-gain and sedative effects. However, in pediatric and adolescent patients, parents can often guarantee compliance. The doses required for successful treatment of anorexia are typically less than those needed for psychosis, usually in the range of 0.625 to 10.0 milligrams per day. Once weight restoration and abatement of symptoms occurs, Zyprexa can be tapered and stopped. In more difficult cases, especially those with unrelenting, coexisting anxiety and/or depression, low doses of a relatively weight-neutral, atypical antipsychotic agent—such as quetiapine, ziprasidone, or aripiprazole—may be helpful adjuncts as recovery progresses.

All of this is speculative and untested, and most patients do not need continued antipsychotic treatment following full weight recovery. The tendency for Zyprexa and other atypical antipsychotics to cause side effects requires careful monitoring, for example Zyprexa has been shown to cause potentially serious blood sugar problems. Patients will also be loath to take them because of their weight gain effects. However, the use of antipsychotic agents should be considered and evaluated in light of substantial medical and psychiatric problems, as well as potential death, associated with persistent cases of anorexia.

Bulimia Nervosa and Medication

The use of psychotropic agents in treating bulimia nervosa has been much more promising than in anorexia nervosa. Most drug trials have involved antidepressants, particularly the newer SSRIs, which have shown significantly more improvement in binge/purge frequency compared to placebo. Antidepressant medication doesn't work for everyone; only some patients (about 20 to 33 percent) have complete remission of symptoms, while others have significant reductions in bingeing and purging behaviors.

The class of antidepressants known as SSRIs, discussed earlier (Prozac, Zoloft, and so on), are the newer versions of antidepressants, the originals being tricyclics and monoamine oxidase inhibitors (MAOIs). Tricyclics such as desiprimine and imipramine were effective but had many side effects, such as weight gain, which were not well tolerated by eating disordered patients. Amitriptyline (Elavil) was studied but was no better than placebo. Additionally, tricyclic overdose is the third leading cause of death in hospital emergency departments and as such is extremely dangerous in depressed patients, the very people it treats most effectively. The lethality of tricyclic overdose is enhanced by the medical effects of eating disorders, especially lowered potassium in the body.

The MAOIs, such as tranylcypromine (Parnate) and phenelzine (Nardil), show efficacy in reducing symptoms of bulimia. However, individuals taking MAOIs must be on a very restrictive low-tyrosine (an amino acid) diet; if any lapse occurs, it can cause a hypertensive crisis (extremely high blood pressure, possibly resulting in serious side effects such as stroke or death). Of the SSRIs, only Prozac has been shown to decrease bulimic symptoms such as poor regulation of hunger and satiety, sensitivity to stress, and obsessive thinking and behavior without undue side effects.

The antibulimic effects of antidepressants have been shown in a number of studies to be independent of the drugs' antidepressant effects per se. Unlike treatment for major depression or anxiety disorders, one cannot generalize from one SSRI to another because not all of them have been studied in bulimia nervosa, and available evidence suggests that they are not equally effective. The only SSRIs that have been seriously studied in bulimia are fluoxetine, sertraline, and fluvoxamine. In a large multicenter study, fluoxetine (Prozac) at 60 milligrams per day was superior to placebo in decreasing both bingeing and purging; a dose of 20 milligrams per day was not effective. Thus, clinicians treating bulimia must realize that higher doses (40 to 80 milligrams per day) are generally required for an effective antibulimic response (which is similar to OCD). Two much smaller studies indicate a positive response to sertraline in bulimia nervosa. Fluvoxamine (Luvox) was not found to be statistically different from placebo in two European trials, although it may help in relapse prevention. Fluoxetine has also been found to decrease relapse rates in bulimia compared to placebo over the course of one year.

Except for bupropion (Wellbutrin), there are no known studies using non-SSRI newer generation agents, such as nefazodone, mirtazapine, and venlafaxine. Although bupropion was effective in one placebo-controlled trial to reduce bingeing and purging, there was a high incidence of seizures, and this drug's use in eating disorders has been contraindicated by the U.S. Food and Drug Administration.

Ondansetron (Zofran) is a potent serotonin receptor antagonist and antivomiting (antiemetic) drug used for treating induced nausea and vomiting caused by chemotherapy. It was found in one placebo-controlled trial to significantly reduce bingeing and purging in bulimics. Although this drug is costly (about $30 per pill), it may be worthwhile in life-threatening cases that have been resistant to other more conventional treatments.

Topiramate (Topamax) is an anticonvulsant (antiseizure) drug that has been reported to reduce bingeing and purging in patients with bulimia when compared to placebo. It also works to reduce bingeing in BED and to reduce weight in non–eating disordered patients with obesity. Topiramate appears to be beneficial to patients with migraines and anxiety, including that from PTSD. However, bothersome side effects can limit its usefulness, and these include numbness and tingling in the extremities, impaired ability to think clearly, and kidney stones. Patients should be advised to drink copious amounts of water. It can be used together with SSRI antidepressants.

Naltrexone (ReVia) is a potentially useful drug for eating disordered patients with coexisting alcoholism and/or self-injurious behaviors. Although naltrexone was not better than placebo in one controlled trial in bulimia, another study reported that it significantly reduced bingeing and purging.

Phototherapy

Exposure to full-spectrum, high-intensity light can be helpful in the treatment of bulimia nervosa, particularly when there is seasonal worsening of symptoms and/or coexisting seasonal affective disorder ("winter depression"). Light therapy is usually well tolerated but requires special lights that emit all of the energy wavelengths contained in sunlight (which normal indoor lighting does not). Phototherapy is thought to act like a drug to increase serotonin function. Dosage is usually half an hour to two hours per day of at least 10,000 lux (a measure of light intensity). Side effects may include eye strain, headache, and manic symptoms.

Binge Eating Disorder and Medication

Research on BED has been growing for several years, and investigators believe that binge eating is less a matter of willpower than of brain chemistry. In some cases, clinicians and researchers are using SSRIs for binge eating disorder for the same reasons they use these medications for bulimia nervosa. Serotonin promotes a feeling of fullness, so it is theorized that people with binge eating may want to eat all the time because they have too little of the neurotransmitter serotonin and thus don't feel satisfied (satiated) after eating.

Placebo-controlled trials have shown BED to be significantly reduced by the SSRIs fluoxetine (Prozac), fluvoxamine (Luvox), sertraline (Zoloft), and citalopram (Celexa). As noted earlier, topiramate (Topamax) also benefits this condition. Recent studies indicate that sibutramine (Meridia) significantly reduces binge eating and has also helped with weight loss in BED when compared to placebo. Although Meridia has shown some promise, most medication trials for BED that have resulted in reduced binge eating have fallen short in reducing weight. Meridia is a stimulant medication and a controlled substance and should only be used under close supervision by a doctor. Side effects include nausea, constipation, dizziness, and in some cases even increase in appetite and suicidal thoughts. More research is needed in this area.

Guidelines for When to Use Medications

Continued research is clearly necessary to improve psychiatric medication management of eating disorder patients, but there are some general guidelines for when to use medications:

- After nutritional rehabilitation has begun
- After a full patient history and medical evaluation are complete
- After a full family history and evaluation
- After review of valid, reliable, published data-based trials
- After psychoeducation and initiation of psychotherapy
- When medication-responsive coexisting conditions are clearly identified, particularly when they predate the onset of the eating disorder

- After receiving informed consent, meaning the patient understands the possible benefits, risks, and side effects of all medications prescribed and consents to take them

Many medications have been tried and continue to be evaluated in our search for improved treatments for eating disorders, but we are far from a medication solution. A group of innovative psychiatrists believe that a new approach in this area is warranted and they have been using an alternative method of assessing and prescribing medication, which is discussed in Chapter 16.

With even the best efforts at therapy, nutrition counseling, and medical and psychiatric interventions some patients will require a level of care that goes beyond what can be accomplished without a structured and controlled environment. Treatment may need to involve removal from ordinary life in order to participate in a partial or full 24-hour program. The next chapter discusses the alternatives available for this purpose.

15

When Outpatient Treatment Is Not Enough

MOST EATING DISORDER treatment takes place on an outpatient basis, but there may come a time when outpatient treatment is insufficient due to the severity of the eating disorder. Treatment in a structured setting may be chosen as a better means than outpatient therapy to facilitate recovery or be required when symptoms are severe, out of control, and/or the medical risks are significant. This chapter provides an overview of various treatment options and guidelines for making an appropriate choice.

Determining Level of Care

The mechanisms for choosing a level of care that is more structured than outpatient treatment vary. In many instances, people are referred to an inpatient setting by one or more of their outpatient clinicians who deem it necessary or optimal. The treatment team should establish criteria for such referrals in advance to avoid panic and confusion. In other cases, individuals with an eating disorder or their family members will choose to try a structured treatment program even though the client is not yet seriously compromised.

I often wonder why treatment programs are not sought earlier. Part of the answer lies in the sad fact that insurance companies often deny coverage for this treatment. I have known clients who did not meet the low weight criteria for inpatient care, so they proceeded to lose enough weight to get the treatment they needed. The newest version of the APA guidelines is attempting to address this issue by eliminating low weight requirements recommended for residential or inpatient care. If a treatment provider suggests this level of care, clients and/or their loved ones might have to fight their insurance company. (The National Eating Disorders Association website at nationaleatingdisorders.org has more information.)

Not a Last Resort

Unfortunately, treatment programs are often regarded as a last resort to be used only when all else fails. Professionals and loved ones should avoid remarks such as, "If you get too bad, or if you don't improve, you are going to have to go into treatment." Treatment programs should not be feared or seen as punishment. It is better for individuals to be told, "If you are unable to battle your eating disorder with outpatient therapy alone, additional help can be found in a treatment program where you will be provided the care, nurturing, and added strength you need to overcome your disorder." Treatment programs can be viewed as a welcome, albeit scary, choice individuals make from the healthy part of them that wants to get better.

Treatment Program Options

A variety of settings provide more intense levels of care than outpatient therapy. When looking for a treatment program, the treatment team and client must understand the difference between the intensity and structure of these different levels. The various options include 24-hour live-in facilities (hospital or residential programs), partial hospitalization or day-treatment programs, intensive outpatient programs, and transitional or recovery houses.

Hospital Facilities

Inpatient treatment, or 24-hour care in a hospital setting, can take place in a medical or psychiatric facility. The cost is usually high, around $1,400 to $1,800 per day or more. Inpatient treatment at a medical hospital is usually a short-term stay to treat medical conditions or complications that have arisen as a result of the eating disorder. Psychiatric hospitals often take eating disorder clients but, unless they have a specialized eating disorder track, should be used only for stabilization purposes (e.g., allowing someone to overcome a suicidal episode). Treatment in a hospital, whether medical or psychiatric, without specialized staff and treatment protocols for eating disorders will not only be unsuccessful, but can cause more harm than good.

Residential Facilities

The majority of eating disorder individuals are not actively suicidal or medically unstable and do not require hospitalization. However, there may be a substantial benefit to these individuals of having supervision and treatment on a 24-hour-a-day basis. Bingeing, self-induced vomiting, laxative abuse, compulsive exercise, and restricted eating do not necessarily lead to acute medical instability and thus, by themselves, do not qualify as criteria for hospitalization. Since insurance coverage often requires the individual to be medically compromised, clients can have many of these behaviors and still not qualify for insurance coverage.

However, eating disorder behaviors can become so habitual or addictive that trying to reduce or extinguish them on an outpatient or even day-treatment basis can be impossible. Residential treatment facilities offer an excellent alternative to hospitals, providing round-the-clock care in a nonhospital setting and are usually less expensive than hospital-based options. Many of these programs are much smaller and feel more personal than hospital programs. Some are housed in former private residences or estates that have been converted into treatment facilities, which allows for a home-like environment.

Residential facilities vary greatly in the level of care provided, so each program must be investigated thoroughly. Some facilities offer sophisticated, intensive, and structured treatment similar to that of a hospital inpatient program but in a less sterile, more relaxed, and more natural setting. Other facilities are less structured, provide far less treatment, and are often centered around group therapy. These programs are closer to transition or recovery houses (see section with this title). The treatment team and patient should thoroughly explore the various levels of treatment and services offered and find out about the expertise of the professionals who provide them.

Residential treatment is becoming increasingly popular as a choice for treating eating disorders. Some individuals go directly to residential treatment programs, while others spend time in a hospital and then transfer to a residential program. Many of these programs offer crucial and important features that are not possible in a hospital setting. Clients have the opportunity to be increasingly involved in meal planning, shopping, cooking, exercise, and other daily living activities that simulate what they will need to do when they return home.

These are problem areas for eating disorder individuals that cannot be practiced and resolved in a hospital or even in a large residential facility. Small, homelike facilities offer treatment and supervision of behaviors and daily living activities, providing clients with increasing responsibility for their own recovery. (See the description of the Monte Nido Treatment Facility at the end of this chapter.)

Partial Hospitalization or Day Treatment

Often individuals need a more structured program than outpatient treatment but do not need 24-hour care. Additionally clients who have been in an inpatient or residential program can often step down to a lower level of care but are not ready to return home and begin outpatient treatment. In these cases, partial hospitalization or day-treatment programs may be indicated and come in a variety of types, usually offering services from five to eight hours a day. Clients are often in the program during the day and return home in the evening, but some of these programs include dinner and evening groups. Day-treatment and partial hospitalization programs are becoming more prevalent, partially because of the cost of full 24-hour inpatient programs and partially because clients can receive great benefits from these programs without the additional burden or stress of having to leave home entirely.

Day treatment programs vary in the amount of structure they provide. Higher success rates have been reported in day-treatment programs where the treatment is intensive and involves clients at least five days a week for approximately eight hours a day. Due to the amount of variation in these programs, it is not possible to give a fee range. One example is the Eating Disorder Center of California, which meets six days per week from five to eight hours a day. Readers can find details of this program at edcca.com.

Intensive Outpatient Programs

These programs offer even less structure and treatment than day-treatment or partial programs, but they are a good step up from outpatient care alone. Intensive outpatient programs (IOPs) vary but usually involve clients three times a week for three or more hours. If tried early, IOPs can be useful when a client is not improving with outpatient treatment or a useful step down as a transition from a higher level of care.

Transitions or Recovery Houses

Some people may confuse a transition or recovery house with residential treatment. Recovery houses have far less structure and are inappropriate for individuals who are still engaging in ongoing behaviors that require supervision. Recovery houses are best used as transitional living situations after residential or inpatient treatment. Generally, recovery homes provide group therapy and/or other recovery meetings and the clients who live there are under the supervision of a "house parent." This option is far less expensive than hospitals or residential facilities, but these programs provide minimal or no treatment unless they are connected to a day-treatment facility that residents are required to attend.

When to Seek 24-Hour Care

It is always the best circumstance when an individual chooses to enter into a treatment program by choice or before it becomes a necessity. A person may decide to seek treatment in a hospital or residential setting to get away from the normal daily tasks and distractions and focus exclusively and intensely on recovery. However, it is often as a result of medical evaluation or a crisis situation that the decision to go to, or put a loved one in, a treatment program is made. To avoid panic and confusion, it is important to establish criteria for and goals of any hospitalization in case such a situation arises. It is essential that the therapist, physician, and any other treatment team members agree on hospitalization criteria and work together so the client sees a competent, complementary, and consistent treatment team. The criteria and goals should be discussed with the client and significant others and, when possible, agreed upon at the beginning of treatment or at least prior to admission. Involuntary hospitalization should be considered only when the patient's life is in danger.

In relation to the specific eating disorder behaviors, the primary goal of 24-hour care for the severely underweight individual is to institute refeeding and weight gain. For the binge eater or person with bulimia, the primary goal is to establish control over excessive bingeing and/or purging. Twenty-four-hour care may be needed to treat coexisting conditions such as depression or severe anxiety that are impairing the individual's ability to function. Furthermore, many individuals with an eating disorder experience suicidal thoughts and behaviors and need to be hospitalized for protection. A person may be hospitalized strictly for a medical condition or complication such as dehydration, electrolyte imbalance, fluid retention, or chest pain, in which case a medical hospital may be sufficient. The decision regarding where to go for treatment must be decided on a case-by-case basis. It is important to look for a residential treatment program or hospital specializing in the care of patients with eating disorders. The following are some reasons why a decision to seek 24-hour care might be made.

Summary of Reasons for Hospital or Residential Care

1. Postural hypotension (low blood pressure)
2. Cardiac dysfunctions such as irregular heartbeat, irregular or prolonged QT interval, ventricular ectopy (A physician should help determine when certain levels of cardiac abnormality should be referred to a hospital setting.)
3. Pulse less than 45 beats/minute (BPM) or greater than 100 BPM (with emaciation)
4. Dehydration/electrolyte abnormalities such as a serum potassium level less than 2 milliequivalents per liter, fasting blood glucose level less than 50 milligrams per 100 milliliters, creatinine level greater than 2 milligrams per 100 milliliters
5. Weight loss of more than 25 percent of ideal body weight (could need 24 hour care with even less weight loss) or rapid, progressive weight loss (1 to 2 pounds per week) in spite of competent psychotherapy
6. Binge/purge behaviors are happening multiple times per day with little or no reduction in outpatient forms of treatment
7. Outpatient treatment failure when client is unable to complete an outpatient trial, for example, can't physically drive to or remember sessions, or treatment has lasted six months with no substantial improvement
8. Observation for diagnosis and/or medication trial
9. Suicidal thoughts or gestures or self harm behavior
10. Chaotic or abusive family situation in which the family sabotages treatment

11. Increases in impulsivity such as shoplifting, risky sexual behavior, and so forth
12. Inability to perform activities of daily living

Hospitalization should not be regarded as an easy or a final solution to an eating disorder. Minimally, hospitalization should provide a structured environment to control behavior, supervise feeding, observe the client after meals to reduce purging, provide close medical monitoring, and, if necessary, provide medical treatment. However, some treatment programs for eating disorders offer an established protocol and a trained staff and milieu that provide empathy, understanding, education, and support, facilitating cessation or dramatic reduction of eating disorder thoughts and behaviors. This kind of treatment should not have to wait until a crises situation and should be discussed early on with some clients and their families.

Letting eating disorder individuals be included in all of their treatment decisions, including when to go to a treatment program, is valuable. Control issues are a consistent theme seen in individuals with eating disorders. It is important not to let a "me against them" relationship develop between the therapist or treatment team and the person with the eating disorder. The more control individuals have in their treatment, the less they will need to act out other means of control, (for example lying to the therapist, sneaking food, or purging when not being observed). Furthermore, if an individual has been included in the decision making process regarding a higher level of treatment, there is less trouble getting compliance when admission is necessary.

Curative Factors of Day Treatment or 24-Hour-Care Treatment Programs

A good eating disorder program provides not only structure and monitoring, but a number of curative factors that facilitate recovery as well.

1. It separates the client from home life, family, and friends.
   - Removing the client from the family may help determine the "role" the client plays in the family, the role the family played in the development of the eating disorder, and secondary gains to having an eating disorder.
   - Being away from normal routines and responsibilities (work, school, children, etc.) can help clients focus attention where it is needed.
2. It provides a controlled environment.
   - Exposing the patient's true patterns and behaviors (e.g., food rituals, mood at mealtimes, food rigidity) is necessary to deal with these issues and find alternative, more suitable behaviors.
   - A controlled, structured environment assists in breaking addictive patterns. Popcorn and frozen yogurt diets cannot be continued. Vomiting is difficult to accomplish when there is supervision after snacks and meals. A healthy, realistic meal plan and schedule can be introduced and practiced.
   - Medication can be monitored for compliance, side effects, and effectiveness, particularly in inpatient or residential settings.
3. It offers support from peers and a healing environment.
   - The camaraderie, support, and understanding of others are well-documented healing factors.
   - Staff members can be positive role models for self-care and can be an example of a healthy "family" system. The treatment team can provide a good experience of the balance between rules, responsibilities, and freedom.

The duration of time spent in a treatment program will depend on the severity of the eating disorder, any complications, and the treatment goals. These programs can help break addictive patterns or cycles and start a new behavioral process for the client, but they are not the cure. Long-term follow-up is necessary. Success rates for treatment programs are scarce, and different facilities have different means of defining recovery. Some do not follow enough clients, some do not follow clients long enough, and others do nothing to track outcome data at all. Besides asking for success rates, there are many aspects to choosing the right program, and the right program may not be the same for everybody.

Questions to Ask When Choosing a Treatment Program

The following questions (not in order of importance) will provide important information to use in deciding on a program. Individuals considering a treatment program for themselves or a loved one should ask these questions and get as much information as they can from various facilities in order to compare options and select which is most suitable. In some cases I have given an indication of what is appropriate, for other questions the individuals asking them will need to satisfy themselves.

- What is the overall treatment philosophy, including the program's position on psychological, behavioral, and addictive approaches? (All good programs should incorporate a variety of approaches, but cognitive behavioral therapy, in order to combat such things as black-and-white thinking, perfectionism, and irrational food fears, must be among them.)
- How are meals handled? Is vegetarianism allowed? What happens if the meal plan isn't followed? Are meal plans individualized in any way? (There should be flexibility in these areas.)
- Is there an exercise component other than walks, such as weight training or yoga? Is there an exercise evaluation and are there certified and trained professionals to assist clients in setting exercise goals and developing appropriate and balanced forms of activity? (There should be an exercise component staffed by qualified professionals.)

- Are there other recreational activities besides exercise, such as team sports, hiking, or dancing?
- What kind of background and qualifications do staff members have? (Staff members and especially the clinical director should be specifically trained in eating disorders.)
- Do you openly utilize staff members who have recovered from eating disorders? (Clients at Monte Nido consistently describe working with recovered staff as an important factor in their recovery; see Chapter 8 for details.)
- Is there a physician at the facility regularly to take care of medical needs and does a psychiatrist perform a psychiatric evaluation, monitor the overall treatment, and prescribe medication when appropriate? (This is a must for any responsible program.)
- What are the arrangements for individual therapy? Who performs it and how often? (Individual therapy is critical. Be cautious of group-based programs with little or no individual therapy.)
- How many and what kind of groups are held during the week and on the weekends? (A variety of groups is important, cognitive behavioral groups are a must.)
- Do clients meet individually with a dietitian at least once a week? (A good program should provide weekly meetings with an experienced eating disorder dietitian.)
- What is the staff-to-client ratio? (In the last few years, many large facilities have opened up, leaving individualized care behind. I am cautious of large programs with a small staff-to-client ratio. Clients often report that they chose large programs in order to more easily get away with their behaviors—and they often did.)
- Is the clinical director involved in client care? (Clinical directors are the most highly trained eating disorder specialists in a treatment program and should not be too busy or unavailable for direct client contact.)
- Is there some kind of body image component to help address the over-evaluation of weight and shape in each client and in our culture? (This is an important factor which should be included.)

- What is the client schedule? How much leisure time is there? How much supervision versus treatment takes place? (Steer clear of cost-cutting programs with little programming or excessive use of Twelve-Step groups substituting for other important therapy groups or individual therapy.)
- What step-down levels of care are provided? (It is best if the program has a tier system to provide clients with increasing responsibility for and hands-on experience with shopping, cooking, independent exercise, and other behaviors that should be practiced before returning home. In addition passes to go into the community and practice skills learned with family, friends or alone are also important as are passes to go home.)
- What are the aftercare treatment and follow-up services? (Every program should be able to delineate what it does to provide or assist clients in getting good aftercare. Programs should also offer an outreach program, alumni services, and outcome follow-ups.)
- What is considered noncompliance, and what are the consequences?
- What is the average length of stay, and why?
- What are the fees? Are there any extra fees besides those quoted?
- What books or literature are given or recommended?
- How are family members involved? (Family members should be involved in the treatment and not just in the assessment phase. Individual family therapy, multifamily groups, and long family weekends should all be included. For adolescents, research has shown that family therapy is critical for recovery, but it is also important for adults unless mitigating factors dictate otherwise.)
- Is it possible to meet with the clinical director from the program and also talk to former clients and/or their family members? (Making a decision about treatment is a difficult choice. Meeting with the clinician in charge and talking to former clients and family members can provide

useful information. Be skeptical of any program that will not arrange for this.)

- Do you conduct outcome data, and if so, what are the results? (Programs should be interested in outcome data to ensure that they are actually helping clients, and they should be able to discuss their data with potential clients.)

The Monte Nido Residential Treatment Center

The following information on Monte Nido—my residential program in Malibu, California—provides an idea of the philosophy and treatment goals of a 24-hour residential facility specializing exclusively in anorexia nervosa, bulimia nervosa, and activity disorder. For more information, contact montenido.com.

Program Overview

All too often a person does well in a highly structured, regimented environment only to relapse upon returning to a less structured situation. Monte Nido is designed to meet the individual needs of clients and their families in a way that gives them a higher level of responsibility and "teaches" them how to recover. The atmosphere at Monte Nido is professional and structured, but it is also warm, friendly, and family-like. Our staff, many of whom are recovered themselves, serve as role models, and our environment inspires people to commit to overcoming obstacles that are interfering with the quality of their lives.

The program at Monte Nido is designed to provide behavior and mood stabilization, creating a climate where destructive behaviors can be interrupted. Clients can then work on the crucial underlying issues that caused and/or perpetuate their disordered eating and other dysfunctional behaviors. We provide a structured schedule with education, psychodynamic, and cognitive behavioral therapy; corrective eating patterns; healthy exercise; life skills training; and spiritual enhancement in a serene natural setting nestled in the foothills, close to Malibu Beach.

Our treatment philosophy includes restoring biochemical function and nutritional balance, implementing healthy eating and exercise habits, changing destructive behaviors, and gaining insight and coping skills for underlying emotional and psychological issues. We believe that eating disorders are illnesses and that, when treated correctly, individuals can become fully recovered, where they can resume a normal, healthy relationship to food.

We recognize nutrition and exercise as crucial areas of recovery. Therefore, we require assessments on nutritional status, metabolism, and biochemistry, and we teach clients what this information means in terms of their recovery. Our fitness trainer performs a thorough assessment and develops a fitness plan suitable for each client's needs.

Every aspect of our program is designed to provide clients with a lifestyle they can continue after leaving our program. Along with traditional therapy and treatment modalities, we deal directly and specifically with eating and exercise activities that can't be adequately addressed in other settings due to size or structure; we feel these activities are crucial to facilitate full recovery.

- **Planning, shopping, and cooking meals are all part of each client's program.** Dealing directly with these activities is a unique part of our program. We believe developing skills in these areas is necessary because they will all have to be faced upon returning home. Clients will have independent, individualized goals in this area and gain increased responsibilities for their own care.

- **Clients participate in exercise according to individual needs and goals.** After an exercise assessment, a fitness trainer, in conjunction with the treatment team, develops an individualized exercise plan for each client. This is continually monitored, evaluated and adapted throughout treatment. Exercise and activity disorders are addressed with the focus on developing healthy, noncompulsive, lifelong exercise and activity habits. We are set up to meet the needs of athletes and compulsive exercisers who require specialized attention in this area.

- **Exercise and leisure activities.** Our goal is to provide a variety of activities that nourish both body and soul. We have scheduled outings two to three times per week and special events periodically. Our recreational outings can involve going to an art studio, to the beach, to a museum, to a miniature golf course, or anywhere that seems appropriate. Occasionally, we attend special events, like dance performances, concerts, and plays. We also utilize a variety of recreational activities that have a direct therapeutic value such as ropes courses and equine therapy.

- **Spirituality and mindfulness.** We believe that in healing eating and exercise disorders we must engender purpose and meaning in our clients' lives by providing nondenominational spirituality. In this aspect of our program, we work with eating and exercise disorder symptoms as the voice of a disconnected soul and we listen carefully and learn from them. At the same time we work to instill soulfulness and a spiritual dimension back into the lives of our clients. Once reconnected to the spiritual, sacred, and soulful aspects of life, the need for the symptoms diminishes.

- **Individual therapy is a critical component of the program.** Clients need individual sessions to work on their own particular problems and issues that have caused or perpetuate their disordered thinking and/or behavior. Clients meet at least three times per week with their primary therapist and also have individual sessions with the clinical director, dietitian, and psychiatrist.

- **Group therapy solidifies the other treatment components.** Through intensive group work, clients receive and offer support, gain insight into their problems, and develop the ability to transform them. Increasing confidence is gained by being able to identify feelings, communicate, deal with conflict, express needs in effective ways, and deal with shame and anger. All of this helps clients develop appropriate skills in order to deal with underlying issues and life's challenges without resorting to eating disorder behaviors.

• **Outings and passes are provided for skill building and to assess each client's growth in handling real-life situations.** Once clients are stabilized and it is determined that they are capable of it, they are allowed to obtain passes to go to restaurants, shopping, participate in social activities, and even go home for several hours or a couple of days (insurance permitting). On returning from an outing or pass, clients process their experience in both individual and group sessions to learn from the experience and plan for the future.

Level System

The Monte Nido level system allows for increased freedom and responsibility as clients progress in the program. All clients have a written contract, which they help create with their therapist and in a special group called "contract group." In this group, all the clients meet with the clinical director or other staff members and discuss together their goals for the upcoming week. The contract shows the current level they are on and spells out the goals for that level. Each client's program is individualized, although there are certain activities, reading assignments, and other standard requirements for every level. A copy of the contract is given to each client, one is posted, and one is kept in the client's chart.

• **Special privileges.** If deemed appropriate, clients may have special privileges spelled out in their contract that allow for things not usually spelled out for their current level. For example, a client may ask for and be allowed to independently cook her own meal on Level III even though this is a Level IV activity.

• **Level changes.** When clients feel they are ready, they can request a move to the next level. Level change requests are discussed in individual sessions and in contract group, where they receive feedback from the staff and peers. The treatment team will make final decisions regarding all contract issues and level requests in the staff meeting. All clients and staff then meet to go over each client's final contract for that week.

Agreement for Participation in a Healing Journey

When clients come to Monte Nido, we have them read and sign the following document which we adapted from information I once received in a workshop. This document, which they sign, invites them to participate in a healing journey with us.

> In coming to Monte Nido I have agreed to begin a new journey toward wellness so that I can fully participate in life on earth. I realize that for this journey I will need a vehicle, a body. In order to have a healthy body, I will need to feed it with appropriate foods. While I'm learning to do this I may stumble along the way, as it is human to do so; but I will forgive myself and I will give myself permission to ask for assistance, guidance, and support. My goal is to abstain from intentionally harming or neglecting my body. I realize that this will be essential in completing my journey to recovery. I will strive to make my relationship with my body one of forgiveness for its imperfections and one of honor for its value. I realize that all of this will be a difficult task. I agree to go forward with these goals and have come to Monte Nido because I have been unable to accomplish them on my own. There will be times when I am afraid, I do not understand, or I do not trust those trying to help me. Nevertheless, since I believe I can find the help I need at Monte Nido, I will be honest, I will listen to the wisdom of those who are here to help me including those who have completed the journey and recovered before me, and I will face my fear with the Monte Nido staff by my side.

This chapter is meant to be a guide for those wishing to explore alternatives to outpatient care. Based on research and experience, treatment programs continue to improve their care. Readers are advised to take their time and be thorough and cautious in their selection. In the last 5 years, there has been a proliferation of programs offering a wide range of eating disorder services. This is both good and bad news. It means there are more choices for a person to get help, but there are also more people needing it. An increasing number of people are also turning to alternative methods of treatment rather than or in addition to traditional methods. An introduction to some of these alternatives is presented in the next chapter, "Alternative Approaches to Treating Eating Disorders."

16

Alternative Approaches to Treating Eating Disorders

(Coauthored by Carolyn Ross, M.D., and Hamlin Emory, M.D.)

It would be a glaring omission to leave out alternative treatments in a sourcebook on eating disorders. People are increasingly turning to alternative treatments and finding benefit in these regimens. There is not enough research to substantiate all of the therapies used, but many are gaining acceptance, and there are promising studies. Acupuncture, chiropractic, herbal medicine, massage, movement therapy, equine therapy, yoga, dietary supplements, and other alternative approaches have been used with eating disorders.

With varying success, most patients do not abandon conventional medicine but add alternative therapies to the more traditional treatments they are receiving. The combination of traditional and alternative approaches can be called *integrative medicine*. Dr. Carolyn Ross has been practicing integrative medicine in the treatment of eating disorders with successful results. In the first section of this chapter, Dr. Ross provides a brief overview of only a few alternative approaches.

The second section of this chapter by Dr. Hamlin Emory is devoted to an alternative method for assessing brain physiology and prescribing treatments suited to each individual's unique brain wave profile. Treatments can consist of either allopathic or naturopathic agents or both. Dr. Emory and colleagues have been using the methodology described since 1986 and are currently experiencing success with eating disorder patients.

Alternative Therapies (Carolyn Ross)

Alternative therapies offer components of healing that are often not available in conventional treatments. Various combinations of the treatments discussed in this section address the whole person—body, mind, and soul—in a way that complements and increases the efficacy of conventional therapies. Integrative medicine offers many benefits to patients with eating disorders. Well-designed research of alternative therapies and integrative medicine is in its infancy; however, in the hands of experienced practitioners, the risk of harm to patients is low. The information provided here is not intended to substitute for medical advice. Readers interested in integrative medicine and alternative therapies should consult a physician trained and licensed in this field.

Nutrition and Nutraceuticals

In every ancient healing system, there are specific prescriptions for diet and exercise. Hippocrates, the father of modern medicine, was quoted as saying, "Let food be thy medicine and medicine be thy food." In every ancient tradition, there were ceremonies and rituals involving food. The guides to health and wholeness saw food and nutrition as sacred. In our busy, fast-paced, fast-food culture, the sacred act of sharing food with others and even of nourishing ourselves has been lost or misplaced by other rituals that are not as healthy.

In an integrative model, food is treated as medicine. There have been documented studies of the effect of nutrient balance on eating disorder behaviors. For example, studies show that consuming a protein supplement before a meal or a nutrient-dense diet—a diet free of blood sugar destabilizers—can reduce bingeing behavior in individuals with bulimia. The following nutraceuticals—defined as vitamins, botanicals, and dietary supplements—are used for therapeutic purposes.

B Vitamins

Folic acid, niacin, thiamine, B_6, and B_{12} are known to improve mood and energy and have been found to be lacking in individuals with anorexia and bulimia in several small studies. The first sign of niacin deficiency is loss of appetite, or "anorexia." Supplementation has been shown to improve appetite and mental state.

Fatty Acids

Omega-3 and omega-6 fatty acids are essential fatty acids (FAs) because they cannot be synthesized by the body and must be obtained through diet or supplementation. Omega-3 FAs are known to have anti-inflammatory benefits, protect the heart, dilate the blood vessels, and prevent blood clots. Omega-6 FAs tend to promote inflammation and blood clot formation. The omega-3 FAs, eicosapentaenoic acid (EPA) and docosahexaenoic acid (DHA) are found in fish and fish oils such as salmon, mackerel, tuna and sardines. Alpha-linoleic acid (ALA) is an omega-3 fatty acid that is found in seeds and oils, green leafy vegetables, walnuts, and soybeans.

Omega-3 FAs offer several benefits in the treatment of eating disorders. Studies have documented benefits that include lowering serum triglyceride; increasing high-density lipoprotein (HDL, or good cholesterol); and reducing the risk of sudden death syndrome caused by arrythmias, or abnormal rhythms of the heart (Covington 2004). Epidemiological data demonstrate that countries in which there is high consumption of fatty fish (which contain omega-3 FAs) have a lower incidence of depression and bipolar disorder.

Several studies have also shown a decrease in levels of omega-3 FAs in patients with depression. Omega-3 fatty acid supplements can be given along with prescription medications for depression and bipolar disorder. EPA was shown in one study to decrease aggressiveness and depression in borderline personality disorder (Natural Medicine Comprehensive Database).

Because metabolism of omega-3 FAs can cause oxidative stress, they should be given with a vitamin E supplement in doses of between 400 and 800 international units (IU) daily. Omega-6 FAs (gamma-linoleic acid and linoleic acid) are readily available in the diet, for example in oils such as borage, corn, cottonseed, grapeseed, peanut, evening primrose oil, safflower, sesame, soybean (has both Omega-3 and Omega-6), and sunflower. Other food sources include egg yolks, meats in general, and organ meats in particular. Interactions and adverse effects for omega-3 FAs include thinning of the blood. However, there are no known cases of abnormal bleeding as a result of omega-3 supplementation even at high doses or in combination with anticoagulant medications. Side effects include a fishy burp or aftertaste and stomach upset. Dosages range from 1 to 3 grams a day for treatment of depression and prevention of heart disease and up to 9 grams for treatment of bipolar disorder.

Zinc

A deficiency of the mineral zinc in eating disorder patients has been reported by several researchers. It is a little-known fact that a zinc deficiency actually causes loss of taste acuity and appetite. In other words, such a deficiency may directly contribute to a reduction in the desire to eat, enhancing or perpetuating anorexia. What starts out as a diet motivated by a desire to lose weight may turn into a physiological desire not to eat when zinc deficiency is induced by restrictive nutritional intake.

Several investigators discovered through a simple taste test reported years ago in the British medical journal *Lancet* that most individuals with anorexia and many with bulimia are zinc deficient. When these individuals were given a supplement containing a specific solution of liquid zinc, many experienced positive results and, in some cases, even remission of eating disorder symptoms. More research needs to be done in this area, but until then, it seems fair to say that zinc supplementation looks promising and, if done appropriately, may provide a substantial benefit with no harm.

Alex Schauss, Ph.D., and Carolyn Costin coauthored a book on this subject, *Zinc and Eating Disorders* (1981), and another, *Anorexia and Bulimia: A Nutritional Approach to the Deadly Eating Disorders* (1997), detailing the research on zinc and many other nutritional supplements useful for individuals with eating disorders. Readers are encouraged to explore these sources for further details.

Herbals/Botanicals

Valerian is an herb with sedative, hypnotic, and anxiolytic properties; it is useful in the treatment of insomnia, anxiety, and benzodiazepine withdrawal. Valerian reduces the time to sleep onset and improves the quality of sleep. Past reports of hepatotoxicity (liver damage) were related to the use of multi-ingredient preparations and were probably idiosyncratic. Common dosages for sleep range from 300 to 600 milligrams of valerian root at bedtime. The dosage for valerian tincture is 2.5 to 5 milliliters. Side effects may include nausea, headache, dizziness, and upset stomach, which were reported in less than 10 percent of subjects.

Probiotics and Digestive Enzymes

Chronic constipation is associated with changes in the flora of the gastrointestinal tract and can cause intestinal permeability and decreased immune response. In several small studies on patients with the full spectrum of eating disorders, the use of plant-based digestive enzymes in combination with the probiotic lactobacillus GG decreased constipation, gas, and bloating during the refeeding period.

Alternative Therapies for Treating Depression

Depression is discussed separately because several supplements are suggested for alleviation of symptoms. Dieting may alter brain serotonin function in women but not in men, and this alteration could contribute to depression and frequency of binges. 5-Hydroxytryptophan (5-HTP) is related to both the amino acid L-tryptophan and to serotonin. In the body, L-tryptophan is converted to 5-HTP, which can then be converted to serotonin. 5-HTP is able to easily cross the blood-brain barrier (gets into the brain easily) and increases the production of serotonin in the central nervous system. Since 5-HTP can increase synthesis of serotonin, it has been used to treat several conditions where serotonin is believed to play a significant role; depression, insomnia, and obesity for example. At higher doses (900 milligrams per day), 5-HTP has been associated with weight loss in obese patients, an increase in early satiety, and a reduction in carbohydrate intake. At lower doses, it has been effective in treating insomnia and refractory depression and has been used to boost the effectiveness of conventional antidepressants. The main side effect is stomach upset. Dosages begin at 50 to 200 milligrams a day for insomnia and depression.

SAMe contributes to the synthesis; activation; and/or metabolism of hormones, neurotransmitters, proteins, and certain drugs. Multiple studies and meta-analyses have shown SAMe to be better than placebo and possibly as effective as or better than some prescription medications in treating depression. It is also useful in the treatment of osteoarthritis, and might be helpful for those eating disorder patients with a history of competitive athletics or compulsive overexercise. The main side effects are stomach upset, mild insomnia, headache, and nervousness. The starting dose is 200 milligrams twice a day.

St. John's Wort can be used in treating depression, seasonal affective disorder, attention deficit hyperactivity disorder, obsessive-compulsive disorder, and anxiety. Several active constituents in St. John's Wort have been identified, including melatonin, hypericin, and hyperforin. Hyperforin is thought to be the ingredient mainly responsible for its actions. Any preparation used should be standardized to 3 percent hyperforin. The starting dosage is 300 milligrams three times a day. More recent studies have supported its use for even moderate to severe depression (Szegedi, A., R. Kohnen, A. Dienel, and M. Kiesser *BMJ* 2005). Drug-herb interactions are possible with either SAMe or St. John's Wort, and their use can precipitate mania in bipolar patients. With all supplements it is important for the treating professional to know everything being taken in order to coordinate effective care and prevent negative interactions and reactions.

Mind-Body Therapies

The following mind-body therapies have been shown to be effective in treating eating disorders.

- **Guided imagery.** Guided imagery (GI) uses the power of the mind's imagination to influence the body. By imagining you are lying on a warm beach, your body responds in much the same way as if it were actually performing this activity. GI uses not just visual images but also taps into the other four senses to promote relaxation and reduce stress. This practice produced a 74 percent reduction in bingeing and a 75 percent reduction in vomiting in a study of women diagnosed with bulimia. Stress management techniques were more effective than nutritional management alone in reducing binge frequency in patients with bulimia. Other benefits included an improvement in body image and a decrease in the symptoms of depression. In a study on obese individuals and those with anorexia, biofeedback decreased overeating and undereating behaviors.

- **Mindful practices.** Mindful practices can include meditation, prayer, or any activity in which one's attention is focused, thereby increasing our inner awareness, our mind-body connection, and our awareness of the external environment. Mindfulness practices can improve one's sense of awe, provide self-soothing for emotional regulation, and be useful as an adjunctive treatment for depression and anxiety. Mindful eating can begin with invocations that connect the person more deeply with the sacred act of self-nourishment.

- **Body therapies.** Body therapies such as qi gong, tai chi, and yoga can help facilitate the mind-body connection and enable patients to recognize their own body's cues, thereby decreasing the sense of disconnection and dissociation often exhibited by their behaviors. Research on yoga demonstrates benefits such as decreasing depression and anger, minimizing obsessive-compulsive behaviors, and reducing drug use and criminal activities in recovering addicts on methadone maintenance. Many eating disorder treatment programs now include yoga as part of their services. Among other things, clients at Monte Nido report that yoga helps them be in their body with increased awareness, provides an alternative to the more compulsive cardio workouts many are used to, and begins to expose them to spiritual ideas concerning reverence for their bodies and the divine and the connection between the two. Yoga is about communicating with your body, asking it to move and stretch, but not pushing it. Through yoga, clients learn how to be grounded, flexible, and balanced. They also learn how to listen to their bodies and accept just where they are. See my book *100 Questions About Eating Disorders* for more information and quotes from clients.

- **Acupuncture.** Acupuncture is an important component of traditional Chinese medicine and comprises the use of fine needles placed on energy channel points to stimulate the flow of vital energy. Western studies have documented benefits of using acupuncture in the treatment of depression when compared to medication and/or placebo. Acupuncture is also effective in treating chronic pain syndromes, chronic anxiety, menstrual problems, and patients going through drug detox. At Monte Nido, we have successfully used acupuncture to assist clients return to menses after months of weight and body fat restoration were insufficient.

- **Massage/touch therapy.** Talk therapy has limitations. Our bodies can store emotions that cannot be released through verbal therapy alone. Touch is one of the best ways to release emotions in the body, but this form of healing must be used wisely and cautiously. Traditional massage can release stress and tension and promote calmness and relations all of which can be useful for a variety of clients. A well-trained massage therapist can help a person release pent-up emotions and tears without going too far into work that is more appropriate for a psychotherapist. A master in touch therapy, such as Ilana Rubenfeld, (see her book *The Listening Hand*) can use a combination of touch and talk to lead people from the prison of the past to freedom in the present. Her method, the Rubenfeld Synergy Method, helps people reframe past experiences and heal old stored-up wounds. The Rubenfeld Synergy Method is just one example of touch therapy that can be used successfully with clients.

An Alternative to Standardized Psychiatric Prescribing (Dr. Hamlin Emory)

In the 12th century, Maimonides observed that asthmatic sufferers showed variable responses to herbal compounds and concluded that there were differences in their physical nature or physiology. He wisely anticipated the necessity of physical subtyping or measurement in the art of healing. Today, scientific medicine is guided by physical measurement. We know that without objective measurement of the organ or system in question, treatment recommendations must be based on opinion.

Until recently, psychiatrists were the only medical specialists who did not have an objective measurement tool to assess the physical function of the organ they treat, the human brain. Substantial technical progress during the 20th century led to sophisticated tests of organ function that are routinely used to assist physicians in distinguishing subtle differences in physical illnesses. Medical specialists use EEGs, x-rays, and EKGs, as well as CT, PET, and MRI scans, to penetrate the outer body and see beyond symptoms and behaviors. It follows that measurement of an individual's brain function is essential to identify whether there is a neurobiological disturbance contributing to their mental disorder. Medications change cellular physiology, and neuroactive medications change brain physiology. A medication can produce negative results in one person, no results in a second person, and positive therapeutic results in a third. Medication that improves a person's neurobiology can be the first step in recovering health.

In this biological century, psychiatric medicine's challenge is to distinguish the functional brain disturbances that contribute to mental disorders. This is the logical path toward personalizing biopsychosocial treatment.

Human Brains Are Different

We tell our children that everyone is different, that everyone is special, and that no two people are alike, yet the psychiatric approach to treatment is standardized from behavioral criteria. Evidence is accumulating that within each eating disorder—anorexia nervosa, bulimia nervosa, and binge eating disorder—there are variations in brain activity from person to person. In addition, modern tools that measure the brain's electrical activity show previously unrecognized brain features that can help clinicians formulate better decisions in these complex illnesses.

EEG Data Identify Brain Differences

In 1986 our neuropsychiatric group decided to seek a way of improving psychiatric treatment decisions. We believe that using descriptive labels such as *anorexia*, *bulimia*, and *binge eating disorder* as the basis for treatment decisions is inadequate. Looking for a better method, we discovered the use of the electroencephalogram (EEG), a technology that quantifies brain waves (QEEG) and compares them with age-matched normal values. When a patient's QEEG values were outside the normal range, we noted the values, classified the QEEG profile, and monitored the patient's response and nonresponse to medical treatments. Examining patients with a broad range of mental disorders, including eating disorders, we found both differences and similarities in the QEEG profiles for each mental disorder. Our clinical research discovered that when a patient shows abnormal QEEG values, selection of medical treatment (including medications, nutritional supplements, and light therapy) to improve the values and normalize the QEEG profile produces more consistently satisfactory therapeutic outcomes. We stored this information in an electronic database for future use.

This novel approach to psychiatric treatment is based on EEG expressions of genetic differences and can help physicians make objective treatment recommendations in complex biopsychosocial conditions such as eating disorders. A patient with normal QEEG values will likely not require neuroactive medication. If a patient's QEEG values are outside the normal range, the QEEG profile is matched with similar database profiles and their known response and nonresponse to medical treatment. When added to clinical information, profile matching and treatment correlation provides objective information to guide a physician's reasoning and recommendations. After medical treatment, reassessing the QEEG profile gives the physician a powerful tool to understand how a medication affects the patient's brain function. Improving an eating disordered patient's abnormal QEEG profile and helping him or her achieve brain wave balance decreases symptoms and enables participation in necessary psychological, nutritional, physical, and sociological treatments.

The current database contains nearly 3,000 patients, their QEEG profiles, and their responses to more than 30 neuropsychiatric medications, more than 10 naturopathic agents (supplements, herbal compounds), and light therapy. Physicians are able to assess and successfully use this information to improve treatment decisions and patient outcomes. This process is consistent with the principles of evidence-based medicine.

EEG Data Improve Management of Eating Disorders

Eating disorders are profoundly damaging. Individuals with these illnesses often cannot work, study, or maintain stable relationships. Their lives are broken, and their families suffer with them. Eating disorders wreak havoc on families; put the mental health of siblings, parents, and significant others at risk; and destroy a family's financial stability. This is a true drama of life.

Our group has assessed and treated nearly 300 eating disorder patients using EEG data to guide treatment decisions. Approximately 85 percent of these individuals had previously undergone treatments that did not work. Although each eating disorder diagnostic group exhibited similar behaviors and voiced similar concerns, their QEEG profiles after nutritional rehabilitation were remarkably diverse. Some patients' profiles often linked with complex or counterintuitive treatments that are not normally recommended for eating disorders. For example, several patients with anorexia nervosa evidenced brain wave patterns consistent with the need for a stimulant medication such as Ritalin or Dexedrine. Subsequent supplementation with a stimulant medication has helped many of these patients calm down, resume eating, and go on to full recovery. Some patients' values were only mildly abnormal or within normal limits. These patients generally responded to naturopathic agents or did not require medicinal compounds. For example, eating disorder patients with brain wave patterns indicative of mild depression have responded to St. Johns Wort and/or a combination of the amino acids tyrosine, phenalalanine, and glutamine.

A growing number of neuroscientists and clinicians are now using EEG technology as a practical tool to improve the treatment of a variety of mental and emotional conditions, including eating disorders. The predictive value of using this information as a laboratory test has prompted the idea that EEG data may become the standard of care in psychiatry. For more information on the use of QEEG, please refer to drhamilinemory.com. The Monte Nido Treatment Center has been using the QEEG since 1996, and readers can find contact information on montenido.com to get more information about this method, our treatment results, and/or to speak with patients who have experienced this approach.

17

Increasing Awareness and Prevention

(Coauthored by Michael P. Levine, Ph.D., FAED)

HEALING PEOPLE ONE person at a time is too consuming and ultimately ineffective to resolve the growing problem of eating disorders. We have to prevent them. For each person we treat several new cases are developing. Eating disorders and related conditions (e.g., negative body image, chronic dieting, chaotic eating patterns) are rampant in our society and many countries around the world, yet adequate prevention programs do not exist. Extensive programs aimed at preventing cigarette smoking, alcohol abuse, and other substance abuse have proved valuable and have been accepted into school curricula. However, very few schools or colleges have systematic programs for preventing eating disorders.

The increase in eating disorders, the high cost of treatment, the longevity of these illnesses, and the high mortality rate make it imperative that programs be implemented to stop them before they occur. Since the vast majority of people who suffer from these disorders report the onset of their illness by age 20, prevention programs should focus on children, young people, and their parents to maximize preventive efforts. With an increasing number of children aged 8 through 13 ending up in eating disorder treatment, the need for early education and prevention programs is crucial.

Prevention information and programming cannot be targeted exclusively at women. It is a mistake to think of body image, weight and shape concerns, and eating disorders as a "female issue." As described in Chapter 2, males do suffer from binge eating disorder, bulimia nervosa, anorexia nervosa, and other eating problems, as well as body image problems such as those that contribute to the abuse of steroids and supplements. Furthermore, we need to educate fathers, male coaches, male physicians, businessmen, and so forth about the significant role they have in preventing eating disorders in the general population. In this regard, millions of men, often without realizing it, objectify females even at an early age, making comments about and overemphasizing looks and weight. Fathers have to learn to relate better to their daughters, husbands to their wives, brothers to their sisters, boyfriends to their lovers, male coaches to their athletes, and so on. We all have to work on changing our cultural emphasis on appearance (and particularly on thinness) as the quintessential feature of female identity if we want to fight eating disorders, body image problems, and weight preoccupation in general.

Primary and Secondary Prevention

There are two basic types of prevention: primary and secondary. *Primary prevention* refers to systemic efforts to reduce the number of new cases of eating disorders. This means it is designed to prevent illness by strengthening health and resilience. Risk factors for eating disorders include internalization of the slender beauty ideal, body dissatisfaction, a tendency to determine one's body image and self-worth through social comparisons, high levels of anxiety and depression, dieting, sexual abuse, and genetic predisposition.

Factors that may serve to prevent eating disorders include high self-esteem, a multifaceted identity, social support, media and propaganda awareness, a focus on health instead of weight and shape, and the use of one's body in active but healthy ways. The "universal" form of primary prevention addresses the systems (e.g., public health education, laws, mass media) that could reduce risk factors and increase protective factors in the general population. The "selective" form of primary prevention focuses on groups such as middle-school girls and boys who are at high risk because this period coincides with the physical, psychological, and social changes of puberty.

Secondary prevention refers to identifying and rehabilitating people who are showing the early signs and symptoms of what could become a severe and chronic eating disorder. There is a fine line between "very high-risk" and "early warning signs," so secondary prevention programs are typically targeted toward or indicated for groups with, for example, an entrenched commitment to the slender beauty ideal, a great deal of body dissatisfaction, and unhealthy forms of weight management.

Programs for Primary and Secondary Prevention

Currently, a variety of programs for elementary- and middle-school children have shown promise for primary-selective prevention. Moreover, several different types of programs for secondary-targeted prevention have been demonstrated to be effective, in the short run at least, for high school and college students. For more information on recent prevention efforts and research, readers can look at M. P. Levine and L. Smolak's *The Prevention of Eating Problems and Eating Disorders* and J. K. Thompson and L. Smolak's *Body Image, Eating Disorders, and Obesity in Children and Adolescents* (2001).

Several organizations include prevention of eating disorders as one of their goals. These organizations are listed in the appendix. Prominent among them is the National Eating Disorders Association, a nonprofit organization that officially began in 1987 (as Eating Disorders Awareness and Prevention, Inc.) in response to the enormous number of individuals suffering from eating disorders and the lack of any organization dedicated exclusively to prevention and education. A task force of mental health professionals from all over the United States, with its headquarters in Seattle, works together with businesspeople and lay volunteers.

NEDA sponsors and organizes Eating Disorders Awareness Week (EDAW), which takes place every year during the last week of February. Each state has a coordinator and steering committee that help to organize community events and activities during EDAW and throughout the year. Scheduled events include workshops, hotlines, radio shows, and media events such as scale bashing or "Fearless Friday" (a day on which everyone refuses to diet). The audience for NEDA's website, materials, and programs has expanded from college students and those who work with them to high school and junior high students and, more recently, to families, particularly through the Parent Family Network (PFN). Anyone can join the PFN by visiting the NEDA website and simply clicking on the PFN section. There are also other categories of membership, for example for students and professionals.

NEDA workers and other professionals have created educational materials for use in schools. Books, curriculum guides, tapes, and workbooks are now available, many of which can be purchased through NEDA or Gürze Books, located in Carlsbad, California. *Your Dieting Daughter* by Carolyn Costin (1996) is one such book useful for not only parents but educators, therapists, and physicians. The recommendations in the following section are for those interested in preventing eating disorders. Not all items will apply to everyone.

Prevention Ideas

The following are some general prevention ideas for a variety of circumstances. Do not get trapped into thinking that you the reader or any individual cannot have an impact. Margaret Meade once said, "Never doubt that a small group of thoughtful, committed citizens can change the world. Indeed it is the only thing that ever has."

- **Educate yourself and others.** In your book clubs, service organizations (e.g., Rotary Club, Kiwanis, Friends of the Library), and other groups, look for ways to learn about and help others learn about healthy lifestyles, stress management, women's history, weight-related prejudice, and so on. Look for ways to integrate relevant stories, art, biography, media literacy, and websites into youth activities such as scouts, 4-H, Future Farmers of America, and other forms of service learning.

- **Be an activist, even if it is only part-time.** Instead of receiving gifts for your birthday, ask your family and friends to give money to NEDA or the local Friends of the Library for the purchase of books and videos that can contribute to preventing eating disorders. Talk to your friends and family about commercials and advertisements that you find offensive because they objectify women or men and glorify slenderness.

Once or twice a year, write to companies to protest offensive or objectifying advertising or to praise positive ads that feature people of diverse size and shape, for example, the Body Shop or ads for Dove Soap. (Unfortunately, Dove then came out with an ad for thigh reduction cream.) Work with your local mental health association and/or your school system to initiate or reinforce EDAW in your community. Identify sexist or weightist prejudices in your workplace and collaborate with others to have them removed. Join a prevention-oriented organization such as NEDA or Dads and Daughters (see the appendix). Two excellent sources of ideas and inspiration for everyday activism are Margo Maine's *Body Wars: Making Peace with Women's Bodies—An Activist's Guide* (2000) and Joe Kelly's *Dads and Daughters* (2002). When you take these small but very important steps, share them with your family, friends, and coworkers and describe what being an activist means to you.

• **Practice taking people in general—and girls and women in particular—seriously, regardless of their size or shape.** Work to surround yourself with, and to connect your loved ones with, "women of substance." These are women who, regardless of size or occupation, take up space in the world and have things of importance to say and do in regard to taking care of themselves and to making the world a better place. Whenever and wherever you can—at home, the library, meetings of clubs and organizations, your place of worship—promote stories of girls and women of character who, regardless of their physical size and shape, resisted negative cultural forces and went on to create laws, art, inventions, and other things of lasting value.

For Parents, Therapists, Doctors, and Teachers

• **Discuss society's thinness mania and myth.** It's important to talk about the cultural pressure to be thin and beautiful. Discuss myths, realities, and uncertainties regarding weight, overweight, and obesity. Connect ignorance, weight-related prejudice, and sexism to the dieting hype and advertising propaganda that promote the myth of thinness as attractiveness and salvation. Talk to young children, peers, and others about these issues and how this misinformation can lead to eating problems, eating disorders, and paradoxically, a worsening of the disturbing trend toward obesity in children and adolescents. Teach others to appreciate and respect people of all sizes. Speak out against the objectification of people in TV shows, movies, videos, beauty pageants, bodybuilding competitions, and so on. Avoid obvious sources of objectification, certain advertisements or magazines such as pornography and sexist films.

• **Educate people about healthy dieting.** Help steer people away from fad or quack diets, diet pills, cigarettes, and so on. Use your own behavior, as well as your words and emotional support, to help people learn to listen to hunger and satiety cues and respond to their body's needs rather than pressure from other people or the media. Dieting and weight-loss myths need to be exposed, challenged, and ultimately discarded or ignored. The phrase "diets don't work" has become a cliché. Provide the necessary information to make people understand that the cliché is a reality. A great source of information and practical ideas for parents is Dianne Neumark-Sztainer's book *"I'm, Like, So Fat!" Helping Your Teen Make Healthy Choices About Eating and Exercise in a Weight-Obsessed World* (2005).

- **Teach and practice good nutrition and exercise habits.** Make it a point to read up on these topics and put your knowledge to use. Share it with others. Many people really don't know much about proper nutrition and exercise. Even doctors have very little knowledge on these subjects. When exercising, focus on coordination, balance, breathing, strength and stamina, enjoyment, and improved health and body acceptance rather than on calories burned or resulting changes in appearance.

- **Avoid criticizing your own body.** If you criticize your appearance, you will perpetuate the message that a body is more important than the person who owns it. Too much emphasis on looks leads to distorted ideas about happiness and what is truly important in life. Don't objectify yourself by frequently weighing yourself; scrutinizing yourself in mirrors; comparing yourself to others; or talking loudly, dramatically, and ashamedly about the need to lose weight. If you can't avoid doing these things, get professional help.

- **Discuss cultural influences.** Using various cultures, time periods, or mass media, discuss cultural influences and pressures placed on people, especially females but increasingly males, to look a certain way. Discuss ways to combat these pressures.

- **Develop self-esteem.** Read books on reducing self-disparagement and raising self-esteem. Learn and practice positive self-talk to boost self-esteem, learn about mindfulness-based stress management techniques that help you come to terms with and thus reject negative messages (those "critical voices") from media, society, parents, and other people, including yourself. Practice listening to and empathizing with others—and telling them directly that you care about and respect them—to help them develop a healthy, resilient sense of self.

- **Love people and make them feel loved for who they are on the inside.** This encourages others to love and be themselves. Model kind and flexible ways to nurture yourself, meet emotional needs, and cope with stress that are not focused on food, weight, appearance, or other self-destructive behaviors. Sometimes it's not "what you are eating" that matters, it's "what's eating you" and how you are dealing with it.

- **Do not push to excel.** Very often people get the feeling that they are loved for their accomplishments or what they are striving so hard to obtain rather than who they are. Children who experience such "conditions of worth" may grow up feeling that if they aren't competing, excelling, or being the best, they aren't lovable or loved. It's okay to encourage kids or others to try hard, but they must feel loved and praised for things other than performance (including living up to appearance standards). Too much anxiety about and stress on performance and perfection can lead a person to rely solely on external, rather than internal validation and motivation. Be sure to validate people for who they are, not what they do.

- **Balance rules and limits as well as freedom and responsibility.** If you are a parent, it is hard to know when to push a child to eat lunch or dinner or to stop eating chips, cake, or candy. A good rule to follow is that it is your responsibility to provide moderate-sized portions of good, wholesome, healthy food, desserts, and treats; it is your child's responsibility to eat them. Being too strict may cause certain "forbidden foods" to attain an elevated status, thus making them more desirable. The book *How to Get Your Kid to Eat . . . But Not Too Much* (1987) by Ellen Satter, as well as the Neumark-Sztainer book mentioned earlier, are good resources on this subject.

• **Avoid making, and confront others who make, sarcastic, prejudicial comments or jokes about weight.** Calling someone "fatty" serves no purpose other than to make the person feel terrible and lose self-esteem, which only perpetuates the problem. Let people know that making fun of fat people is cruel and offensive. Show your dislike for tasteless items such as greeting cards or bumper stickers saying things like "no fat chicks." If anyone objectifies others by judging their appearance, explain why it bothers you and ask them to stop.

• **Focus on health, not weight.** Even if someone has been advised to lose weight by a doctor or dietitian, the focus should be about being healthier, not thinner. Talk about healthy foods, foods with life force, not just fattening ("bad") versus nonfattening ("good") foods. Promote the message that there are no bad or fattening foods, only bad eating habits. Ice cream is not a bad food; eating it for breakfast, lunch, and dinner would be a bad eating habit. One's health and vitality are far more important than one's weight. Even in a weight-loss program, the focus should be on the person's relationship to food and health. Get rid of the scale—even if weight loss is recommended for health reasons, losing fat rather than just indiscriminate weight is the goal, and this cannot be determined by a number on a scale.

Keep in mind that people are often misled into thinking they need to lose weight for health reasons, when in fact the real motivation behind the suggestion has to do with appearance. Educate yourself, learn the facts, and face them. Read books like Glenn Gaesser's *Big Fat Lies* (1996) and Frances Berg's *Underage & Overweight* (2004) to help dispel the myths about weight and weight loss. Subscribe to *Health at Any Size*, coedited by Jon Robison and Karen Miller.

One last note: The dieting industry has proven to be a colossal moneymaking venture that fails the people who try it, leaving them to blame themselves for the failure while continuing to resort to fad diets, pills, laxatives, and other unhealthy methods to beat the odds. Researchers have identified a few risk factors for eating disorders, the interlocking problems of body dissatisfaction and dieting are two of them.

- **Love, regardless of looks.** Looks and attractiveness play a part in most relationships, but the degree or extent is important. Appearance should not mean more than other inner qualities. Moreover, style comes in many forms, and it has a lot to do with authentic individual expression and creativity. The notion that only "thin" or "lean and muscular" are attractive and appealing is clearly preposterous. In general, try not to gossip, positively or negatively, about your own looks or the appearance of others.

- **Communicate effectively.** Good communication is important for healthy, happy relationships. This can't be emphasized enough. Be open and honest and allow others to be the same. Learn assertive communication skills to express feelings rather than "stuffing" or denying them. Read books, take courses, and get counseling early if you have any problems in this area.

- **Help others to help themselves.** Help others cope with their problems by reaching out to them and letting them know you are there in a nonjudgmental way to listen and offer guidance whenever you can. Be supportive and encouraging. Help them seek further help for themselves if they need to do so. Assist them in locating a therapist, group, counselor, dietitian, and so on.

- **Provide literature for your children, students, patients, and so on regarding healthy eating, exercise, self-esteem, dieting, and eating disorders.** Carefully scrutinize any material, because many books and articles are misguided. They give people ideas and advice that contradict the principles in this chapter and can thus promote poor health and disorder instead of prevention. Get ideas from the resources listed in this chapter.

• **Help promote strong, multifaceted role models for girls and women.** For example, help young girls turn their focus away from external female qualities to internal ones. This means reclaiming certain "masculine" qualities such as being physically fit, knowing how to use tools, and being assertive in solving problems. It also means exploring and valuing "feminine" qualities such as patience, resilience, intuition, flexibility, expression of emotions, and nurturing. Parents, grandparents, and family friends can buy (perhaps as gifts for children and adolescents or as contributions to libraries and churches) books and posters that feature powerful women who are respected for qualities other than their appearance.

• **Spend time developing your soul and spirit, and remember what is truly sacred.** Promote this practice in others. Our society makes it easy to focus on accomplishments and material things, thereby losing touch with what is truly important. People stay late at the office and end up with no time to have dinner with their family or to read a book to a child. Often the amount of money people make or the type of car they drive seems more valuable than whether they gave to charity or were kind to neighbors. With the continual advance of technology, we no longer need to leave our homes or cars and connect with others to do our banking, shopping, or eating. We need to stop and ponder where this is all going. Read *Care of the Soul* (1992) and *The Re-Enchantment of Everyday Life* (1996) by Thomas Moore. Devote time to nurturing and enhancing (instead of starving) your soul and your spirituality.

Prevention in Schools

• **Collaborate.** Effective prevention requires a good deal of time, effort, and advocacy. Consequently, a teacher or counselor who is committed to prevention must work with various other people. Teachers can work with other teachers and with interested students to form a resource and study group. This group could be the catalyst for EDAW at the school and in the community. In conducting an EDAW, the group can collaborate with local business groups (e.g., the Rotary Club) and work with newspapers, television, and radio to promote public health. The group may also work with school administration to establish and enforce a no-teasing policy at the school. Finally, the group can also collaborate with a Parent-Teacher Organization, local service group, or local mental health association to sponsor guest speakers to educate school staff and parents about subjects such as body image, dieting, cultural propaganda, and eating disorders.

- **Educate and train.** Work with principals and other administrators to arrange teacher in-service training and peer leadership training about eating disorders and, most important, about what adults and young people can do and be to prevent these disorders. Work with librarians, nurses, and school-based social workers to provide (and publicize) high-quality books, pamphlets, and videos about healthy lifestyles and the spectrum of disordered eating. Make sure these are available at school for students, teachers, and parents.

Schools need to have informative materials, including referral resources, available for students to casually pick up in the nursing office, library, or counselor's office. Students often don't want to admit to having a problem—or they don't want to "get my friend in trouble"—but they will pick up literature to read anonymously. The appendix, list of reading materials, and bibliography can suggest many resources. Note that local service groups (e.g., a retired teachers association) can be a source of financing.

- **Curriculum.** Contact an eating disorders organization such as NEDA or ANAD, or go to the Gürze books website (gurze.com) to consider the excellent curricula that are available for primary and secondary schools. *Full of Ourselves*, a book and a program developed by Catherine Steiner Adair and Lisa Sjostrum, has been shown to be effective in prevention. Look for ways to integrate preventive education into the general curriculum. Levine and Smolak (2006) have reviewed ways that prevention can be infused into media studies, biology, English, psychology, history, and the creative arts. It is exciting to contemplate how student creations (e.g., survey-based research projects, posters, newspaper articles, public service announcements) can become part of EDAW or adorn the walls in classrooms and hallways.

• **Conduct an ecological analysis.** Conduct a survey of materials and practices that may inadvertently promote negative body image and disordered eating or, conversely, that do a good job of promoting health and resilience. Does the school have posters in the halls or classrooms that demean fat people? Are there contests that reward people who can eat the most or lose the most weight fastest? Are there explicit or implicit size regulations for who can be a cheerleader or a dancer? In the classrooms, are all the pictures of eminent scientists, historical figures, authors, leaders, and so on pictures of men? Research, dialogue, and activism in this area can be an excellent source of prevention as well as leadership, respect, and citizenship.

• **Identification and referral.** Determine whether or not the school or school system has a policy and a set of procedures that govern the process by which students with the warning signs of an eating disorder or body image problem (e.g., steroid abuse) are identified and referred for evaluation. Whether this policy needs to be affirmed, revised, or established for the first time, the following guidelines should be followed:

- Be sure staff know how to speak respectfully but firmly with the affected person and with family and friends. The emphasis is on caring, identifying problems, and effective referral for evaluation.
- Administrators, teachers, counselors, and school psychologists should know who is responsible for speaking to the student who is affected and when it is necessary for the right person to speak to parents.
- Identify and work with local or nearby resources for professional evaluation and treatment. Organizations

such as NEDA and edreferral.com can often provide these resources.
- Have a mechanism in place whereby teachers and other "front-line" people can be informed of how well they did in initiating a referral, of how the student they care about is doing, and what they can do to be of support.

Overcoming the factors that promote and reinforce eating disorders will require significant personal and social changes. Nevertheless, we should not despair, as such changes are possible. Witness the dramatic efforts in the past 30 to 40 years to reduce cigarette smoking and drunk driving, and to promote seat belt use and girls' and women's participation in athletics. Prevention, whether it unfolds at home, at school, or in the public domain, will be facilitated by attention to the 4 Cs (Levine and Smolak 2006):

- Consciousness-raising
- Connections between people
- Competence-building
- Collaborative action for constructive Change

Above all else, do not be discouraged or deterred. At Monte Nido, there is an old Greek proverb hanging on the wall that says "A civilization flourishes when its citizens plant trees under whose shade they may never sit."

Appendix

Eating Disorder Organizations and Websites

THE FOLLOWING LISTS of organizations are provided to give readers additional sources for information and guidance. These organizations and web sites are only a sample of all that is available. They offer information about the nature and treatment of eating disorders, activism and advocacy, and prevention programs. Some of the organizations sponsor specific activities and programs such as "Eating Disorders Awareness Week" put on by NEDA or support groups as promoted by ANAD. Other organizations like ED Referral exist to provide information to consumers for better access to treatment providers. The Eating Disorder Coalition is involved in lobbying and other political action at the national level. There are a variety of organizations out there to help with understanding, awareness, advocacy, treatment and prevention. It is useful to be familiar with them. Following the organizations and websites is a list of several journals and newsletters dedicated to eating disorders and related issues.

Organizations

Academy for Eating Disorders (AED)
60 Revere Dr.
Northbrook, IL 60662
Phone: (847) 498-4274
Fax: (847) 480-9282
http://aedweb.org

About-Face
P.O. Box 77665
San Francisco, CA 94107
Phone: (415) 436-0212
about-face.org

Body Image Coalition of Peel
c/o Peel Health, 9445 Airport Rd.
3rd Floor, West Tower
Brampton, ON L6S 4J3
Canada
bodyimagecoalition.org
info@bodyimagecoalition.org

Dads and Daughters
2 West 1st St., Suite 101
Duluth, MN 55802
Phone: (888) 824-DADS (824-3237)
dadsanddaughters.org

Eating Disorders Coalition for Research, Policy, and Action
611 Pennsylvania Ave.
Washington, DC 20003-4303
Phone/Fax: (202) 543-9570
eatingdisorderscoalition.org

International Association of Eating Disorder Professionals (IAEDP)
427 Whooping Loop #1819
Altamonte Springs, FL 32701
Phone: (800) 800-8126
iaedp.com

The Massachusetts Eating Disorders Association (MEDA)
92 Pearl St.
Newton, MA 02458
Phone: (617) 558-1881
medainc.org

National Association of Anorexia Nervosa and Associated Disorders (ANAD)
Box 7
Highland Park, IL 60035
Phone: (847) 831-3438
Fax: (847) 433-4632
anad.org

National Eating Disorders Association (NEDA)
603 Stewart St., Suite 803
Seattle, WA 98101
Phone: (206) 382-3587
Treatment referral: (800) 931-2237
nationaleatingdisorders.org

National Eating Disorder Information Centre (NEDIC)
CW 1-211, 200 Elizabeth St.
Toronto, ON M5G 2C4
Canada
Phone: (416) 340-4156 (in Toronto)
Fax: (416) 340-4376
nedic.ca

Overeaters Anonymous (OA)
World Services Offices
P.O. Box 44020
Rio Rancho, NM 87124
Phone: (505) 891-2664
oa.org

Websites

Andrea' Voice Foundation
Started after the death of Andrea Smeltzer by her parents to raise awareness and promote prevention.
andreasvoice.org

Eating Disorder Referral and Information Center
"The Eating Disorder Referral and Information Center provides information and treatment resources for all forms of eating disorders. If you need to find a treatment center or private practitioner specializing in eating disorders anywhere in the United States or internationally, this site may be the best resource of its kind on the Web." From the television show "NOVA" on PBS.
edreferral.com
edreferral@aol.com

BodyPositive.com
This is a great source of information and resources (including links to other websites) to promote a positive body image in people of all ages.

Gurze.com or bulimia.com
Books, videos, articles, journals, and more. An excellent resource.

Mirror-mirror.org/eatdis.htm
The Eating Disorders and Getting Help sections contain a wealth of solid, introductory information.

Natural Medicine Comprehensive Database
A comprehensive site on the level of effectiveness for natural products for various medical conditions and tells you the potential interactions between any natural product and any drug.
naturaldatabase.com

Something Fishy
A website dedicated to raising awareness and providing support to people with eating disorders and their loved ones. An excellent source of all kinds of information from prevention to online support to medical issues and finding help.
somethingfishy.org

Journals and Newsletters

- ***Dads and Daughters: How to Inspire, Understand and Support Your Daughter When She's Growing Up So Fast*, editor Joe Kelly. Dads and Daughters, Deluth, Minnesota.** (This newsletter is geared for dads but good for everyone. Whether dads live with their daughters or not, they will find excellent guidance for having good relationships with her—and the rest of the family.)

- ***Eating Disorder Review*, editor in chief, Joel Yager, M.D. Gürze Books, Carlsbad, California.** (This bimonthly newsletter presents current clinical information for the professional treating eating disorders. This easy-to-read newsletter features summaries of relevant research from journals and unpublished studies. Lay persons might find this useful as well as professionals.)

- ***Eating Disorders: The Journal of Treatment and Prevention*, editor Leigh Cohn. Taylor & Diorders: The Francis, Philadelphia, Pennsylvania.** (Geared to therapists, treatment facilities, clinical researchers, and educators, this journal presents a wide range of practical, informative viewpoints from many of the most respected professionals involved internationally in the treatment of eating disorders. It features articles on prevention, feminist theory, research, multicultural issues, treatment, multidisciplinary perspectives, and much more. Each issue contains metaphorical stories, book and film reviews, "How I Practice," and questions and answers.)

- ***Eating Disorders Today*, editor in Chief, Joel Yager, M.D. Gürze Books, Carlsbad, California.** (This is a newsletter for recovering individuals and their loved ones. It combines clinical facts and self-help advice related to recovery. Practical suggestions on a variety of topics are included.)

- ***Health at Every Size*, editors: Wayne C. Miller, Ph.D., and Jon Robison, Ph.D., M.S. Gürze Books, Carlsbad, California.** (Previously known as the *Healthy Weight Journal*, this offers research, theory, and practice supporting the Health at Every Size [HAES] movement and is written to help health professionals understand and practice this compassionate and effective nondieting approach to resolving weight and eating-related concerns.)

- ***International Journal of Eating Disorders*, editor in chief Michael Strober. John Wiley and Sons, Wiley Publishing, Inc., Indianapolis, Indiana.** (This journal publishes basic research and clinical and theoretical articles of scholarly substance on a variety of aspects of anorexia nervosa, bulimia, obesity, and other atypical patterns of eating behavior and body weight regulation in clinical and normal populations.)

Suggestions for Further Reading

I HAVE INCLUDED in the bibliography those books that have informed this sourcebook. Several of these books are demarcated with an * that means they are also on my list as recommended reading. There are other eating disorder books that I believe to be valuable but were not used directly in writing this book. Some of them are listed here. I have also included several books that have been influential in my own understanding of people, eating disorders, and healing. I wanted to share these because I believe they have been useful in my own continued growth and my work as an eating disorder therapist.

Fallon, P., M. Katzman, and S. Wooley. *Feminist Perspectives on Eating Disorders.* New York: Guilford Press, 1994.

Fodor, Viola. *Desperately Seeking Self, An Inner Guidebook for People with Eating Disorders.* Carlsbad, Calif.: Gürze Books, 1997.

Johnston, Anita. *Eating in the Light of the Moon.* Carlsbad, Calif.: Gürze Books, 2000.

Latimer, Jane E. *Living Binge-Free: A Personal Guide to Victory Over Compulsive Eating.* Boulder, Col.: LivingQuest, 1988.

Maine, Margo. *Father Hunger.* Carlsbad, Calif.: Gürze Books, 1991.

Moore, Thomas. *Dark Nights of the Soul.* New York: Gotham Books, 2004.

Paulson, T., and J. M. McShane. *Because I Feel Fat.* Lincoln, Neb.: Tony Paulson, 2004.

Reiff, D. W., and K. K. Reiff. *Eating Disorders: Nutrition Therapy in the Recovery Process.* New York: Aspen, 1997.

Roberts, Monty. *The Man Who Listens to Horses.* New York: Random House, 1998.

Robison, John. *The Spirit and Science of Holistic Health.* Bloomington Ind.: Authorhouse, 2006

Roth, Geneen. *Appetites.* New York: Plume, 1996.

———. *When Food Is Love: Exploring the Relationships Between Intimacy and Eating.* New York: Dutton, 1991.

Siegel, Daniel J. *The Developing Mind: Toward a Neurobiology of Interpersonal Experience.* New York: Guilford Press, 1999

Waterhouse, D. *Like Mother, Like Daughter: How Women Are Influenced by Their Mothers' Relationship with Food—And How to Break the Pattern.* New York: Hyperion, 1997.

Bibliography

Agras, W., and R. Apple. *Overcoming Eating Disorder (ED): A Cognitive-Behavioral Treatment for Bulimia Nervosa and Binge-Eating Disorder Therapist Guide.* San Antonio, Tex.: The Psychological Corporation, 1997.

Agras, W. S., E. M. Rossiter, B. Arnow, et al. "Pharmacologic and Cognitive Behavioral Treatment for Bulimia Nervosa: A Controlled Comparison." *American Journal of Psychiatry* 149 (1992): 82–87.

Alcoholics Anonymous. *Alcoholics Anonymous, The Big Book.* New York: Alcoholics Anonymous World Services, 1995.

American Psychiatric Association. *Diagnostic and Statistical Manual of Mental Disorders.* 4th ed. (Text revision; *DSM-IV-TR*). Washington, D.C.: American Psychiatric Association, 2000.

Andersen, A. K., P. J. Woodward, and N. LaFrance. "Bone Mineral Density of Eating Disorder Subgroups." *International Journal of Eating Disorders* 18 (1995): 335.

Andersen, Arnold. *Males with Eating Disorders.* Philadelphia: Brunner/Mazel, 1990.

Andersen, Arnold, Leigh Cohn, and Thomas Holbrook. *Making Weight: Men's Conflicts with Food,Weight, Shape and Appearance.* Carlsbad, Calif.: Gürze, 2000.

Anderson, A., and J. Holman. "Diagnosing and Treating Bone Mineral Deficiency." *Eating Disorder Review* 8, no. 1 (1997): 1.

Andreasen, N. C., J. Rice, J. Endicott, T. Reich, and W. Coryell. "The Family History Approach to Diagnosis." *Archives of General Psychiatry* 43 (1986): 421–29.

Anorexics and Bulimics Anonymous. *Anorexics and Bulimics Anonymous.* Edmonton: Anorexics and Bulimics Anonymous Friesens Book Division, 2002.

Armstrong, Roth. "Attachment and Separation Difficulties in Eating Disorders: A Preliminary Investigation." *International Journal of Eating Disorders* 8, no. 2 (1989): 141–55.

Baran, S., T. Weltzin, W. Kaye, et al. "Low Discharge Weight and Outcome in Anorexia Nervosa." *American Journal of Psychiatry* 152, no. 7 (1995): 1070–72.

Becker, A., R. Burwell, S. Gilman, D. Herzog, and P. Hamburg. "Eating Behavior and Attitudes Following Prolonged Exposure to Television Among Ethnic Fijian Girls." *British Journal of Psychiatry* 180 (2002): 509–14.

Becker, Daniel. *This Mean Disease.* Carlsbad, Calif.: Gurze Books, 2005.

Bell, Rudolf. *Holy Anorexia.* Chicago: University of Chicago Press, 1987.

Bemis, K. "'Abstinence' and 'Non Abstinence' Models for the Treatment of Bulimia." *International Journal of Eating Disorders* 4 (1985): 389–406.

*Berg, Frances M. *Underage & Overweight: America's Childhood Obesity Crisis—What Every Family Needs to Know.* Long Island City, N.Y.: Hatherleigh Press, 2004.

Bergen, A. W., M. Yeager, R. A. Welch, et al. "Association of Multiple DRD2 Polymorphisms with Anorexia Nervosa." *Neuropsychopharmacology* 30, no. 9 (2005): 1703–10.

Bernstein, Jerrold G. *Drug Therapy in Psychiatry.* 3rd ed. St. Louis, Mo.: Mosby-Year Book, 1995.

Biederman, J., T. Rivinius, K. Kemper, et al. "Depressive Disorders in Relatives of Anorexia Nervosa Patients with and without a Current Episode of Nonbipolar Major Depression." *American Journal of Psychiatry* 142 (1985): 1495–97.

Bloom, C., A. Gitter, S. Gutwill, L. Kogel, and L. Zaphiropoulos. *Eating Problems, A Feminist Psychoanalytic Treatment Model.* New York: Basic Books, 1994.

*Bolen, Jean. *Close to the Bone.* New York: Scribner, 1996.

Bonjour, J., G. Theintz, B. Buchs, D. Slosman, and R. Rizzoli. "Critical Years and Stages of Puberty for Spinal and Femoral Bone Mass Accumulation During Adolescence." *Journal of Clinical Endocrinological Metabolism* 73 (1991): 555.

Booth, Christopher. "Technology and Medicine." *Proceedings of the Royal Society of London. Series B, Biological Sciences* 224, no. 1236 (1985): 267–85.

Brewerton, T. D., B. S. Dansky, D. G. Kilpatrick, and P. M. O'Neil. "Bulimia Nervosa, PTSD And 'Forgetting': Results from The National Women's Study." In *Trauma and Memory*, edited by L. M. Williams and V. L. Banyard, 127–38. Durham, N. C.: Sage Publications, 1999.

Brewerton, Timothy (ed). *Clinical Handbook of Eating Disorders.* New York: Marcel Dekker, 2004.

———. "Toward a Unified Theory of Serotonin Dysregulation in Eating and Related Disorders." *Psychoneuroendocrinology* 20 (1995): 561–90.

Brisman, J., and M. Siegal. "Bulimia and Alcoholism: Two Sides of the Same Coin?" *Journal of Substance Abuse Treatment* 1 (1984): 113–18.

Brody, C. *Women's Therapy Groups.* New York: Springer Books, 1987.

Bruch, Hilda. *Eating Disorders: Obesity, Anorexia Nervosa, and the Person Within.* New York: Basic Books, 1973.

———. *The Golden Cage: The Enigma of Anorexia Nervosa.* New York: Vintage Books, 1979.

*Brumberg, Joan J. *Fasting Girls: The History of Anorexia Nervosa.* New York: Plume, 1989.

Bryant-Waugh, R., and B. Lask. *Eating Disorders: A Parents' Guide.* Rev. ed. London & New York: Brunner-Routledge, 2004.

Bulik, C. M., P. F. Sullivan, F. Tozzi, et al. "Prevalence, Heritability, and Prospective Risk Factors for Anorexia Nervosa." *Archives of General Psychiatry* 63, no. 3 (2006): 305–12.

Bulik, C. M. "Role of Genetics in Anorexia Nervosa, Bulimia Nervosa and Binge Eating Disorder." *Clinical Handbook of Eating Disorders.* Timothy Brewerton (ed). New York: Marcel Dekker, 2004.

Butler, S., and C. Wintram. *Feminist Group Work.* London: Sage Publications, 1992.

Chassler, Lynda. "Understanding Anorexia Nervosa and Bulimia Nervosa from an Attachment Perspective." *Clinical Social Work Journal* 25, no. 4 (1997): 407–23.

Chernin, Kim. *The Hungry Self.* New York: Harper and Row, 1986.

———. *The Obsession.* New York: Harper and Row, 1994.

Colbert, Ty. *Blaming Our Genes: Why Mental Illness Can't Be Inherited.* Tustin, Calif.: Kevco Publishing, 2001.

Conterio, K., and W. Ladder. *Bodily Harm: The Breakthrough Treatment Program for Self-Injurers.* New York: Hyperion, 1998.

Costin, Carolyn. *100 Questions About Eating Disorders.* Sudbury, Mass.: Jones & Bartlett, 2007.

Costin, Carolyn. "Soul Lessons: Finding the Meaning of Life." *Eating Disorders: The Journal of Treatment and Prevention* 9 (2002): 267–73.

*Costin, Carolyn. *Your Dieting Daughter.* New York: Brunner/Mazel, 1996.

Costin, Carolyn, Ali Borden, Anna Kowalski, Jeff Radant, and Norah Wynne. "Books for Families and Significant Others." *Eating Disorders, the Journal of Treatment and Prevention*, vol. 13 no. 4 (Summer 2005): 433–45.

Covington, Maggie B. "Omega-3 Fatty Acids." *American Family Physician*, vol. 70 no. 1 (2004).

Crowther, J. H., D. L. Tennenbaum, S. E. Hobfoll, and M. A. P. Stephens (eds). "Epidemiology of Bulimia Nervosa." In: *The Etiology of Bulimia*

Nervosa: The Individual and Familial Context, 1–26. Washington, D.C.: Taylor & Francis, 1992.

Dansky, B. S., T. D. Brewerton, P. M. O'Neil, and D. G. Kilpatrick. "The National Women's Study: Relationship of Crime Victimization and PTSD to Bulimia Nervosa." *International Journal of Eating Disorders* 21 (1997): 213–28.

Darby, P., P.E. Garfinkel, J. Vale., et al. "Anorexia Nervosa and Turner Syndrome: Cause or Coincidence?" *Psychological Medicine* 11 (1981): 141–45.

Davidson, S., and M. Davidson, (eds.) *Behavioral Medicine: Changing Health Lifestyles*. New York: Brunner/Mazel, 1980.

Dolan, B. "Cross-Cultural Aspects of Anorexia Nervosa and Bulimia: A Review." *International Journal of Eating Disorders* 10, no. 1 (1991): 67–78.

"Dual Hormone Therapy Prevents Bone Loss." *Eating Disorders Review* 9, no. 6 (1998): 8.

Duncan, B., S. Miller, and J. Sparks. *The Heroic Client*. San Francisco: John Wiley & Sons, 2004.

Eaves, I. J., N. G. Martin, A. C. Heath, and K. S. Kendler. "Testing Genetic Models for Multiple Symptoms." *Behavioral Genetics* 17 (1987): 331–41.

Eaves, L. J. "Including the Environment in Models for Genetic Segregation." *Journal of Psychiatric Research* 21 (1987): 639–47.

Elston, R. C., and K. C. Yelverton. "General Models for Segregation Analysis." *American Journal of Human Genetics* 27 (1975): 31–45.

Emory, H., M. J. Schiller, and S. Suffin. "Referenced EEG in the Treatment of Eating Disorders." Poster presentation, NIMH National Clinical Drug Evaluation Unit Conference, Phoenix, Ariz., June 2004.

Epling, W. F., W. E. Pierce, and L. Stefan. "A Theory of Activity-Based Anorexia." *International Journal of Eating Disorders*, 24 (1998): 27–46.

Fairburn, C. G., and S. L. Welch. "Child Physical Abuse and Bulimia Nervosa." *Archives of General Psychiatry* 54 (1997): 509.

Fairburn, C. G., R. Jones, R. C. Peveler, R. A. Hope, and M. O'Conner. "Psychotherapy and Bulimia Nervosa. Longer Term Effects of Interpersonal Psychotherapy, Behavior Therapy, and Cognitive Behavioral Therapy." *Archives of General Psychiatry* 52 (1993): 304–12.

Fairburn, Christopher, Marsha D. Marcus, and Terrence Wilson. "Cognitive-Behavioral Therapy for Binge Eating and Bulimia Nervosa: A Comprehensive Treatment Manual." *Binge Eating: Nature, Assessment, and Treatment*. Christopher Fairburn and Terrence Wilson (eds). New York: Guilford Press, 1993.

Fairburn, C. G., Z. Cooper, H. A. Doll, P. Norman, and M. O'Conner. "The Natural Course of Bulimia Nervosa and Binge Eating Disorder in Young Women." *Archives of General Psychiatry* 57 (2000): 659–65.

Fairburn, Christopher. *Overcoming Binge Eating.* New York: Guilford Press, 1995.

Fairburn, Christopher, and G. Wilson, (eds.) *Binge Eating: Nature, Assessment, and Treatment.* New York: Guilford Press, 1993.

Fairburn, Christopher, and Timothy Walsh. "Atypical Eating Disorders." In *Eating Disorders and Obesity*, Christopher Fairburn and Kelly D. Brownell, et al., (eds), 171–77. New York: Guilford Press, 1995.

Fichter, M. "Symptomatology, Psychosexual Development, and Gender Identity in 42 Anorexic Males." *Psychological Medicine* 17 (1987): 409–18.

Fichter, M. M., and N. Quadfling. "Six Year Course of Bulimia Nervosa." *International Journal of Eating Disorders* 22 (1997): 361–84.

Fichter, M. M., N. Quadflieg, and A. Gnutzman. "Binge Eating Disorder: Treatment Outcome Over a 6 Year Course." *Journal of Psychosomatic Research* 44 (1998): 385–405.

Fichter, M. M., and R. Noegel. "Concordance for Bulimia in Twins." *International Journal of Eating Disorders* 9 (1990): 255–63.

Fluoxetine Bulimia Nervosa Collaborative Study Group. "Fluoxetine in the Treatment of Bulimia Nervosa: A Multicenter, Placebo-Controlled, Double Blind Trial." *Archives of General Psychiatry* 49 (1992): 139–47.

*Gaesser, Glenn. *Big Fat Lies.* New York: Ballantine Books, 1996

Garfinkel, P., H. Moldofsky, and D. M. Garner. "The Heterogeneity of Anorexia Nervosa." *Archives of General Psychiatry* 37 (1980): 1036–40.

Garner, D. M., M. P. Olmsted, Y. Bohr, and P. E. Garfinkel. "The Eating Attitudes Test: Psychometric Features and Clinical Correlates." *Psychological Medicine* 12, no. 4 (1982): 871–78.

Garner, D. M., P. E. Garfinkel, and M. O'Shaughnessy. "Validity of the Distinction Between Bulimia with and Without Anorexia Nervosa." *American Journal of Psychiatry* 142 (1985): 581–87.

Gelenberg, Alan J. *The Practitioner's Guide to Psychoactive Drugs.* 3rd ed. New York and London: Plenum Medical Book Company, 1991.

Geller, J., and D. L. Drab. "The Readiness and Motivation Interview: A Symptom Specific Measure of Readiness for Change in the Eating Disorders." *European Eating Disorders Review* 7 (1999): 259–78.

Gordon, R. A. *Anorexia and Bulimia: Anatomy of a Social Epidemic.* New York: Blackwell, 2000.

Grabowski, A. "Recovered? What's That?" *The Awakening Center* newsletter, vol 8 no. 2.

Grinspoon, S., H. Baum, K. Lee, E. Anderson, D. Herzog, and A. Klibanski. "Effects of Short-Term Recombinant Human Insulin-Like Growth Factor I Administration on Bone Turnover in Osteopenic Women with Anorexia Nervosa." *Journal of Clinical Endocrinological Metabolism* 81 (1996): 3864–70.

Hall, R. C. W., L. Tice, T. P. Beresford, B. Wooley, and A. K. Hall. "Sexual Abuse in Patients with Anorexia Nervosa and Bulimia." *Psychosomatics* 30 (1992): 79–88.

Hammer, L. D., H. C. Kraemer, D. M. Wilson, P. L. Ritter, and S. M. Dornbusch. "Standardized Percentile Curves of Body Mass Index for Children and Adolescents." *American Journal of Diseases of Children* 145 (1991): 259–63.

Hanich, Lydia. *Honey, Does This Make My Butt Look Big?* Carlsbad, Calif.: Gurze Books, 2005.

Harper-Giuffre, H., and K. R. MacKenzie. *Group Psychotherapy for Eating Disorders.* Washington, D.C.: American Psychiatric Association Press, 1992.

Hatsukami, D., P. Owen, R. Pyle, and J. Mitchell. "Similarities and Differences on the MMPI Between Women with Bulimia and Women with Alcohol or Drug Abuse Problems." *Addictive Behaviors* 7 (1982): 435–39.

Herrin, Marcia, and Nancy Matsumoto. *The Parent's Guide to Eating Disorders.* New York: Henry Holt and Company, 2002.

Herrin, Marcia. *Nutrition Counseling in the Treatment of Eating Disorders.* New York: Brunner-Routledge, 2002.

Herschman, Jane, and Carol Munter. *When Women Stop Hating Their Bodies.* New York: Ballentine Publishing Group, 1995.

Hoek, H. W. "The Distribution of Eating Disorders." In *Eating Disorders and Obesity: A Comprehensive Handbook*, K. D. Brownell and C. G. Fairburn (eds), 207–11. New York: Guilford Press, 1995.

Hoffman L., and K. Halmi. "Psychopharmacology in the Treatment of Anorexia Nervosa and Bulimia Nervosa." *Psychiatric Clinics of North America* 16, no. 4 (1993): 767–78.

Hongisto, S. M., L. Paajanen, M. Saxelin, R. Korpela, et al. "A Combination of Fibre-Rich Rye Bread and Yoghurt Containing Lactobacillus GG Improves Bowel Function in Women with Self-Reported Constipation." *European Journal of Clinical Nutrition* vol. 60, no. 3 (2006): 319–24.

Hsu, L. K. G. "Outcome Studies in Patients with Eating Disorders." In *Psychiatric Treatment: Advances in Outcome Research*, S. M. Miren et al. (eds), 159–80. Washington, D.C.: American Psychiatric Association Press, 1991.

Hubble, M., B. Duncan, and S. Miller. *The Heart and Soul of Change.* Washington D.C.: American Psychological Association, 1999.

Jennings, James and Elizabeth L. *12 Steps for Overeaters: An Interpretation of the 12-Steps of Overeaters Anonymous.* Center City, Minn: Hazelden, 1993.

Johnson, C., and C. Costin. "Been There Done That: The Use of Clinicians with Personal Recovery in the Treatment of Eating Disorders." *Eating Disorders, The Journal of Treatment and Prevention* 10, no. 4 (2002): 293–303.

Johnstone, J., J. Gunkelman, and J. Lunt. "Clinical Database Development: Characterizing EEG Phenotypes." *Clinical EEG Neuroscience* 36, no. 2 (2005): 99–107.

Kajander, K., K. Hatakka, T. Poussa, M. Farkkila, and R. Korpela. "A Probiotic Mixture Alleviates Symptoms in Irritable Bowel Syndrome Patients: A Controlled 6-Month Intervention." *Alimentary Pharmacology and Therapy* 22, no. 5 (2005): 387–94.

*Kater, K. *Real Kids Come in All Sizes: 10 Essential Lessons to Build Your Child's Body Esteem*. New York: Broadway Books, 2004.

Kaye, Walter, G. Frank, and C. McConahan. "Altered Dopamine Activity After Recovery from Restricting-Type Anorexia Nervosa" *Neuropsychopharmacology*: 21 (1999): 503–6.

Kaye, Walter. "Neurobiology and Temperament." Paper presented at the Eating Disorder and Advocacy and Research meeting of the National Institute of Mental Health, Bethesda Maryland, December 1998.

Kearney-Cooke, A. "Group Treatment of Sexual Abuse among Women with Eating Disorders." *Women and Therapy* 7 (1988): 5–22.

Keddy, D., and T. Lyon. "Assessing Nutritional Status." *Eating Disorders Review* 9 no. 5 (1998): 5.

Keel, P. K. *Eating Disorders*. Upper Saddle River, N.J.: Pearson/Prentice Hall, 2005.

Keel, P. K., and K. L. Klump. "Are Eating Disorders Culture-Bound Syndromes? Implications for Conceptualizing Their Etiology" *Psychological Bulletin* 129 (2003): 747–69.

Keel, P. K., and J. E. Mitchell. "Outcome in Bulimia Nervosa." *American Journal of Psychiatry* 154, no. 3 (1997): 313–21.

Kelly, Joe. *Dads and Daughters: How to Inspire, Understand and Support Your Daughter When She's Growing Up So Fast*. New York: Broadway Books, 2002.

Kendall, P. C., and S. D. Hollon (eds). *Cognitive Behavioral Interventions: Theory, Research and Procedures*. New York: Academic Press, 1979.

Kennedy, S. H., and D. S. Goldbloom. "Current Perspectives on Drug Therapies for Anorexia Nervosa and Bulimia Nervosa." *Drugs* 41, no. 3 (1991): 367–77.

Khalif, I. L. "Alterations in Colonic Flora and Intestinal Permeability and Evidence of Immune Activation in Chronic Constipation." *Dig Liver Dis* 37, no. 11 (2005): 838–49.

Kilbourne, J. *Deadly Persuasion: Why Women and Girls Must Fight the Addictive Power of Advertising*. New York: Free Press, 1999.

*Knapp, Caroline. *Appetites*. New York: Counterpoint, 2003.

*Kornfield, Jack. *A Path with Heart*. New York: Bantam Books, 1993.

Krebs, C., K. Huttmann, and C. Steinhauser. "The Forgotten Brain Emerges." *Scientific American* 15, no. 4 (2004): 40–44.

Kriepe, R. E., D. G. Hicks, R. N. Rosier, and J. E. Puzas. "Preliminary Findings on the Effects of Sex Hormones on Bone Metabolism in Anorexia Nervosa." *Journal of Adolescent Health* 14 (1993): 319–24.

Lee, Sing. "Anorexia Nervosa in Hong Kong: A Chinese Perspective." *Psychological Medicine*, 21 (1991): 703–11.

Lee, Sing, T. P. Ho, and L. K. G. Hsu. "Fat Phobic and Non-Fat Phobic Anorexia Nervosa: A Comparative Study of 70 Chinese Patients in Hong Kong." *Psychological Medicine*, 23 (1993): 999–1017.

Levenkron, Steven. *The Best Little Girl in the World*. New York: Warner Books, 1981.

———. *Cutting: Understanding and Overcoming Self-Mutilization*. New York: W.W. Norton, 1998.

———. *Treating and Overcoming Anorexia Nervosa*. New York: Warner Books, 1997.

*Levine, M. P., and L. Smolak. *The Prevention of Eating Problems and Eating Disorders: Theory, Research, and Practice*. Mahwah, N.J.: Lawrence Erlbaum Associates, 2006.

———. "Primary Prevention of Body Image Disturbances and Disordered Eating in Childhood and Early Adolescence." In *Body Image, Eating Disorders, and Obesity in Youth: Assessment, Prevention, and Treatment*, J. K. Thompson and L. Smolak (eds), 237–60. Washington, D.C.: American Psychological Association, 2001.

Levine, M., and M. Marcus. "Psychosocial Treatment of Binge Eating Disorder." *Eating Disorders Review* July/August 2003 Vol. 14 /NO. 4: Gürze Books, 2003.

Levitt, J., R. Sansone, and L. Cohn, eds. *Self Harm Behavior and Eating Disorders*. New York: Taylor & Francis, 2004.

Linder, R. *The Fifty Minute Hour*. New York: Holt, Rinehart, and Winston, 1955.

*Linehan, Marsha. *Cognitive Behavioral Treatment of Borderline Personality Disorder*. New York: Guilford Press, 1993.

*Lock, James, and D. Le Grange. *Help Your Teen Beat an Eating Disorder*. New York: Gilford Press, 2005.

Luo, J. "A Prescription to Improve Drug Regimens?" *Current Psychiatry Online* 4, no. 8 (August 2005).

Lyon, Tami J. "Resumption of Menses in Teens with Anorexia Nervosa." *Eating Disorders Review* 9, no. 1 (1998): 6–7.

*Maine, Margo. *Body Wars: Making Peace with Women's Bodies—An Activist's Guide*. Carlsbad, Calif.: Gürze Books, 2000.

*Maine, Margo, and Joe Kelly. *The Body Myth: Adult Women and the Pressure to Be Perfect*. Hoboken, N.J.: John Wiley & Sons, 2005.

Maisel, Richard, David Epston, and Alisa Borden. *Biting the Hand That Starves You*. New York: W. W. Norton & Company, Inc., 2004.

Malenbaum, R., D. Herzog, S. Eisenthal, et al. "Overeaters Anonymous: Impact on Bulimia." *International Journal of Eating Disorders* 7 (1988): 139–43.

Marlatt, G. A. *Alcohol Use and Problem Drinking: A Cognitive Behavioral Analysis*. New York: Academic Press, 1979.

Marlatt, G. A., and J. R. Gordon. "Determinants of Relapse: Implications for the Maintenance of Behavior Change." In *Behavioral Medicine: Changing Health Lifestyles*, P. O. Davidson and S. M. Davidson (eds). New York: Brunner/Mazel, 1980.

Mehler, P. S., and M. J. Krantz. "QT Dispersion in Anorexia Nervosa." *American Journal of Cardiology* vol. 96, no. 7 (2005): 1034.

Miller, M. N., and A. J. Pumariega. "Culture and Eating Disorders: A Historical and Cross-Cultural Review." *Psychiatry* 64, no. 2 (2001): 93–110.

Minuchin, Rosman. *Psychosomatic Families: Anorexia Nervosa in Context*. Cambridge, Mass.: Harvard University Press, 1978.

Moore, Thomas. *Care of the Soul*. New York: Harper Collins, 1996.

Moore, Thomas. *The Re-Enchantment of Everyday Life*. New York: Harper Collins, 1992.

Morin, C. M., U. Koetter, and C. Bastien. "Valerina-Hops Combination and Diphenhydramine for Treating Insomnia: A Randomized Placebo-Controlled Trial. *Sleep* 28, no. 11 (2005): 1465–71.

Morton, Richard. *Phthisiologia: Or a Treatise of Consumptions*. London: Smith & Walford, 1694.

National Institutes of Health (NIH) Consensus Development Panel On Optimal Calcium Intake. "Optimal Calcium Intake." *Journal of the American Medical Association* 272 (1994): 1942–8.

*Neumark-Sztainer, D. *"I'm, Like, So Fat!" Helping Your Teen Make Healthy Choices About Eating and Exercise in a Weight-Obsessed World*. New York: Guilford, 2005.

Nielson, S., S. Moller-Madsen, T. Isager, J. Jorgensen, K. Pagsberg, and S. Theander. "Standardized Mortality in Eating Disorders: A Quantitative Summary of Previously Published and New Evidence." *Journal of Psychosomatic Research* 44 (1998): 413–34.

Oppenheimer, R., K. Howells, R. L. Palmer, and D. A. Chaloner. "Adverse Sexual Experiences in Childhood and Clinical Eating Disorders: A Preliminary Description." *Journal of Psychiatric Research* 19 (1985): 157–61.

———. *Just for Today*. Los Angeles: Overeaters Anonymous, 1979.

———. *Questions & Answers About Compulsive Overeating and the OA Program of Recovery*. Los Angeles: Overeaters Anonymous, 1979.

———. *The Tools of Recovery*. Los Angeles: Overeaters Anonymous, 1981.

———. *To the Newcomer*. Los Angeles: Overeaters Anonymous, 1979.

Pinker, Steven. *The Blank Slate: The Denial of Human Nature*. New York: Viking Penguin, 2002.

Pope, H. G., and K. I. Hudson. "Is Childhood Sexual Abuse a Risk Factor for Bulimia Nervosa?" *American Journal of Psychiatry* 149 (1992): 455–63.

Pope, H. G., Jr., K. A. Phillips, and R. Olivardia. *The Adonis Complex: The Secret Crisis of Male Body Obsession.* New York: The Free Press, 2000.

Preskorn, S. H. "Beyond *DSM-IV*: What Is the Cart and What Is the Horse?" *Psychiatric Annals* 25 (1995): 53–62.

Robison, Jonathon, and Karen Carrier (eds). *Health at Every Size.* Carlsbad, Calif.: Gürze Books. (This is a journal published every year; cited as a resource only.)

Root, M. P., and Patricia Fallon. "The Incidences of Victimization Experiences in a Bulimic Sample." *Journal of Interpersonal Violence* 3, no. 2 (1988): 161–73.

Rosen, Jonathan. *Eve's Apple.* New York: Random House, 1997.

Rosen, L. W., and D. O. Hough. "Pathogenic Weight-Control Behaviors of Female College Gymnasts." *Physicians and Sports Medicine Journal* 17 (1994): 176–88.

Rosenthal, N. E. *Winter Blues: Seasonal Affective Disorder—What It Is and How to Overcome It.* New York: Guilford Press, 1993.

Ross, Colin. *The Trauma Model.* Richardson, Tex.: Manitou Communications, 2000.

Roth, Geneen. *Breaking Free from Compulsive Overeating.* New York: Penguin Group, 1984.

Rubenfeld, Ilana. *The Listening Hand: How to Combine Bodywork, Intuition, and Psychotherapy to Release Emotions and Heal Pain.* London: Piatkus Books, 2001.

Ryan, Joan. *Little Girls in Pretty Boxes.* New York: Doubleday, 1995.

Sansone, Randy, and Craig Johnson. "Integrating the Twelve Step Approach." *Eating Disorder Review* 4, no. 2 (1993): 1–3.

*Satter, Ellen. *How to Get Your Kid to Eat . . . But Not Too Much.* Palo Alto, Calif.: Bull Publishing Company, 1987.

Schaefer, Jenni, and Thom Rutledge. *Life Without Ed: How One Woman Declared Independence from Her Eating Disorder and How You Can Too.* Chicago: McGraw-Hill, 2004.

Schauss, Alexander, and Carolyn Costin. *Anorexia and Bulimia: A Nutritional Approach to the Deadly Eating Disorders.* New Caanan, Conn.: Keats Publishing, 1997.

———. *Zinc and Eating Disorders.* Los Angeles: Keats Publishing, 1981.

Schwartz, M., and L. Cohen. *Sexual Abuse and Eating Disorders.* New York: Brunner/Mazel, 1996.

Serpell, Lucy, and Janet Treasure. "Treatment Recommendations for Osteoporosis in Anorexia Nervosa." *Eating Disorders Review* 9, no. 1 (1998): 7.

Shinomiya, K., K. Fujimura, Y. Kim, and C. Kamei. "Effects of Valerian Extract on the Sleep-Wake Cycle in Sleep-Disturbed Rats." *Acta Medica Okayama* 59, no. 3 (2005): 89–92.

Shisslack, C. M., M. Crago, and L. S. Estes. "The Spectrum of Eating Disturbances." *International Journal of Eating Disorders* 18, no. 3 (1995): 209–19.

Siegal, Dan. *Parenting from the Inside Out.* New York: Putnam, 2003.

*Siegel, M., J. Brisman, and M. Weinshel. *Surviving an Eating Disorder: Strategies for Family and Friends.* Rev. ed. New York: Harper Perennial, 1997.

Simeon, D., and E. Hollander. *Self-Injurious Behavior: Assessment and Treatment.* New York: American Psychiatric Association, 2001.

Solomon, M., and D. Siegel. *Healing Trauma, Attachment, Mind, Body and Brain.* New York: W.W. Norton, 2003.

Spitzer, R. L., M. Devlin, and B. T. Walsh, et al. "Binge Eating Disorder: A Multisite Field Trial of the Diagnostic Criteria." *International Journal of Eating Disorders* vol. 11, no. 3. (1992) 191–203 (20 ref).

*Steiner Adair, Catherine, and Lisa Sjostrum. *Full of Ourselves: A Wellness Program.* New York: Teachers College Press, 2006.

Steinhausen, H.-C. "Outcome of Anorexia Nervosa in the 20th Century." *American Journal of Psychiatry* 159, no. 8 (2002): 1284–93.

Strober, Michael, R. Freeman, and W. Morrel. "The Long-Term Course of Severe Anorexia in Adolescents: Survival Analysis of Recovery, Relapse and Outcome Predictors Over 10–15 Years in a Prospective Study." *International Journal of Eating Disorders* 22 (1997): 339–60.

Stunkard, Albert. "A Description of ED in 1932." *American Journal of Psychiatry* 147, no. 3 (1990): 263–68.

Suffin, Stephen C., and Emory W. Hamlin. "Neurometric Subgroups in Attentional and Affective Disorders and Their Association with Pharmacotherapeutic Outcome." *Clinical Electroencephalography* 26, no. 2 (1995): 76–83.

Sullivan, P. F. "Mortality in Anorexia Nervosa." *American Journal of Psychiatry* 157 (1997): 1073–76.

Szegedi, A., R. Kohnen, A. Dienel, and M. Kiesser. "Acute Treatment of Moderate to Severe Depression with Hypericum Extract WS 5570 (St. John's Wort): Randomised Controlled Double-Blind Non-Inferiority Trial Versus Paroxetine." *BMJ* 330 (5 March 2005): 503, doi; 10.1136/bmj.38356.655266.82 (originally published online 11 February 2005).

Tannen, D. *Gender and Discourse.* New York: Oxford University Press, 1994.

Tessina, T. "Recovery Beyond Recovery: The Real Thirteenth Step." *The California Therapist*, November/December 1991, 47–48.

Thompson, J. K., and L. Smolak. *Body Image, Eating Disorders, and Obesity in Children and Adolescents: Theory, Assessment, Treatment, and Prevention.* Washington D.C.: American Psychological Association, 2001.

*Tolle, Eckhart. *The Power of Now.* Vancouver, British Columbia: Namaste Publishing, 1999.

Treasure, Janet. "Anorexia Nervosa: New Markers Track Bone Resorption, Formation." *Eating Disorders Review* 8, no. 1 (1997): 5.

*Tribole, Evelyn, and Elyse Resch. *Intuitive Eating: A Revolutionary Program That Works*. 2nd ed. New York: St. Martin's Press, 2003.

Tyre, Peg. "Fighting Anorexia, New Research into Its Origins—and Its Youngest Victims." *Newsweek*, 5 December 2005, 50–60.

"Valeriana Officinalis." *Alternative Medicine Review* 9, no. 4 (2004): 438–441.

Van Den Broucke, S., and W. Vandereycken. *Eating Disorders and Marital Relationships*. New York: Routledge Chapman Hall, 1997.

Vandereycken, W. "The Addiction Model in Eating Disorders: Some Critical Remarks and a Selected Bibliography." *International Journal of Eating Disorders* 9 (1990): 95–101.

Waltos, D. L. "Historical Perspectives and Diagnostic Considerations." *Occupational Therapy in Mental Health* 6, no. 1 (1986): 1–13.

Wampold, B.E., G. W. Mondin, M. Moody, F. Stich, K. Benson, and H. Ahn. "A Meta Analysis of Outcome Studies Comparing Bonafide Psychotherapies: Empirically, 'All Must Have Prizes'." *Psychological Bulletin* 122 (1997): 203–215.

Warren, M. P., N. Perlroth, L. W. Rosen, et. al. "Pathogenic Weight-Control Behavior in Female Athletes." *Physician and Sports Medicine Journal*, 14 (1986): 79–86.

Whitehouse, A.M., P. J. Cooper, C. V. Vize, C. Hill, and L. Vogel. "Prevalence of Eating Disorders in Three Cambridge General Practices: Hidden And Conspicuous Morbidity." *British Journal of General Practice* 42 (1992): 57–60.

Wolf, Naomi. *The Beauty Myth*. New York: William Morrow, 1991.

Wonderlich, S. A., T. D. Brewerton, Z. Jocic, B. S. Dansky, and D. W. Abbott. "Relationship of Childhood Sexual Abuse and Eating Disorders." *Journal of American Academic Child and Adolescent Psychiatry* 36 (1997): 8.

Wooley, Susan. "Sexual Abuse and Eating Disorders, the Concealed Debate." In *Feminist Perspectives on Eating Disorders*, Patricia Fallon, Melanie Katzman and Susan Wooley (eds), chapter 9, 171–211. New York: Guilford Press, 1994.

Worcester, S. "rEEG System Helps Guide Prescribing." *Clinical Psychiatry News* 33, no. 2 (2005): 1–6.

Yager, J. (ed). "The Twelve-Step Approach and Psychotherapy: An Integrated Model." *Eating Disorders Review* 4 (1993): 1–3.

Yates, Alayne. *Compulsive Exercise and the Eating Disorders*. Philadelphia: Brunner/Mazel, 1991.

*Zerbe, Kathryn J. *The Body Betrayed*. Carlsbad, Calif.: Gürze Books, 1993.

Index

About the Author

Carolyn Costin, M.A., M.Ed., M.F.T., has been a specialist in the field of eating disorders for nearly thirty years. The owner and director of the Monte Nido Residential Treatment Facility in Malibu, California, and all of its affiliates, she is also is the clinical advisor to the Parent Family Network of the National Eating Disorder Association, and an editor of *Eating Disorders: The Journal of Treatment and Prevention*. She speaks nationally on the treatment and prevention of eating disorders and is known for her position that people with eating disorders can be fully recovered. She is also the author of *Your Dieting Daughter* and *100 Questions About Eating Disorders*.